THE GOTHAM LIBRARY OF THE NEW YORK UNIVERSITY PRESS

The Gotham Library is a series of original works and critical studies published in paperback primarily for student use. The Gotham hardcover edition is primarily for use by libraries and the general reader. Devoted to significant works and major authors and to literary topics of enduring importance, Gotham Library texts offer the best in literature and criticism.

Comparative and Foreign Language Literature:
Robert J. Clements, Editor
Comparative and English Language Literature:
James W. Tuttleton, Editor

Greek Months 154

1 Hecatombaeon, first month in the Attic year, answering to the last half of our July & the first ½ of August: in it the Hecatombaea were held (festivals in wh. hecatombs were offered

2 Metageitnion, 2d month, answering to the Boeotian Panemos & Laconian Karneios; also to the latter ½ of our August & to the first ½ of Sept. (Said to be from μετα, γειτων, because then people flitted & changed their neighbours.

3 Boedromion, 3d Attic month = ½ Sept. & ½ Oct. Boedromia celebrated, i.e. games in memory of the defeat of the Amazons by Theseus.

4 Pyanepsion, 4th month = ½ Oct. & ½ Nov. Pyanepsia, feast in honour of Apollo said to be so called from a dish of beans, or peeled barley & pulse then cooked & eaten.

5 Maimakterion, 5th month = ½ Nov. & ½ Dec. Festival of Zeus Maimaktes, boisterous, stormy.

6 Poseideon, 6th month = ½ Dec. & ½ Jan.

7 Gamelion, 7th month = ½ Jan. & ½ Feb. So called because it was the fashionable time for weddings

8 Anthisterion, 8th Attic month = ½ Feb. & ½ March Anthisteria, the feast of flowers, the three days' feast of Dionysus at Athens.

9 Elaphebolion = ½ March & ½ April. Elaphebolia held; the festival of Artemis.

10 Munychion = ½ April & half May. Festival of Munychian Artemis. Munychia harbour adjoining Piraeus

11 Thargelion = ½ May & ½ June. Feast of Apollo & Artemis

12 Scirophorion, 12th Attic month = ½ June & ½ July. The festival of Athena Skiras. Skiron, a white parasol, borne by the priestesses in this festival; thence called τα σκιρα, or τα σκιροφορια

Page 154 of George Eliot's *Commonplace Book:* Greek Months. Reprinted by permission of Jonathan Ouvry and the Beinecke Rare Book and Manuscript Library, Yale University.

The Triptych and the Cross

The Central Myths of George Eliot's Poetic Imagination

Felicia Bonaparte

New York · New York University Press · 1979

Library of Congress Cataloging in Publication Data
Bonaparte, Felicia.
The triptych and the cross.

(The Gotham library)
Includes bibliographical references and index.
1. Eliot, George, pseud, i.e., Marian Evans, afterwards Cross, 1819-1880. Romola. 2. Myth in literature. 3. Florence in literature. 4. Savonarola, Girolamo Maria Francesco Matteo, 1452-1498, in fiction, drama, poetry, etc.
I. Title.
PR4668.B6 823′.8 78-20542
ISBN 0-8147-1012-3
ISBN 0-8147-1013-1 pbk.

Manufactured in the United States of America

for E.J.H.
who, like George Eliot, recalls the myths

Acknowledgements

I began my study of *Romola* several years ago when I determined finally to settle for myself at least the long disagreement about the book between George Eliot and her readers. Like most of her readers, I had always held *Romola* to be the least inspired of Eliot's works. But it had become increasingly difficult to take comfort in numbers when Eliot herself, as formidable a critic as she was a novelist, had called *Romola* the product of her "best blood." If Eliot was not mistaken—and it seemed difficult for me to believe that she was—there was something in *Romola* that her readers had not yet suspected. I had no idea when I began what that something might be, and to the very end, long after I had formulated my general conclusions, every discovery was a revelation. Indeed, the exploration of this book has been for me that happiest of enterprises, an unpredictable and joyful journey. Rewarding that journey would have been under any circumstances. But it has been made far more rewarding, and far easier, by those whose generous help I take great pleasure in acknowledging here.

The first draft of my manuscript, which attempted to integrate into a coherent thesis my copious notes on the book's imagistic patterns, found in my colleagues Professors Alice Chandler and Morton N. Cohen of the City University of New York two patient and thoughtful readers. To their ample marginal suggestions, I owe many wise revisions. I was fortunate to find for the second draft an equally sympathetic and demanding reader in Professor George Levine of Livingston College, Rutgers University. In attempting to answer his questions and to meet his objections, I came to see in my own arguments many subtle implications, especially in the relationship between the novel and the epic forms, that I might otherwise not have perceived. For that, and for his generous encouragement, I am deeply grateful. I am grateful too to the members of several groups to which I had the privilege of reading papers on my work in progress: the Friday Night Speakers Club of the City College of New York; the faculty and students of the Ph.D. Program in English at the City University of New York, and among them particularly Professors Irving Howe and Allen Mandelbaum; the Seminar on Generic Approaches at the meeting of the Modern Language Association of December 1975; the Harvard Victorians, especially Professor Jerome H. Buckley; and my class in Myth and Religion at the Bread Loaf School of English in the summer of 1978. Their provocative questions and vigorous discussions helped to shape the final version of the manuscript.

In the final version, I incorporated considerable material from a number of Eliot's unpublished manuscripts: Journal, 1854-1861 (no. 1 in the George Eliot Collection), Journal, 1858-1860 (no. 2), Journal, July 1861-December 1877 (no. 3), Commonplace Notebook (no. 6), and the Notebook marked "Quarry" (no. 18), all at the Beinecke Library at Yale University; and the Quarry for *Romola* (Additional Manuscript no. 40768) at the British Library in London. For granting me access to these manuscripts, I am greatly indebted to both libraries, and for their invaluable assistance, to many people associated with them. I wish especially to thank Ann Payne and Timothy A.J. Burnett, Assistant Keepers in the Department of Manuscripts at the British Library, and Marjorie G. Wynne, Research Librarian at the Beinecke Rare Book and Manuscript Library. Their kind help and special efforts on my behalf are deeply appreciated.

For their generous permission to quote from these unpublished manuscripts, I am very grateful to the British Library, to the Beinecke Library, and to Jonathan G. Ouvry, the literary executor of George Eliot's estate. I am additionally indebted to the Beinecke Library and to Jonathan G. Ouvry for permission to reproduce page 154 of Eliot's Commonplace Notebook at the front of this volume.

Finally, I wish to thank the Research Foundation of the City University of New York for a grant which made it possible for me to obtain photocopies of the manuscripts at the British and Beinecke Libraries.

Contents

The Triptych and the Cross:

The Central Myths of George Eliot's Poetic Imagination

1.

Introduction

It is a very curious fact, whose implications have not sufficiently troubled us, that of George Eliot's seven novels we have very much disliked no less than half. Even her most enthusiastic admirers have invariably concluded that while Eliot wrote three and a half of the best novels in the English language, she also wrote three and a half very misguided books. She wrote *Felix Holt,* a tangled political melodrama whose subtitle, *The Radical,* remains to this day a mystery to us. She wrote *Silas Marner,* a work of uncertain form and dubious perspective. And she wrote the Daniel half of *Daniel Deronda,* a book so infuriating that it drove Samuel Butler's aptly named friend Eliza Savage to remark that she had had to buy a dictionary to read it in the original. Never, of course, did Eliot disappoint us as utterly as she did in *Romola,* a book that contemporary reviewers greeted, as George Henry Lewes reports, "with a universal howl of discontent," [1] and that, in the hundred years since, escaped our censure only when it secured our neglect.

Yet astonishingly enough, Eliot herself considered *Romola* her best work.[2] She said so many times, and she said so again in January 1877 when, looking back as it happened on all the fiction she was ever to write, she remarked to her friend and publisher John Blackwood [3] about *Romola:* "There is no book of mine about which I more thoroughly feel I could swear by every sentence as having been written with my best blood" *(Letters,* VI, 335-36). It pained Eliot but it did not surprise her that so few of her readers shared her judgment. The "howl of discontent" was just what she had anticipated. To her friend Sara Hennell, Eliot wrote that "of necessity, the book is addressed to fewer readers than my previous works, and I myself have never expected—I might rather say *intended*—that the book should be as 'popular' in the same sense as the others." Indeed, Eliot saw only too clearly that after the publication of her first works her readers had formed such inflexible expectations that they could never accept anything really new from her. Again to John Blackwood she wrote that she wanted *Romola* to appear without her name. "I need not tell you the wherefore of this plan," she added prophetically; "you know well enough the received phrases with which a writer is greeted when he does something else than what is expected of him" *(Letters,* III, 330). She wrote *Romola,* she said, not because she thought her readers would like it, but because, as in conclusion she remarked to Sara Hennell, she refused to be "a machine always grinding out the same material" and because she insisted on enough artistic "freedom to write out one's varying unfolding self" *(Letters,* IV, 49).

That "varying unfolding self," it seems to me, had been moving for some time considerably beyond the narrow realism we have always assumed to be the limit of Eliot's art. Eliot meant, as she had promised to do in the famous seventeenth chapter of *Adam Bede,* to go on telling the truth as she saw it. But the truth Eliot saw was becoming more complex, less accessible, with every word, and Eliot had no sooner articulated what we have taken to be her doctrine of realism than she began to discover that the old forms could no longer express her unfolding vision. Eliot did not, of course, repudiate realism. In one sense at least, the principles that inspired her first work inspired her last. But I believe she felt increasingly that to give that "faithful account of men and things" she had once undertaken required a mirror far subtler than verisimilitude. Uncertain at first perhaps of her direction, with *The*

Mill on the Floss she began to experiment with the form and substance of her fiction in radical and striking ways until the realistic narrative, which she never abandoned, became only the prose half of a rich and encompassing poetic vision.

Poetry is not something we have ever acknowledged in Eliot's fiction. We have often observed that Eliot had what we have called poetic aspirations, but it is these aspirations that we have generally held responsible for what we have assumed to be the great blunders of Eliot's books. With Laurence Lerner, we have always believed that "even in prose, Eliot is primarily a novelist, not a poet." [4] Lerner's "even" seems to me to be significant. For perhaps we have allowed our judgment of Eliot's verse to determine our estimate of her novels. Yet the two must not be confused. Eliot's verse, as everyone knows, is poor stuff at best. Who has read *The Spanish Gypsy* without embarrassment? Clumsy and ponderous, its only merit seems to lie in the power of mind that conceived the argument, a power that does not always survive the poem's lame and halting lines. Yet in writing about *The Spanish Gypsy* to a friend, Eliot remarked that in it she seemed "to have gained a new organ, a new medium that my nature had languished for" *(Letters,* IV, 465). If Eliot was wrong about the poem's success, she was not wrong about the need she confesses, the need she had long felt for a new, a poetic voice. The error in Eliot's estimate of the poem is not, of course, negligible. But Eliot may have given us a clue to her difficulties in her essay, "Notes on Form in Art," whose date, 1868, suggests a close connection with *The Spanish Gypsy,* which was completed in that same year. The essay, which is actually a set of notes probably not intended for publication, at least not in the form in which we have it, seems an exercise in which Eliot sorted out her thoughts on the nature of poetry and verse. While not quite inconsistent, in this essay Eliot is clearly drawn in two quite different directions. On the one hand, she is inclined to the conclusion, on which she comes to rest again and again, that the chief, indeed the only, function of poetry is to express emotion. Although a common enough view to a Victorian, for which reason perhaps Eliot holds it, it is one altogether alien to her own philosophic perspective. Thus, Eliot forces herself to distinguish, by no means convincingly, between "poetic form," which, she claims, "begins with a choice of elements . . . as the accordant expression of emotional states," and "poetry," which "begins when passion weds thought by finding expression in an image."

It seems clear in the essay that Eliot identifies "poetic form" with verse, while "poetry," although it inspires "poetic form," is a far larger category, which includes "all literary production" in which "passion weds thought by finding expression in an image." Thus, although verse does not exclude thought, its end is ultimately lyrical. With such an end in mind, it is little wonder that Eliot's attempts in verse failed. It was not "emotional states," in this sense at least, that inspired Eliot. Eliot's poetic imagination was not at all lyrical but, like her realistic imagination, philosophic. Its philosophical bias is, in fact, what we have always cited as the great flaw in Eliot's verse, the burden that weighs too heavily on her poetry. Yet surely it is not Eliot's thought that is itself the flaw, but a flaw only because it subverts her attempt to achieve an opposite, a lyrical effect. The problem with Eliot's verse is not that she was too much a philosopher to be a poet but that in her verse she tried to be something she was not. When she did not aim for the lyricism of "poetic form," when she gave up writing verse, she wrote poetry that was not divided in purpose but that allowed her poetic imagination to express itself in its own natural idiom. The result is not poetic prose, not merely prose heightened by poetry, but prose poetry, or poetry in prose if we will—poetry, that is, which, although not verse, is precisely the poetry of one of Eliot's favorite poets, Dante, poetry in which thought and feeling have not only a common origin and a common end but are conceived as one. It was certainly her own poetic imagination Eliot was describing when in "Notes on Form in Art" she defined that larger category of "poetry" as characterized by the image in which passion and thought are wedded, for it was precisely in such images that Eliot wrote.

Although I obviously disagree with Thomas Pinney's interpretation of this essay in his introduction to it, I think he is right to be disturbed by it, for it does, as he suggests, ask us to reconsider our firm and long established conviction that Eliot argued for realism in fiction in the strictest, narrowest sense.[5] Indeed, the essay offers not only a summary of what may have been Eliot's long reflection on this subject but a retrospective description of her own development. Eliot's poetic imagination, which is not incompatible with realism in its broader sense, was born almost simultaneously with it. It stirred already in *Adam Bede;* in *The Mill on the Floss* it struggled to escape the boundaries of verisimilitude; and in *Silas Marner* it usurped fully half the book. But in none of these did Eliot yet find its final form. It was not until *Romola* that she discovered the full scope and power of her poetic voice. Perhaps it was the exuberance of that discovery that inspired Eliot to her repeated use of the word "image," and sometimes "symbol," in *Romola,* words that are themselves a clue to her poetic intentions and that appear often in the passages I quote from the book.

It is precisely because *Romola* is a poem that it has always displeased us most. For like Eliot's contemporaries, we too have insisted on our own very strict notion of what an Eliot novel ought to be. Assuming, as we have, that Eliot was not only a realistic novelist but always and only a realistic novelist, we have, not surprisingly, found ourselves puzzled and irritated by everything in her fiction that has not met our expectations. We have only to change our expectations, however, to discover some very remarkable things. Most of what we have taken to be the failures of Eliot's realism are, in fact, the triumphs of her poetry. It is Eliot's poetry that has troubled us in the countless quarrels we have had for over a century with *Adam Bede, The Mill on the Floss,* and even *Middlemarch.* It is Eliot's poetry that has made *Silas Marner, Felix Holt,* and *Daniel Deronda* so largely unintelligible to us. And it is because we have not recognized the relationship between realism and poetry in Eliot's work that we have divided her fiction into two very distinct halves, admiring the one, regretting the other. But Eliot's fiction is a coherent whole. If it has not seemed so to us, it is only because we have taken realism to be the end, the *telos,* of Eliot's genius. That end we have always held fulfilled in *Middlemarch,* and it is *Middlemarch* we have always used as the measure and type of Eliot's accomplishment. Yet *Middlemarch* too is as much the product of Eliot's poetic, as of her realistic, imagination, and even as such cannot hold the pivotal place in Eliot's fiction. If in Eliot's view it was not *Middlemarch* but *Romola* that was her finest achievement, it was, in part at least, because in *Romola* and nowhere else, Eliot brought the two currents of her imagination into a single stream. Whether or not we come in the end to accept Eliot's judgment of *Romola,* we must come to see it as her central work, the work—appropriately the middle of her seven novels—on which her evolution as an artist turned.

Eliot realized that with *Romola* she had entered a new stage in the development of her creative imagination. She spoke of *Romola* always as her most ambitious project, a remarkable distinction when we consider what the contenders for that superlative are. Indeed, *Romola* proved to be the most demanding and the most exhausting task she was ever to undertake.

Its composition was unusually long and difficult. In a letter to Alexander Main (the enthusiastic admirer who collected her "Wise, Witty, and Tender Sayings"), Eliot described *Romola* as "a book which was an intense occupation of my feeling as well as thought for three years before it was completed in print" *(Letters,* V, 174). In every other case, the order of publication follows the order of conception. But while the idea for this book came to her while she was still writing her first novel,[6] *Romola* was not Eliot's second, or her third. Through the end of *Adam Bede,* through *The Mill on the Floss,* through *Silas Marner,* the idea struggled in her mind, not without some effect on those works, especially on *Silas Marner,* which "thrust itself," Eliot wrote in her Journal on November 28, 1860, "between me and the other book I was meditating" *(Letters,* III, 360). It was, in fact, just before she began *Silas Marner* that Eliot had decided to start her "Italian story," as she had begun by calling *Romola (Letters,* II, 463). Returning with Lewes from their first trip through Italy from March to June 1860, Eliot wrote to John Blackwood: "When we were in Florence, I was rather fired with the idea of writing a historical romance—scene, Florence—period, the close of the fifteenth century, which was marked by Savonarola's career and martyrdom. Mr. Lewes has encouraged me to persevere in the project, saying I should probably do something in historical romance rather different in character from what has been done before" *(Letters,* III, 339). It is no surprise, however, that although "fired" by Lewes's idea, Eliot wrote *Silas Marner* first, for while *Silas Marner* did interrupt her historical romance, it did not interrupt her artistic evolution. To

John Blackwood, Eliot wrote that *Silas Marner* "came to me first of all, quite suddenly, as a sort of legendary tale." "I have felt all through," she added, "as if the story would have lent itself best to metrical rather than prose fiction ... except that, under that treatment, there could not be an equal play of humour" *(Letters,* III, 382). In essence, we have here again, of course, Eliot's distinction between poetry and poetic form, and if Eliot rejected metrical treatment for *Silas Marner,* she allowed the "legendary tale" to take its own natural poetic course. In this sense, *Silas Marner* was a preliminary exercise that "thrust itself between" her and her Italian story because Eliot was not yet ready not only to execute but to conceive the intricate pattern that her poetic imagination would require in *Romola.*

Fruitful as that exercise was, and much as Eliot learned from it, on finishing *Silas Marner* she was by no means prepared to begin writing *Romola,* for although Eliot did not yet have a precise notion of what she would attempt in her next work, she knew already that it was to be a far more complex and taxing enterprise. The more she thought of it, the more diffident she became. To John Blackwood again, Eliot wrote: "I am quite without confidence in my future doings, and almost repent of having formed conceptions which will go on lashing me now until I have at least tried to fulfil them" *(Letters,* III, 339). It was not unusual for Eliot to doubt herself, but never before or after did she experience such agonies of despair. The reason seems clear in retrospect. *Romola* was to prove to be Eliot's most radical and daring experiment, a work of a kind she had never fully attempted before. From Florence, to which she had returned to absorb the physical culture of the city, Eliot wrote again to John Blackwood on May 19, 1861: "I feel very brave just now and enjoy the thought of work—but don't set your mind on my doing just what I have dreamed. It may turn out that I can't work freely and fully enough *in the medium I have chosen*" *(Letters,* III, 417; my italics). Indeed, on returning to England, the dream seemed further away than ever. "Terribly depressed and hopeless," Eliot noted in her Diary on July 23, 1861.[7] July and August 1861, in fact, nearly saw the end of the project. On July 30, Eliot wrote in her Diary that she had been "dwelling with much depression on the probability or improbability of my achieving the work I wish to do. . . . I am much afflicted with hopelessness and melancholy just now" [8] On August 1, she was still "struggling constantly with depression" (Cross, II, 245). And on August 12 she was ready to concede defeat: "Got into a state of so much wretchedness in attempting to concentrate my thoughts on the construction of my story, that I became desperate, and suddenly burst my bonds, saying, I will not think of writing!" (Cross, II, 245).

The chief difficulty was that as an experiment *Romola* required not only the usual construction that preceded writing but formal definition as well. Until the very moment she set down the first words, and for a time thereafter as she revised the opening, Eliot was continually engaged in conceiving and reconceiving the book, not merely in substance, but generically. Time and again, her Diary entries suggest entirely new beginnings. On August 15, 1861, for example, three years after she had first noted the germ of the idea, Eliot wrote in her Diary that she had discussed the plot with Lewes and "struck out an idea with which he was thoroughly satisfied as a 'backbone' for the work" (Yale MS 3). But characteristically, the new idea, disclosing as it must have new possibilities, created even more problems than it solved. Never did Eliot procrastinate as deliberately as she did now, to such a degree, in fact, that Lewes could hardly contain his impatience. " 'The Book,' " he wrote to John Blackwood, possibly not without some irritation in his capitals, "is slowly crystallizing into what will be a magnificent programme. Until quite lately I thought she would relinquish altogether in despair, her singular diffidence being exaggerated in this case. But now I think it will really be written. *If only I could see the first chapter!" (Letters,* III, 446; my italics).

It was to be nearly another two months, however, before Eliot even attempted a first chapter, and that attempt was to prove abortive, for the moment Eliot began to write her health failed her. One can hardly doubt that Eliot's physical condition always depended greatly on her state of mind; she was seldom as ill as when she was troubled by anxiety over her work. None of her novels was written in perfect health, but through none did she complain so often and so much of general debility as through *Romola.* At the end of October 1861, she wrote in her Diary: "Not very well. Utterly desponding about my book" (Cross, II, 250). The coincidence of ill health and despondency is not accidental. Exhausted and depressed, in fact, Eliot was once more on the brink of giving the book up. On November 6, she wrote in her Diary: "So utterly dejected that in walking with G. in the Park, I almost resolved to give up my Italian novel" (Yale MS 3).

Whether or not something specific happened in the next few days to inspire her anew we do not know, but on November 10 her Diary entry reveals a new and more confident purpose. "New sense of things to be done in my novel," she wrote (Cross, II, 250). Perhaps it was because, as she wrote in her Diary on the same day, the "Italian scenes returned upon me with fresh attraction" (Yale MS 3). But it was not only memory rekindled, I think, that stirred Eliot in these last months before she began the book's final writing. She returned to her work with new vigor chiefly because after so long a struggle she had at last found the form and substance she had so long been striving to imagine. As though she had never discussed the subject with Lewes before, Eliot wrote in her Diary early in December: "I told him my conception of my story, and he expressed great delight" (Cross, II, 253). In a sense, the "conception," in its full and final form, was really new. This is evident, I think, from the Diary entries that follow and that suggest that only now has Eliot grasped her own intention. For example, on December 11 she noted, "In the morning I wrote a scheme of my book" (Yale MS 3). The "scheme" must have come to her in a flash that synthesized all her earlier thoughts, for on the next day she recorded that although it needed revision, the plot of her book was finished (Cross, II, 253). On January 1, 1862, as though in fulfillment of a New Year's resolution, and as though recalling no earlier beginnings, Eliot wrote triumphantly, *"I began my Novel of Romola"* (Yale MS 3; Eliot's italics).

Although the final writing took a year and a half—a full half year longer than did the final version of *Middlemarch*—and although illness, depression, and despair returned many times, so much so that at one point she wondered whether she had "ever before felt so chilled and oppressed" *(Letters,* IV, 17)—Eliot now wrote at least certain of her vision. She wrote with mounting intensity and came near to frenzy as she reached the last chapters. When the book was finished, she was, not surprisingly, entirely drained. Many years later she told John Walter Cross that she had begun *Romola* a young woman and had finished it an old one. It had marked the transitional moment of her life (Cross, II, 277).

That long, ardent struggle is intelligible only when we realize that *Romola* was for Eliot the book in which she discovered and fulfilled her full intellectual and artistic powers. In his splendid and seminal article, "'Romola' as Fable," George Levine has suggested that we consider various scenes and relationships in the book, not literally, but symbolically.[9] But to understand *Romola* completely, and to understand its pivotal place in the evolution of Eliot's fiction, we must do considerably more. For *Romola* is not merely a poetic novel but, in its entirety, a poem. It is a work, that is, in which the prose narrative is at the same time a symbolic narrative in which every character, every event, every detail—every word, in fact—is an image in an intricate symbolic pattern. It is indeed only through the poem that the prose acquires meaning, and only in the imagery, therefore, that all the difficulties we have so long regretted can be resolved.

Nothing, for example, has troubled us as much in *Romola* as its historical setting. Eliot's contemporary readers were as puzzled and distressed by it as we have been. The writer who noticed it in the *Westminister Review* felt quite overwhelmed by what struck him as an oppressively ample account of Florentine history and offered in explanation the view that Eliot's mind was so analytic that it needed the inspiration of direct experience, the vitality of memory, to give it a concrete foundation.[10] His view was echoed by countless others. Even the far more sympathetic Leslie Stephen saw no purpose at all to Eliot's choice of period and remarked more generally that the historical novel "is a literary hybrid which is apt to offend opposite sides. Either the historian condemns it for its inaccuracy, or the novel-reader complains of its dulness."[11]

Certainly much of the historical material in the book is for most readers remote and unfamiliar. Perhaps one of the difficulties the modern reader shares with his nineteenth-century counterpart is his scanty knowledge of the age, at least in the detail in which Eliot explored it. Ignorance breeds contempt. Yet surely the historical world cannot be more alien than a wholly invented fictional one. And surely Renaissance Italy was of all historical periods the most welcome to the Victorian reader. Italy was, indeed, in Elizabeth Barrett's words, the "siren song" of the nineteenth century, and nothing in Italian history so fascinated Eliot's contemporaries as the Renaissance. What has really troubled Eliot's readers, I suspect, then and now, is not that there is too much history but rather that we do not know what to make of it. We feel that Eliot has asked us to amass information that seems to have no bearing on the action of the book, and naturally we resent it.

We have usually blamed Eliot's scholarly inclinations for this apparent excess of erudition. We know Eliot was never satisfied to know enough. She wanted to know everything. In truth, Eliot did arm herself for this work with enviable zeal. It would be impossible to comment on all the research Eliot undertook in preparing to write *Romola.* Despite the ample notes and bibliographies in Eliot's Diaries, in her *Quarry* for *Romola,* and in her *Commonplace Book,* and despite the references and allusions in her letters, much of which I will have occasion to cite in specific instances, we do not know everything Eliot studied. The text itself suggests a far more exhaustive reading list. The knowledge that informs *Romola* is not merely the knowledge Eliot acquired in her immediate research. In a sense, Eliot had been preparing herself for *Romola* all her life. More than any other of her books, *Romola* is the product of everything Eliot thought and knew, which, as everyone has long acknowledged, was nothing less than formidable. Yet even so, she did not feel ready for this special task she had set herself. Part of her constant depression during the book's composition was her fear that she did not yet know enough to accomplish her ends. She read, reread, and read again both before and after she had begun her final writing. On her trips to Florence, especially on her second, from April to June 1861, she immersed herself in the life, idiom, literature, art, and history of the city. She and Lewes haunted the bookstalls for old volumes and read regularly in the Magliabecchian Library in records that had gathered centuries of dust. On her return to England, she continued her research in the London Library and at the British Museum, as well as in her extensive library at home, to which she added a considerable collection at this time on Italian literature and history. In that task she even engaged the goodwill of friends, who brought her books she had been unable to find herself. Above all, of course, she relied on Lewes, who read with and for her, made notes, and suffered himself to be dispatched to various libraries and museums on her behalf. Hearing of her work, John Blackwood reported to his brother that Eliot seemed "to be studying her subject as subject never was studied before" *(Letters,* III, 474). Although it seemed to Lewes that Eliot had "immensely more knowledge" of the period "than any writer who has touched it," she continued her studies at a staggering pace, prompting Lewes to urge John Blackwood to speak to her and to "discountenance the idea of a Romance being the product of an Encyclopaedia" *(Letters,* III, 474). Quite uncharacteristically, Eliot had been extremely secretive about her plans for *Romola,* and perhaps at this time not even Lewes imagined what kind of work Eliot hoped to write.

It was not because Eliot had forgotten the difference between history and fiction that she had undertaken so exhaustive a preparation. To R. H. Hutton, one of the book's better reviewers, Eliot wrote that "there is scarcely a phrase, an incident, an allusion" in *Romola* "that did not gather its value to me from its supposed subservience to my main artistic objects" *(Letters,* IV, 97). But what could those artistic objects have been that persuaded her to so risk alienating the sympathies of her readers? The issues she attacked in *Romola* were recognizably as true of the modern world as of the Renaissance. The reviewer of the *Westminster Review* regretted the historical background in part because he found it unnecessary, since it seemed to him that Eliot was probing distinctly contemporary issues.[12] In his review, R. H. Hutton noted the many points of resemblance between Romola's era and his own.[13] More recently, Carole Robinson has rightly remarked that Romola "is readily identified with the Victorian intellectual."[14] And Leslie Stephen, who thought of Romola as Maggie Tulliver's cousin, wondered why Eliot had removed Romola out of her century, the nineteenth, into the Renaissance.[15]

These questions, which have always been some of our most serious quarrels with *Romola,* are the very questions that provide a clue to the answer, an answer that Eliot herself provides, and precisely where she should, in the first paragraph of the Proem. This Proem has itself puzzled us no less than the work it introduces, and indeed it does seem a strange beginning for a novel, for it appears to have little if anything to do with the book that follows. That is perhaps why we have never listened very carefully to what Eliot tells us in it. Yet here Eliot suggests not only what the subject of her book will be but, implicitly, how we are to read it. The opening lines introduce us to an "angel of the dawn," [16] a figure that implies an interest in origins, and, as this angel surveys the continent of Europe from the Levant to the Pillars of Hercules, we realize that he is following exactly the geographic migration of Western civilization, from its beginnings in Asia Minor to its later development in the Western Isles, and even—for we learn early that the opening date of the action is 1492—across the Atlantic to the American continent. It is important to remember these opening lines when we turn to the first chapter of the book proper and find ourselves suddenly in late fifteenth-century Florence. They prepare us to see that it is not, after all, Florence in 1492 that Eliot is writing about but rather the whole history of Western civilization, of which late-fifteenth-century Florence must somehow be the symbolic representation.

Such a subject, of course, is hardly the appropriate province of a novel, and had we realized what Eliot's purpose was we would soon after have discovered that a novel is not all *Romola* is. It is not surprising that most of our arguments with *Romola* have been that it does not fit our notion of what a novel ought to be. We have articulated our discomfort in various ways. We have objected to certain scenes that seem to escape even our most generous definition of the novel form. We have complained that much of the material in the book fails to contribute to the narrative development. And we have very much disliked the way Eliot handled certain characters who seem not to belong in a novel at all. Romola herself, in fact, has always been cited as the chief offender. Nowhere have our preconceptions about Eliot's fiction so blinded us to our own insights as in our discussion of the main character. Jerome Thale, for example, restating some of the traditional arguments against Romola, and adding not a few of his own, ends by calling Romola "too epical." And the "epical," Thale concludes, raising once more the ghost that haunts the minds of Eliot's readers, "simply will not do in a realistic novel." [17] Indeed not. But it will do very nicely in an epic. For an epic is precisely what Eliot wrote. How appropriate that among the book's first readers it was Robert Browning, himself aspiring to epic vision, who understood what Eliot had done. *Romola,* Browning declared, is "the noblest and most heroic prose-poem" *(Letters,* IV, 96).[18]

I do not mean to suggest that *Romola* is not also a novel. But the novel in *Romola* is only one facet of the epic and is entirely dependent on the epic for its meaning, It was, I think, because Eliot was moving toward the epic form, that she called *Romola* a romance. The term was first suggested by Lewes, who recorded in his Journal on May 21-23, 1860: "This morning while reading about Savonarola it occurred to me that his life and times afford fine material for an historical romance. Polly at once caught the idea with enthusiasm" *(Letters,* III, 295).[19] Eliot readily accepted the term. What "historical romance" meant to Lewes it is impossible to tell from this passage, but what a work that could be so described meant to Eliot is clear from the final form *Romola* assumed, and it is not a romance, in the loose sense, which merely happens to have a particular historical setting. The words "historical" and "romance" seem to me, in fact, to point to the convergence of two traditions which together shaped the realistic novel in England. Although it has long been evident that the realistic novel in England did not, as it did in France, for example, achieve that dispassionate detachment so much commented on in the narrative stance of Flaubert, we have always read the English realistic novel much as we have read the French, holding—F. R. Leavis excepted—its passionate attachment, its moral voice, as the flaw in a purpose somehow unrealized. Yet if generic traditions are embedded in the history of the people who speak and read a particular language, it is clear that such influences as Puritanism and Evangelicalism in England carried long past the Middle Ages the allegorical impulse of the medieval romance, so strongly and so pervasively that it came even to form part of the tradition of the realistic novel. In "Realism, or In Praise of Lying," and later in "Realism Reconsidered," George Levine takes up this question, otherwise so generally neglected, and suggests that the English realistic novel was moving toward becoming a new romance, one that assimilated yet transcended realistic conventions.[20] I agree. But we must, I think, take Levine's argument considerably further.

We have of course always thought of the realistic novel as the child of the Enlightenment, engendered by the same empirical thought that inspired the historicism of the eighteenth and nineteenth centuries. It seems to me, however, that the realistic novel is not only the analogue of the historical impulse but, in fact, its heir. The large number of historical novels, as well as those novels that specify a particular historical moment in the action, whose rise coincided with the development of the realistic novel, point to a predominant concern that in greater writers became the attempt of a disinherited age—an age that was, in its own favorite fictional image, "orphaned"—to examine its own past and to determine whether that past could provide a valid creed for the present confusion. In the great novelists of nineteenth-century England, history in short was not merely a context but a subject, as indeed it became increasingly for Eliot.

It was this very interest in history that transformed for Eliot, and later for Hardy and Lawrence, the realistic into the symbolic novel. The offspring of empiricism, the realistic novel, like history, has always seemed to us concerned only with the individual and the particular, both antithetical to the eternal and transcendent inherent in the allegory of romance. Yet if the particular and the individual were the great discoveries of empiricism, the eternal and the transcendent were its great loss. And it is in just such a loss that symbolism is born. It is just when religion—the world of the eternal and transcendent—no longer commands faith, as in the skepticism of an empirical age it no longer did, that it becomes mythology, the property not of the priest but of the poet. Thus, allegory, which can speak only in the voice of certainty, is replaced by mythology, whose very genesis is doubt; and the romance becomes the symbolic novel, the romance of a secular and skeptical age.

Nothing could be more appropriate for the "historical romance" Eliot wished to write than the imagery of mythology. The poetic expression of a culture, as Vico had called it, mythology is history already in literary form, the eternal and the transcendent of religion transformed in fact by history itself into a metaphor. That on occasion Eliot enlightens a perception with a mythological allusion we have always known, and recently we have begun to suspect that those mythological allusions are not merely transient images but indeed poetic equivalents for the literal action. What we have not yet realized, however, is that there is a complex and extensive mythological structure that carries its own substantive and formal significance not only in *Romola* but in all of Eliot's books, and that through this mythological structure Eliot placed the realistic narrative in an epic persepctive.

Mythology interested Eliot long before she thought of writing fiction. The earliest letters we have of hers, written before she was twenty, allude to mythological figures, often, of course, in a studied way, designed perhaps to impress her correspondents. By the time she came to publish in the *Leader,* in September 1855, her short piece, "German Mythology and Legend," Eliot was already well acquainted with mythologies of all kinds, especially with classical mythology. Although the significance she attached to mythology is nowhere more evident than in *Romola,* it is implied very succinctly in her portrait in *Middlemarch* of Edward Casaubon. If Casaubon is a sad and often laughable figure, it is not because he aspires to find the Key to All Mythologies, but because his search is doomed. The search itself is the central metaphor of the book: it is the most important of all quests. While Casaubon will never write the book he projects, he has stumbled on the right title for it. A "Key" is just what mythology is. Like Lydgate, who seeks to find the primal tissue which is the secret of biological life, Casaubon, although he does not know it, searches for nothing less than the secret of life's meaning, a metaphor through which mankind attempts communally to order the chaos of experience and so to shape a coherent vision of human existence.

If Eliot knew not only that Casaubon was ill-suited to his task but precisely in what ways he was ill-suited, it is, of course, because she herself was not. Indeed, in the myths with which she was especially concerned in *Romola,* the Christian—and Eliot did take Christianity as a myth, as we shall see in the next chapter—and the Graeco-Roman, she had an impressive background. As I shall have reason to discuss in Chapters II and VII, Eliot's religious history made her thoroughly acquainted with every aspect of Christianity.

About that there has never been any question. We have been far less certain, however, of Eliot's familiarity with, and relationship to, the classics. Yet the evidence, not only in her letters and essays, in her Diaries and Notebooks, but on the pages of her fiction,[21] in the countless echoes, allusions, and quotations (many of which are merely incorporated into her own prose), suggests that Eliot's knowledge of the classics was remarkable. We know that she began to study Latin no later than 1839 *(Letters,* I, 29) and Greek no later than 1843 *(Letters,* I, 168), and we know that both languages and their literatures remained a lifelong passion. For Eliot, the classics became not only a body of knowledge; they entered the texture of her mind, so that the mythology of the ancients both informed her vision and was a means of expressing it.

This should not surprise us in an intellectual and scholarly Victorian. Not since the Renaissance had the classics enjoyed so extensive a revival as in the nineteenth century, which was a second Renaissance for the ancients, and never since antiquity had mythology been taken so seriously. With the exception of Vico, and in part of Herder, it was not until the nineteenth century that mythology ceased to be regarded as heresy and superstition and began to be considered, as Eliot considered it, a symbolic expression of the collective human consciousness. It is that revived interest in mythology in fact that Eliot records in Casaubon's enterprise.

Casaubon, of course, reminds us that the nineteenth century did not always hold what we consider to be the right view of the ancients—the right view being, needless to say, our own. It is true that in some instances our judgment is preferable, not always because we know more but because in certain ways we are closer today to the ancients than our Victorian ancestors and thus can read them more sympathetically. This is certainly the case with Euripides, whose psychology is far more acceptable to a world accustomed to Freudian analysis than it could have been to the ordinary Victorian mind. But Euripides, we should recall, did not fare all that well with his contemporaries either, and if nineteenth-century scholars did not fully appreciate him it was not always because they were incapable of understanding the classical mind. George Eliot cannot, in any case, be wholly identified with her contemporaries. In this as in other matters she relied chiefly on her own judgment. While she studied the works available in her time on the subject of mythology, she had read Herder and the even more radical Vico, as we shall see in Chapter II, and returned, above all, to the primary testimony of the ancients themselves.

When Eliot began to plan *Romola,* she knew the classics far better than she knew Florentine history, and therefore we do not find in her immediate preparations for the book as much concentrated study of the ancients as of the Florentine Renaissance. Yet that the ancients were constantly on her mind during these years of contemplation and composition we can be sure, for throughout her Diaries and Notebooks she recorded that she had read or more likely reread one work or another, and time and again we find her commenting, as she did in her Diary entry for November 25-29, 1862, that she was engaged in "looking up various things in the classical antiquities" (Yale MS 3). In one note in her "Recollections of Berlin," Eliot confirmed, although a text like *Romola* hardly requires it, that she understood myths as symbols. Her Journal of that journey, from November 1854 to March 1855, shows an already extensive knowledge of the classics and records a considerable acquisition of more in a country that was, of course, in the vanguard of the classical revival. It was here that Eliot first saw many Greek sculptures, that she first read Lessing, and that she sharpened her eye and appetite for the visual image that plays so important a part in *Romola,* as indeed in all her work. Having attended a performance of Gluck's *Orpheus and Eurydice,* Eliot returned to speculate, as she noted in her Journal, "about *symbolism*—how far it prevailed among the Greeks" (Yale MS 1). Although she did not grant us her speculations, the question itself is suggestive enough.

Thus, what Eliot wished to write was a novel in which the literal and the symbolic carried distinct although related stories, a realistic novel whose symbolism, however, embodied history in an eternal and transcendent form. Her purpose was not very different from Hawthorne's, and it may have been Hawthorne whom Eliot took, in some sense, as her model. Eliot had known Hawthorne long before she had begun to write fiction, and she had admired him immensely from the first. "Hawthorne," she had written in

1852, "is a grand favorite of mine" *(Letters,* II, 52). She had read *The Scarlet Letter* in 1857 *(Letters,* II, 311, n. 5) and was, therefore, acquainted with Hawthorne's discussion, in the chapter on the custom-house, of that "neutral territory" that was the special province of the romance, the territory "where the Actual and the Imaginary may meet." Undoubtedly she understood, as I think Hawthorne intended, "Imaginary" in both of its senses—to include, that is, the notion of an image. As Hawthorne explained at great length in the Prefaces to *The Blithedale Romance,* whose review in the *Westminster Review* may have been written by Eliot (although, as Haight suggests, the ascription is uncertain; see *Letters,* II, 55, n. 6), and to *The Marble Faun,* a book Eliot was eagerly looking forward to reading even as she was preparing to write *Romola (Letters,* III, 300), that "neutral territory," that "fairy precinct" is nothing else than the middle ground in which the literal and the imagistic coincide. Romance, then, as Hawthorne understood it, is the union of prose and poetry, and it is not insignificant that it was to find a setting appropriate for that union that Hawthorne chose Italy as the scene of *The Marble Faun.* Indeed, in describing "The Maypole of Merry-mount"—a work which has much in common with *Romola* in theme, subject, and treatment—as a "philosophic romance," Hawthorne provided a key to understanding both his own and Eliot's fiction: both attempted in the symbolic narrative to explore the philosophic context of the literal, a context that for Eliot, however, assumed historical dimensions.

All this Eliot suggests in the very title of her book. Whatever else an epic may be, it is, first, a work that tells the story of a people. If we read, not the literal, but the symbolic level of Eliot's narrative, we discover that the two major figures other than Romola herself, Tito and Savonarola, are not only the ordinary characters of a realistic novel but also embodiments of Bacchus and Christ. It is through these figures that Eliot represents the pagan and Christian worlds; for it was these two worlds, of course, that shaped the culture of Western civilization, the heritage that, as Eliot had announced in the Proem, was to be the epic subject of her work. This we should have guessed from Romola's name. Gordon Haight is right to wonder that Romola's name has aroused so little interest.[22] I do not think, however, that Eliot appropriated Romola's name from the name of one of the mountains that encircle Florence, as Haight suggests. For although, as Haight remarks, that mountain is included in the list entered in her *Quarry,* Eliot told us that the name of this mountain was not her source when she wrote to Alexander Main that he had correctly assumed Romola's name to be the Italian equivalent of Romulus *(Letters,* V, 174), the mythological founder of Rome.[23] Rome, the city that so haunted the imagination of the Victorians, had for Eliot not the usual romantic associations but a far more precise and substantive significance, a significance stated very clearly in *Middlemarch,* in which Eliot called Rome "the city of visible history." To "those who had looked at Rome," Eliot continued, "with the quickening power of a knowledge which breathes a growing soul into all historic shapes, and traces out the suppressed transitions which unite all contrasts, Rome may still be the spiritual centre and interpreter of the world." I think it is for this reason that Eliot named her character after the mythical figure that gave Rome its name. In Rome we are witness to "the past of a whole hemisphere" *(Middlemarch,* chap. XX), to the history, that is, of Western civilization. For it was in Rome that Greece survived and Christianity flourished, and it was from Rome, in one way or another therefore, that the Western world inherited its consciousness.

That Romola is the heir to the two great traditions of Western civilization is suggested in the fact that she receives in the course of the narrative two symbolic gifts, each a representation of one of the two cultures: from Tito she receives on the day of her betrothal a triptych on which is depicted the legend of Bacchus; from her brother Dino she receives a crucifix. These two gifts, which are also the two major metaphors of the book, identify Romola as the traditional epic hero whose character and fate encompass the life of a people. If by the conventional standards of realistic fiction Romola has seemed to us unreal, it is because Eliot did not draw her realistically but in epic and heoric proportions. To Sara Hennell, Eliot wrote: "You are right in saying that Romola is ideal. . . . The various strands of thought I had to work out forced me into a more ideal treatment of Romola than I had foreseen at the outset" *(Letters,* IV, 103-4). Undoubtedly in her earliest conception, Romola had begun as the heroine of a novel, but by the time

Eliot had worked out her epic intentions, the character had changed, had become ideal, larger than life. As a character, Romola had become as well different from life in just the way a symbolic figure differs from a realistic one. That is, the focus had shifted from verisimilitude, which Eliot did not entirely abandon, to another kind of truth—the truth that describes the course, not of an individual life but of the collective life of Western man—a collective life in which, however, the individual life is mirrored. In tracing that historical journey, *Romola* is formally indebted to the *Odyssey,* for just as Odysseus makes a real journey that has figurative significance, so Romola makes a figurative journey that has a real historical significance.

That Homer was one of the epic poets Eliot especially wished us to remember in reading *Romola* is clear from her allusions to him in the text. She reminds us in the Proem that Homer "was among the early glories of the Florentine press." The early history of printing was of considerable interest to Eliot, for the invention of the printing press, with its incalculable consequences, was a crucial event in the development of civilization, and therefore one of the many threads in Eliot's epic story. Perhaps Eliot had read Christian Friederich Harless's *Die Litteratur der ersten Hundert Jahren nach der Erfindung der Typographie,* a volume in the Eliot/Lewes library; [24] but many of the books Eliot consulted for *Romola* included information on early printings, and she often jotted down such information in her notes for *Romola.* Thus, we find in her *Quarry* the note from which she took the textual reference to Homer in the Proem; there she recorded that a "Fine copy of Homer," the "first considerable Greek book printed in Italy," was "printed at Florence in 1488."

Eliot knew Homer very well. After 1855, which seems to be the date of her first reading of Homer in Greek, as scattered entries in her Diary in June suggest (Yale MS 1), she returned to both the *Iliad* and the *Odyssey* countless times. The holdings of their library attest to the interest both Eliot and Lewes took in Homeric studies. Editions of the two epics, each in Greek with a Latin translation, and each marked and underlined in Eliot's hand (nos. 1051, 1052), are followed by commentaries such as Charles Frédéric Franceson's *Essai sur la Question, si Homère a connu l'usage de l'écriture et si les deux poèmes de l'Iliade et de l'Odyssée sont en entier de lui* (no. 752), Karl Lachman's *Betrachtungen über Homers Ilias. Mit Zusätzen von Moritz Haupt* (no. 1196), and Alexis Pierron's *La Clef d'Homère. Odyssée* (no. 1692). Eliot's love of etymological studies, which often led her to use words in her writing not in their common but in their etymological sense, sometimes to the bewilderment of the inattentive reader, must have found Lewes's copy of Philipp Karl Buttman's *Lexilogus; or A Critical Examination of the Meaning and Etymology of Numerous Greek Words and Passages, intended principally for Homer and Hesiod. Tr. and edited, with Notes, &c., by J. R. Fishlake* (no. 350) a great delight and undoubtedly very useful in deciphering some of Homer's archaic and non-Attic forms. To Lewes also belonged another book Eliot must have looked at, George Heinrich Bode's *Geschichte der epischen Dichtkunst der Hellenen bis auf Alexandros den Grossen* (no. 253), and she may have acquired knowledge of its contents from him, as was certainly the case in many other instances. It is particularly important to keep in mind that Eliot and Lewes often exchanged information and insights when we find Eliot familiar with material that, to our knowledge at least, only Lewes seems to have studied or when, for example, in examining the volumes in their library, we cannot identify which of the two acquired or read an individual entry. The contents of many volumes that carry Lewes's name or annotations appear in Eliot's fiction, and it is likely that Lewes helped Eliot in her research at home even as he was accustomed to do when he haunted various libraries for her and brought home ample notes for her work. Thus, although we do not know who bought them, it seems reasonable to assume that Eliot knew something of the material in three more general volumes on Greek literature in their library: the somewhat elementary *Les Auteurs Grecs expliques d'apres une méthode nouvelle par deux traductions Français* (no. 880); the *History of the Literature of Ancient Greece; from the Foundation of the Socratic Schools to the Taking of Constantinople by the Turks* by John William Donaldson (no. 601); and the considerably more interesting *Etudes sur l'antiquité, précédées d'un essai sur les phases de l'histoire littéraire, et sur les influences intellectuelles des races* by Philarete Chasles (no. 415).

Similarly, we assume that Eliot was familiar with another volume in the Eliot/Lewes library, Gottfried Bernhardy's *Grundriss der griechischen Litteratur; mit einem vergleichenden Überblick der römischen.* Although the library contains only the second volume, on Greek poetry (no. 200), perhaps the Leweses had originally acquired the complete work; certainly a comparison between Greek and Roman literature would have been of enormous interest to Eliot, since such a comparison would suggest essentially a comparative study of Greek and Roman culture. We know that she was concerned with the study of Roman literature while she was preparing for *Romola,* since in April 1862 she recorded in her Diary that she was reading Jean Marie Nisard's *Etudes des moeurs et de critique sur les Poètes Latins* (Cross, II, 265), undoubtedly in the well-marked copy in the Eliot/Lewes library (no. 1564). Although Eliot seems to have been especially interested in Nisard's account of the poets of the Roman decadence (Yale MS 3), in whom she may have seen reflected decadent Florentine poets like Luigi Pulci, to whom I shall return in Chapter V, there is no doubt, from the text and other sources, that Latin poets of every period contributed to the argument of the book. Not surprisingly, however, among the most important was Virgil, or one should perhaps write "Vergil," for as Nello the barber points out to Tito, the "e" spelling had so far gained the favor of the Florentines that those who preferred the "i" spelling were well advised to keep silent on that subject (III, p. 37). Like Homer, Virgil too was one of the early glories of the Florentine press. From William Roscoe's *Life of Lorenzo de' Medici,* Eliot noted in her *Quarry* that Bernardo Cennini, father of the Domenico Cennini, who is a character in *Romola,* and one of the great Florentine goldsmiths, had taken up printing when the art had been brought to Italy from Germany and had published a Virgil in Florence in 1472, historical details that are in part cited in the text (see IV, p. 42). Eliot knew Virgil as well she knew Homer, and perhaps better. Certainly she had started reading Virgil earlier. Although in September 1842 she was just beginning to enjoy the *Aeneid (Letters,* I, 147), a firmer grasp of Latin soon made Virgil one of Eliot's favorite poets. Her first copy of Virgil's *Works,* marked in her hand, remained in her library (Appendix I, no. 566) alongside Lewes's copy (no. 2242); and to Virgil, as to Homer, Eliot returned many times throughout her life.

If in one sense the journey of Odysseus informs Romola's pilgrimage, in another Eliot's conception of Romola was analogous to Virgil's conception of Aeneas. When Virgil rescued Aeneas from the obscure ranks of the Trojan army where Homer had all but forgotten him, he did so because he wanted a figure for his epic who could become an embodiment of a nation's spirit, not as Romulus had embodied it—although Aeneas, like Romola, is connected to that legendary hero as well—but as Virgil conceived that spirit at the height of Rome's greatness. Roman mythology had no such hero, and Virgil knew that to express his vision of the Roman character, of the Roman ideal, of Rome's mission, he would have to invent one. Eliot knew that too. The cultures that made up Western civilization each had its own heroes, but there was no representative of the whole that these cultures finally created. Like Virgil, Eliot had no choice but to invent a new symbol out of the old myths.

But the old myths were vital to Eliot's purpose, not only because they represented the distinct elements of Western culture, but because myths, as William Morris once remarked, were the Bibles of the people, and it was, after all, the people's story Eliot wanted to tell. Indeed, through these myths the people of the Western world spoke for themselves, and most eloquently. That alone would have been sufficient reason for Eliot to turn to mythology in her epic purpose. But mythology was essential for another and even more encompassing reason. In the same Proem in which Eliot had first announced her epic subject, the narrator had also commented on the "broad sameness of the human lot," suggesting that the human condition, in its large outlines, had presented to all men always the same experiences, the same conflicts. Human history, that is, could be seen not only as a progression of events but as in some sense a continuous reenactment of the same essential story: "hunger and labour, seed-time and harvest, love and death" (p. 1). Here, of course, Eliot has taken us beyond the historical level to the universal, to the level at which, because we speak of all time, we speak timelessly. Each of us, singly and collectively, is a variation on the eternal theme of everyman. And as Eliot's literal narrative becomes symbolic of the whole of Western history, so history itself becomes symbolic of the timeless human condition. Here, mythology was indispensable. It was only in mythology that Eliot could express in one image both the historical and the universal levels, since it is the peculiar character of mythology that it embodies both. As we have always entrusted to myth that history that we have wished to keep in our common memory, so have we always invested in myth our most profound and elusive perceptions of the essential truths of our existence. Mythology, in short, is the very idiom of the romance, for it is in myth that the actual and the imaginary meet, and in which we find the means to probe the depth of our common nature. It is for this reason that a "historical romance"—the term Lewes had first suggested to Eliot—is essentially an epic. Whether we take "historical" in its strictest sense, as an account of events that actually happened, as in *The Lusiads* of Camoëns, or in its looser sense, as an account of events that claim not actual but mythological credibility, as in Milton's *Paradise Lost,* when we root the allegory of the universal in some sort of historical narrative, we have the framework of an epic.

I have argued elsewhere that Eliot found the essence of the universal human condition in the eternal conflict between man's spontaneous passion for joy and the experience of sorrow that he discovers to be his human destiny.[25] That conflict is enacted in *Romola,* as it is in all of Eliot's fiction, in the conflict between Bacchus, the god of joy, and Christ, the Man of Sorrow. Here, in fact, we have the traditional divine level of the epic. We are accustomed to finding that divine level in gods who are called by their proper names and who are distinct from the human characters, but this is one of the areas in which we must give the poet latitude to find his own best means of expression. Eliot had good reason for this synthesis of the human and divine; it enabled her to explore, as nothing else could have, the universal implications of every concrete moment and the concrete significance of every universal symbol.

The concrete and the universal levels are even more intimately connected in another way. In the Proem, Eliot spoke of a night-student who questions "the stars or the sages, or his own soul, for that hidden knowledge which would break through the barrier of man's brief life, and show its dark path, that seemed to bend no whither, to be an arc in an immeasurable circle of light and glory" (p. 1).[26] Like the night-student—like man himself—Romola is engaged in a quest, a universal quest whose fulfillment is atemporal but one that began with the dawn of civilization and that continues still. Eliot was not, as this metaphoric approach to history might suggest, careless of the hard facts. She was too much an empiricist for that. But she did believe that the concrete facts of history embodied the universal myths, precisely as she embodied the epic poem in the historical novel. Here, as always in *Romola,* form and substance are one.

In this, Eliot's purpose clearly echoed Dante's. Like Homer and Virgil, Dante too held a special place in Eliot's regard. Eliot had learned Italian early and had begun reading in Italian by the summer of 1840 *(Letters,* I, 53). We do not know when she first read Dante. The Dante holdings in the Eliot/Lewes library are not only of little help in this respect, but are actually misleading. The *Opere minori* in the library was published in 1855-57 (no. 532), but that date seems too late for a first acquaintance. The date of the *Divine Comedy,* 1865, and the fact that it is a translation in English (no. 533), are certainly no guide to Eliot's knowledge of Dante, for we do know that she reread—and she was very specific in her entries that this was not a first reading—the *Purgatorio* in Italian through the fall of 1862 and in January 1863 (Yale MS 3)—while she was writing *Romola.* And it seems difficult to believe that the two volumes on Dante in the library, Cesare Balbo's *Vita di Dante* (no. 111) and Frédéric Antonine Ozmanam's *Dante et la Philosophie Catholique au treizième siècle* (no. 1619), were the only works Eliot had consulted on so important a poet.

As Eliot recalls Homer and Virgil early in the book, so in the first lines of the opening chapter she reminds us that we are now in the city that gave Dante birth. It is in the tradition of these three epic poets that Eliot wished her own work to be placed, not only generically, but also historically. In a significant sense, every epic speaks for its time. That is one of the missions of an epic. In each, the poet conceives his universal vision from the perspective of his own age and expresses it in the idiom of his own culture. Yet Homer, Virgil, and Dante are unique among the rest in that they spoke not only for their immediate contemporaries but for world visions that became the dominant cultures of the Western world, the cultures whose uneasy partnership it would be Eliot's purpose to explore. Although their cultures are to some degree reflected in their contemporaries as well, it is to Homer we turn if we wish to understand the essence of the Greek mind; to Virgil if we wish to distinguish the Roman mind from the Greek; and to Dante, heretic and humanist though he may have been, if we wish to grasp not merely the doctrine but the spirit of the world view of the medieval Christian vision. Similar as in some respects these three poets are, their poems are very different; in the time that separated them, Europe had been each time revolutionized by persepctives unknown to the earlier civilization.

As Virgil knew that Homer's world had passed, as Dante knew that Virgil's had passed also, so Eliot knew that in the nineteenth century Western civilization had entered a new and very different era. Another revolution had created another world that required its own epic vision. Eliot wished to speak for that modern era, as Homer, Virgil, and Dante had for theirs, and like those three great epic poets she realized that a new vision must be expressed in the forms indigenous to the world it encompassed. Had Eliot imitated the older poets more mechanically, we might more easily have discerned her purpose, but we would not then have, as we do have in *Romola,* the first distinctly modern epic. The characteristic voice of the modern age is the voice of the novel, and only in that form could Eliot articulate the vision of her time.

If it is true, then, that Eliot intended to speak for the modern world rather than for the Renaissance, we may well ask why she did not set the action of her book in the nineteenth century, a question, as I suggested earlier, we have been asking for some time, but one to which we may now formulate a very different answer. Eliot meant *Romola* to be a prophetic book, a prospectus for the future progress of Western civilization. Prophecy, of course, implies memory. Every age, as Eliot suggested in the Proem, is a point on the arc of experience whose direction can be discerned only by tracing the curvature of the arc itself. Civilization is a cumulative process. To Sara Hennell, Eliot once wrote: "I hope we are well out of that phase in which the most philosophic view of the past was held to be a smiling survey of human folly, and when the wisest man was supposed to be one who could sympathize with no age but the age to come" *(Letters,* III, 437). It was indeed part of Eliot's argument in *Romola* that in forgetting the past we inevitably lose the future. And in connection with *Romola,* Eliot remarked that "religious and moral sympathy with the historical life of man" is "the larger half of culture" *(Letters,* IV, 97).[27] Indeed, Eliot defined "culture" as the "verbal equivalent for the highest mental result of past and present influences" *(Letters,* IV, 395). Like Romola, we have inherited precious gifts, and we repudiate them only at our peril.

It was Eliot's intention, therefore, to examine the present in the context of all history, and especially in the context of Western history. Although she could not trace the entire record of some three thousand years, she could find that still point in Western history around which the millennia turned. That point could be none other than the Renaissance, for in the Renaissance, all streams converged. It was in the Renaissance that the two cultures that shaped Western civilization collided, and they collided most fruitfully in Florence. Here, the pagan world, newly rediscovered by some of the greatest men of the Renaissance, came to a bitter confrontation with a Christianity suddenly revitalized by religious movements, and one led by possibly the greatest religious figure of his age, Savonarola. Thus, in the late fifteenth century, Florence seemed to be the scene of a sudden reenactment of the currents that had separately fashioned the past and were together to fashion the future. For if the Renaissance was in one sense the culmination of two great traditions, it was also the beginning of a third. It was in the Renaissance too that the peculiarly modern perspective was born, for which, indeed, we are indebted to no single source as much as to the city of Florence. In returning, therefore, to that point at which the pagan and Christian traditions met, and in which the modern world had its origins, Eliot found the one pivotal moment in history. Thus, by setting the action of *Romola* in the Renaissance, Eliot opened her epic quite traditionally *in medias res,* in the middle, that is, of the historical period she intended to explore.

Romola is not the only epic conceived, for the subject that shapes *Romola*'s epic outlines, the progress of civilization, was a subject that increasingly preoccupied her thoughts. The poetic, mythic imagery of *Middlemarch,* foreshadowed in *Romola* and to a lesser but no less obvious extent in *The Mill on the Floss,* extends the historical context of the Reform Bill to the same millennial limits. Although in *Middlemarch* the epic does not dominate the novel, as it does in *Romola,* it is an equal and indispensable current in the book's theme. Similarly, that irritating half of *Daniel Deronda* takes up, in the same mythic and poetic way that *Romola* does, the spiritual pilgrimage of the Judeo-Christian tradition of which the English half, like the six years of Florentine history in *Romola,* is only the concrete, novelistic aspect. It is not surprising that the pattern Eliot was later to use in *Daniel Deronda* first occurred to her while she was writing *Romola:* it is the same pattern Eliot experimented with in *Silas Marner,* the story that "thrust itself" between her and her Italian book. Both *Silas Marner* and *Daniel Deronda* differ from *Romola,* however, in that in the former the novel and the epic are distinct. Although their development is parallel, the two are on the whole embodied in separate narratives that touch only at certain points. In *Romola* the two are one, whole and seamless. Perhaps it was for this reason that in retrospect Eliot though of *Romola* as her perfect book. It was the book in which the two currents of her imagination—prose and poetry, novel and epic—completely coincided.

Although Eliot was the first to use the novel in this way, she was not the last. There was to be another work very much like *Romola* in the twentieth century, Thomas Mann's *The Magic Mountain.* Mann's purpose was precisely the same as Eliot's, to explore the present in the context of the past, and to probe, at the same time, the eternal human condition. Like Eliot, Mann wished to understand the heritage of the Western world, and like her too he found the most meaningful embodiment of that legacy in Greek and Christian mythology. Mann knew very well that he was writing an epic, but he knew just as well that the modern epic must take the form of a novel.

I do not compare Eliot's book with James Joyce's *Ulysses,* despite the obvious analogies, since in many ways Joyce's purpose and method are very different. But in one respect, Joyce too is a pertinent parallel. I think it is important, not only to our study of Eliot, but to our understanding of the development of the novel in the last two centuries, to trace the evolution of the epic form through its fictional transformations. It was not merely the old conviction, never entirely abandoned, that the epic was the greatest of literary forms that persuaded nineteenth- and twentieth-century novelists to attempt epic novels. That conviction may have encouraged them, but novelists such as Eliot, Mann, and Joyce—and others too—required epic forms because they conceived epic visions, just as Homer, Virgil, and Dante had.

That it should have been Thomas Mann who wrote the work that can most fruitfully be compared with *Romola* is no accident. The two writers have far more in common than one might at first suppose. If Eliot was deeply rooted in the tradition of the English novel, as indeed she was, we must not forget that she was also profoundly influenced by German thought. That influence should be traced, not only where we have always traced it, in the philosophic content of her fiction, but where we have not, in the subjects that concerned her, in her approach to those subjects, and in the formal structures in which those subjects found expression. When she spoke of "culture" as the "verbal equivalent for the highest mental result of past and present influences," she attributed her view to her long and intimate acquaintance with the Germans *(Letters,* IV, 395). The tradition that produced Thomas Mann was in part the tradition that produced Eliot as well. If she wrote characteristically English fiction—as certainly she did in some sense—she wrote also characteristically German fiction, amazingly enough perhaps at one and the same moment.

The design of Eliot's epic is admittedly not an easy one to trace. But there is no reason that it should be. Eliot's was not a simple mind, and the progress of Western civilization is not an easy subject. The question we must ask is not why *Romola* is a difficult and complex book but rather whether it is worth the effort to understand it. For several reasons, I believe that it is.

It is worth the effort, first, not only because *Romola,* like *The Magic Mountain,* is a magnificent book, but because, like Mann's work too, it is a great humanistic document. In all her fiction Eliot had frank designs on her readers' souls, but nowhere did she pursue her ministry with such ardor as in *Romola.* We do not, of course, think of literature in such terms today, or if we do we do not like to admit it. The ridicule suffered by the Victorians' moral mission in the last decades of the nineteenth century and the first decades of the twentieth still haunts us, and not even F. R. Leavis has managed to convince us that great literature requires great moral passion. But that is precisely what Eliot offers us. It is not her only virtue, but it is the informing center of her genius, and in *Romola* we are granted perhaps its deepest and most encompassing expression.

It is worth the effort too because as an epic *Romola* is a landmark in the development of the novel, especially the English novel, and as such it may lead us to a very much-needed reassessment of the formal aspect of Eliot's art. We have never thought of Eliot as a writer particularly concerned with form. Form, in fact, is not something we have generally granted her. But through *Romola* we may come to see that Eliot had, in all her fiction, what is surely the most meaningful interest in form—form that is the shape of substance. Perhaps it is true that Eliot would not have engaged in formal experimentation for its own sake, but in looking for a way to express what is undoubtedly the most complex vision in English fiction, she did extend the limits of the novel form in unique and striking directions.

Some of Eliot's readings in the *Romola* years suggest that she may have been searching very consciously for her new form. On August 4, 1861, for example, Eliot noted in her Diary that she had begun Edward Bulwer-Lytton's *Rienzi,* "wishing to examine his treatment of an historical subject" (Yale MS 3). But the book did not satisfy her, and on August 21 she recorded that she had run through the volume and left it with a mere survey (Yale MS 3). Lewes had predicted that Eliot would "do something in historical romance rather different in character from what has been done before" *(Letters,* III, 339), and models like *Rienzi* proved entirely inadequate. Although here, as in Thomas Adolphus Trollope's *Beata,* which she read in the second half of 1861 (Cross, II, 254), and in Agostino Ademollo's *Marietta de' Ricci,* which she read in the Magliabecchian Library in Florence,[28] Eliot may have found something of the Italian flavor she was constantly looking for in various sources, nowhere among historical novels did there seem to be a prototype for her own work. It may also have been at this time that Eliot read Giovanni Battista Cereseto's *Della epopea in Italia considerata in relatione colla storia della civilta,* which is in the Eliot/Lewes library (no. 404), a book that must certainly have appealed to her imagination in its examination of the epic in the context of the history of civilization. We know that it was toward the end of 1861 that Eliot was reading Pierre-Louis Ginguené's *Histoire littéraire d'Italie,* also in the Eliot/Lewes library (no. 806), and that on November 19 she studied his account of the Roman epic (Yale MS 3). It was in those same months that Eliot read George Lillie Craik's *History of English Literature* through the end of the fifteenth century (Yale MS 3), possibly as part of her general research on background, but perhaps also because she was looking in English literature for a form contemporary with her historical setting, a form that might inspire her own efforts. One other interesting source in this connection is recorded in Eliot's *Quarry* for *Romola.* It is Sir Anthony Panizzi's *Introduction to Boiardo and Ariosto.* It was Panizzi who rescued Boiardo from centuries of oblivion, and in tracing the influence of Boiardo's *Orlando Innamorato* on Ariosto's *Orlando Furioso,* Panizzi examined the forms that contributed to both: the Arthurian romance; various classical sources; the influence of Dante, Petrarch, and so on, all of which united at last to shape the form of the two epics, a synthesis Eliot herself was attempting.

It is by recognizing the epic and poetic form of Eliot's novels that we may at last lay to rest our most disturbing suspicion about her fiction. Profoundly as we have admired Eliot, we have not yet been entirely quieted in our fears that, hide it as she would, she was at bottom a preacher. We have only to turn to Jerome Thale's discussion of *Romola* to hear, for example, that one of the chief failures of the book is its didacticism,[29] or to Carole Robinson to hear what is far worse, that the problem with *Romola* lies "in the novelist's uncertain faith in the affirmation she proposes in her effort to satisfy doubt"[30]—the didactic intention that failed, as it were. It is not only *Romola* that has suffered under such criticism, for we have said much the same thing, in varying degrees, about all of Eliot's fiction. At best, we have excused her as sinning only in her time, since no one in the nineteenth century, we have conceded, could escape the temptation to lecture.

But the fact is that Eliot did escape. And it is to settle this argument perhaps more than any other that the question of poetry must be seen as the single most important of the yet unresolved issues in Eliot's fiction. If we have thought Eliot didactic, it is only because we have not probed her moral vision far enough. It is wise to remember that Eliot's moral vision has seemed to us increasingly subtler, less didactic, as we have moved in the past hundred years from the surface of her fiction—where it once seemed to us that she was preaching the simple Christian truisms—to its less obvious implications. The deeper we go, the clearer it is that it is not maxims and aphorisms that Eliot offers us, nor even, in fact, philosophic propositions, but perceptions so elusive that they must forever, as the narrator of *Romola* says, remain inarticulate (XXXVII, p. 341).

It was precisely because the perceptions Eliot wanted to convey were of necessity inarticulate that she became a poet. What cannot be said must be implied. Eliot spoke the truth obliquely because the truth itself is oblique. The faithful account that Eliot wished to give of things-as-they-are was beyond the grasp of literal prose. It was realism, after all, that lied, and poetry that called things by their proper names. Not paradoxically, it was the literal narrative that was the metaphor, and the metaphor that was the thing itself, the center through which the literal narrative could be rightly understood.

If the key to Eliot's fiction is poetry, as I believe it is, the key to Eliot's poetry is *Romola,* not only because *Romola* is her most complete venture in poetry, but because in *Romola,* and nowhere else, can we find what I hope to provide in the chapters that follow, a methodological approach to the full range of Eliot's poetic imagination, and a quarry of all the myths that were the central poetic images of her fiction.

2.

The Greek, Roman, and Christian Worlds

Like the night-student of the Proem who hopes to discover that his life, the life of mankind, is an arc in an immeasurable circle of light and glory, and indeed like many great epic heroes, Romola is engaged in a journey and a quest. The stages of that journey are foreshadowed in Piero di Cosimo's sketch of the three masks. This pictorial prophecy, given to us very near the opening of the book, is also a clue to Eliot's method in *Romola* in that it asks us from the beginning to think in images. That images, and especially pictorial images, should characterize a work set in Renaissance Florence, one of the greatest artistic centers in Western history, can be no surprise. The study of Florentine art was a major enterprise in Eliot's preparation for Romola. In Florence, Eliot spent much of her time in museums and in wandering the streets that displayed so much of the art and architecture of the Renaissance (see, for example, the account in Cross, II, 167-79). In England, too, Eliot took advantage of what was available to her, especially at the British Museum, and above all in her own library. In the Eliot/ Lewes library we find such general histories of art as Jean Jacques

François Coindet's *Histoire de la Peinture en Italie* (no. 257), Sir John Charles Robinson's *Italian Sculpture of the Middle Ages and Period of the Revival of Art: A Descriptive Catalogue* (no. 1851), and Jean Baptiste Louis George Seroux's *History of Art by its Monuments, from its Decline in the Fourth Century to its Restoration in the Sixteenth* (no. 1994). Alexis François Rio's *De la Poésie Chrétienne dans son Principe dans sa Matière et dans ses Formes de l'art, peinture* (no. 1831) must have been of special interest to Eliot, as she herself attempted to suggest the Christian vision through pictorial images. And the *Memoire dei piu insigni Piltori, Scultorie e Architetti* as well as the *Scritti vari* of Vincenzo Marchese (nos. 1387, 1388), whom Eliot was studying in the second half of 1861 (Cross, II, 254), were probably among her major sources. The library also contains many specialized works, such as Rio's study of Leonardo da Vinci and Marchese's account of San Marco; and Eliot's *Quarry, Commonplace Book,* and Diaries are filled with notes on artists and their works, as well as commentaries on them, including extensive notes from Ruskin's *Stones of Venice* on the influence of Greek, Roman, and Arabic forms on Christian architecture, a subject that in a small way parallels Eliot's interest in tracing cultural currents (Yale MS 6).

Eliot did not, of course, neglect the most obvious source, Vasari's *Lives,* which she cited in one of the bibliographies in her *Quarry,* and from whose account of Piero di Cosimo she seems to have taken her characterization of the painter. Piero is not the only artist we meet in *Romola.* Many of the artists alive and in Florence between 1492 and 1498, the terminal dates of the action, make at least a brief appearance, and some who do not, like Leonardo da Vinci, assume an indirect but important role in the book's argument. Much of the narrative itself is pictorial, and although Eliot's paintings of her scenes is so eclectic that we cannot always identify them with any single work, echoes of various paintings, sometimes acknowledged or suggested, haunt her descriptions and allusions (see, for example, Chapters IV, V, and VII).

As far as we know, for Piero's canon is by no means certain, Piero di Cosimo did not produce anything exactly like the sketch of the three masks, and certainly it is reasonable that for so central a metaphor Eliot would have wished to invent her own symbolic pattern. William J. Sullivan has recently rescued this important image from the neglect to which it had been abandoned and has corrected some of the casual interpretations it has been given. Piero's sketch is a subtle prediction, a riddle which only the narrative of Romola's, and mankind's, history can unravel.

The three masks in the sketch are: "one a drunken laughing Satyr, another a sorrowing Magdalen, and the third, which lay between them, the rigid, cold face of a Stoic" (III, p. 36). Tito, utterly incapable of grasping the meanings of symbols, clever though he is, significantly misreads the sketch. But for the reader too it is a difficult parable that functions on many levels. It is dangerous, as Sullivan warns us, to rest an interpretation of the sketch on equations of these masks with single characters in the book; rather, they represent different visions of life.[1] But these visions are associated with individual characters, and particularly so from the point of view of Romola's development.

The first mask, since the satyr is a Bacchic figure, suggests Tito. The second, in Piero's sequence, seems to allude to Bardo, who is a Stoic. The third is a more difficult and complex symbol. Certainly it must be seen primarily as a general representation of the Christian vision to which Romola will be converted by Savonarola. In some sense, in fact, it will be Romola herself who will become the sorrowing Magdalen. But the image points in an ironic way to Savonarola as well. As the symbol of the redeemed sinner, Magdalen is the very essence of the Christian religion for which Savonarola speaks. On another level, however, Savonarola is also the pure prostitute, as we shall see in Chapter VIII. For now, let us return to Romola. If I interpret the masks correctly, they announce at the very start of the book, not only the worlds of the three men who dominate the first three periods of Romola's life, but, in their placement, the relationship these worlds have to one another. In the center, the Stoic's mask mediates between the Bacchic and Christian figures on either side. Thus, the first stage of Romola's life, the Bardo stage, will provide the rational criteria by which Romola will later evaluate both Tito and Savonarola. For, as the sketch also implies, it will be the other two who will compete for her allegiance.

For the fourth stage of Romola's life there is no mask in Piero's sketch. In itself, a mask suggests both a revelation and a disguise. Like theatrical masks, those of Piero's sketch capture the characteristic expression of the three figures they represent, and so focus on their essential natures. Yet at the same time they obscure the subtler, living flesh beneath, and it is this deeper, more elusive substance that Romola will touch in her final phase when she confronts at last the ultimate, inarticulate, empirical fact. This too is foreshadowed in Piero's work in the Christ child on whose lap the three masks rest.

Thus, the first three stages of Romola's life will finally prove to be experiments that prepare her for the last, and something of the moral value of these experiments is immediately suggested in the appearance of the masks themselves. For they are drawn, clearly, in very different styles, and in the order in which they are placed they trace a progression. The first experiment, Bacchus, is represented in caricature as a drunken, laughing satyr in whom we recognize the potential corruption of the Bacchic life. This sketch is indeed the only one that truly resembles a mask, and very appropriately, for the mask is a conventional element of the Bacchic ritual. The second, the Stoic, in the rigid, cold face that recalls a marble statue, stands, as we might expect, apart from the others, in impassive indifference to what surrounds it. The third, the Christian image, most nearly resembles a portrait. It is in this face of the sorrowing Magdalen that we perceive the first human note, the note that will be at last fulfilled in the figure of the Christ child who guides the last steps of Romola's pilgrimage. Piero's sketch, therefore, is a pictorial synopsis of the history of Western civilization on which the remainder of the book will elaborate.

Like Western civilization, Romola has her beginnings in the Graeco-Roman world. This entire period that precedes Romola's conversion to Christianity represents, on the historical level, the whole of the pagan era of civilization. In this portion of the book Eliot tells the first part of her epic story, and her chief concern here is to explore and assess the first of the two cultures that shaped the Western world. The dominant characteristic of this world is light, for it is light, as Baldassarre remarks when he regains his memory for a brief moment, that is the mother of the distinguishing features of the ancient Western civilizations, knowledge and joy (XXXVIII, p. 346). And it is indeed knowledge and joy that mark the two most important pagan figures of the book, Bardo and Tito.

We are introduced first to Bardo's world, the world not of joy but of knowledge. In using Bardo as both a Renaissance and a pagan figure, Eliot followed her habitual practice, as we shall see throughout *Romola,* of suggesting historical parallels by embodying in one figure two distinct historical periods. Bardo is, in fact, a real historical figure who belonged to an illustrious Florentine family, the Bardis, whose history Eliot studied in several accounts. Some of the material she used in *Romola* comes from the *Trattato delle famiglie nobili fiorentine* by Scipione Ammirato, a sixteenth-century Florentine, author of a number of histories and other works, whom Eliot was reading through December 1861 (Yale MS 3), just before she began the final writing of the book. A more important source, however, was the *Osservatore fiorentine* by the eighteenth-century writer Marco Lastri, whose book, although chiefly a guide to the monuments of Florence—and as such an invaluable treasure of information on the city's architecture—contained as well ample accounts of other historical material. Eliot began Lastri in the summer of 1861, "intending to go regularly through it," a task she apparently accomplished if her Diary entries are any indication (Yale MS 3). How useful the book was for her may be gathered from the pages and pages of notes from Lastri we find in her *Quarry* and from the fact that she returned to Lastri while she was reading Ammirato, in December 1861, and even in January 1862 (Yale MS 3), just as she was writing Bardo's story. It was neither Ammirato nor Lastri, however, who was her main source of information on the Bardi family. Eliot acknowledged in the text of *Romola* that her greatest debt, at least for the earlier history of the family, was to Giovanni Villani (V, p. 47), a late-thirteenth- and early-fourteenth-century Florentine historian. The copy of Villani's *History of Florence* in the Eliot/Lewes library was marked by Eliot (no. 2225), and it is clear, from a letter to T. A. Trollope, for example, that the book was not only an important part of her research but that she read it with the utmost care *(Letters,* III, 431). Little wonder. Like so many of Eliot's sources, Villani shared her own perspective.

Although it focuses on Florence and on the events of his own time, his book is a universal history that attempts to understand the contemporary world in terms of the past that created it. And one might add here, in support of the quality of Eliot's scholarship, that like most of her sources again, Villani is the best historian for the period, and has not yet, in fact, been superseded.

Although Bardo's world lacks much to make it attractive, there is a good deal to be said for it. Bardo himself is in many ways a fine man, one whose "proud sincerity and simplicity of life . . . made him one of the few frank pagans of his time" (XV, p. 161). "Pagan" is a deliberately encompassing word, for in Bardo, Eliot united one aspect of the entire ancient world. Although Bardo is primarily a Roman and represents primarily the Roman world, as Tito represents the Greek, Eliot took great care to remind us in countless ways that Roman culture was, in some vital respects at least, a reincarnation, or more accurately an Italian translation, of Hellenic culture. Here we begin to trace the currents of Western civilization which, in passing from Greece to Rome to Florence, created in the Renaissance Bardo a characteristic Roman with clear Hellenic features.

As the embodiment of the world of knowledge, Bardo is the chief spokesman, not of reason which is more abstractly represented in Nello, but of the rational life. We might call Bardo a Roman Apollonian. In some ways, he recalls the Greek ideal, however far he may be from attaining it. His pride, his fierce individualism, his passion for learning are his Hellenic heritage. So too is his love of preeminence (V, p. 48), which grows out of a desire to gain the respect of his fellow citizens. Homer would have said that Bardo strove after *arete,* the achievement of excellence that is rewarded by public recognition. *Arete* was of paramount importance to a Greek: Agamemnon fought for it, even when it meant the sacrifice of his own daughter; Achilles chose to die for it in the prime of his youth; and when he was not awarded the armor of Achilles, Aias went mad because he thought he had lost it. It is important to remember this if we wish to understand why it is so crucial to Bardo to leave his library as his memorial in Florence, and why that request is so binding an obligation on Romola. When Tito betrays his promise to fulfill that wish, he not only robs Bardo of the only immortality Bardo believes in, but even more, he obliterates forever the visible evidence that proved Bardo's worth.

In his ethics, Bardo is characteristically Roman; he is, like the characteristic Roman, a Stoic. Eliot's knowledge of Western philosophy, from ancient times to modern, has long been granted, and there is no need therefore to present her philosophic credentials here. Neither is it necessary to establish that Eliot's fiction is profoundly informed by her philosophic perspective. But in *Romola* philosophy not only informs Eliot's thought; it is itself a subject in the book. Eliot took up many philosophic traditions in the course of the narrative, from Platonism to Utilitarianism, and she made Bardo a Stoic, not merely to characterize his temperament, but to introduce one of her major themes.

It was surely because philosophy was to be a major theme that we find Eliot reading and rereading philosophical works as she prepared for *Romola.* Through November and December 1861, again just as she was about to begin writing the Bardo section, Eliot devoted considerable time to the study of the great Stoic manual, the *Enchiridion* of Epictetus (Yale MS 3), from which, in fact, Bardo himself often quotes (see, for example, V, p. 59). The Eliot/Lewes library contained three copies of Epictetus, two in Greek with Latin translations (nos. 664, 665), and a third in Greek only, which must have been the text Eliot used, since it is marked and annotated in her hand (no. 666). In these same months Eliot read the work of another Stoic, Cicero's treatise on duty, the *De Officiis* (Yale MS 3), her copy of which is also marked with her notes (Appendix I, no. 521). Cicero is well represented in the Eliot/Lewes library, and most of the volumes seem to have been acquired by Eliot. Indeed, although the English translation of selections from Cicero appears to have been their common property, the Latin volumes carry the signature "Mary Ann Evans," which suggests an early acquisition. We find that signature not only on the flyleaf of the *De Officiis* but in a copy of Cicero's *De Natura Deorum* (Appendix I, no. 520) and in a volume of his complete works (Appendix IV, p. 255). It is likely that the work of another Stoic, Marcus Aurelius, was an even earlier acquisition. Eliot's copy of his *Meditations,* underlined by her with marginal notes (no.

85), is in an English translation, a substitute for the original which Eliot would not have preferred after she had learned to read Latin well.

Characteristically, Eliot's study of Stoicism traces a historical progression which marks the evolution of an idea, an idea that is brought up to the period of the Renaissance in Eliot's reading of Poggio Bracciolini, whose *Epistolae* she studied in December 1861 (Yale MS 3), probably in the annotated copy of that work in the Eliot/Lewes library (no. 2365). In some ways, Poggio is a gloss on Bardo. Bardo himself, who seldom approves of anyone in whom he does not recognize his own reflection, acknowledges the affinity when, despite some minor reservations, he pronounces Poggio "admirable" (V, p. 55). Although not entirely a Stoic, Poggio had strong Stoical inclinations and shared with Bardo not only a militant humanism but a consuming interest in the collection of ancient manuscripts. Indeed, Poggio accomplished much of what Bardo hoped to; he was responsible for the discovery of many classical manuscripts and thus left as his memorial a great scholarly library.

Bardo's Stoicism is evident in his discipline, his honesty, and his sense of justice. Committed to a life of reason and moderation, Bardo reminds us of the simplicity of the Roman in the days of the republic, before the corruption that led to the fall of the empire. The judgment Romola passes on her father at the end of the book is a fair assessment of his character. "My father," she says, "had the greatness that belongs to integrity" (Epilogue, p. 599).

It is that integrity that makes the greatest legacy of Stoicism, and one of the greatest legacies of Rome, in Eliot's view, and it is that legacy that Bardo has, ironically, passed on not to his son, in whom he had hoped to see himself reborn, but to his daughter. But Romola has inherited Bardo's Hellenic virtues as well. Like her father, she has a true love of homage (XIII, p. 143); and like the old Greek heroes Bardo so admires, she is endowed with a "man's nobility of soul" (V, p. 57). It is difficult for Bardo to concede that comparison, for he does not take girls very seriously, and surely there is considerable feminist militancy in Eliot's portrait of Romola and of her relationship to her father. Like so many of Eliot's women, Romola dreams of becoming more than she is allowed to be. She would like, she says at one point, to become as learned as Cassandra Fedele (V, p. 56), a figure about whom Eliot copied into her *Quarry,* from William Roscoe's *Life of Lorenzo de' Medici,* "one of the first scholars of the age—corresponded with Politian." The education of women was a subject of great interest to Eliot, and perhaps in connection with Romola she consulted Jules Michelet's *Introduction à l'histoire universelle, suivie du discours d'ouverture pronouncé en 1834 a la Faculté des Lettres et d'un fragment sur l'èducation des femmes au moyen-âge.* The volume (no. 1455 in the Eliot/Lewes library) is heavily marked by Lewes, and this may be one case among many in which Eliot relied for information on a book that shows only Lewes's hand.

Although Romola never does rival Cassandra Fedele, she is far better educated than most young women of her day and, although not a scholar, she is able to read and understand the classics well enough to internalize them. That, of course, is Eliot's chief point. If classicism does not in Romola become scholarship, it becomes something far more important, a clear critical intelligence, as R. H. Hutton rightly observed in his review of the book, which acts as a tool that helps her always to sift the true from the false.[2] For it was that critical intelligence, in all its many forms, that was, in Eliot's view, the highest gift of the ancients.

In Bardo's world, there is no deliberate cruelty, no corruption of the soul. Yet Bardo is not fortunate, and he is acutely aware of that fact. Listening to Tito tell of his travels through Greece with Baldassarre, Bardo impatiently interrupts to ask: "Was he fortunate?" (VI, p. 69). The question echoes the final line of *Oedipus Tyrannos,* which itself echoes Solon's words to Croesus in Herodotus, "Count no man happy until he is dead," words that so fully express the Greeks' sense of the mysteries of fortune. But Bardo's misfortunes are not entirely inexplicable, since he is in part responsible for them. If he fails to meet even his own standards, it is not for the reasons he gives. That "great work," he says to Romola, "in which I had desired to gather, as into a firm web, all the threads that my research had laboriously disentangled, and which would have been the vintage of my life, was cut off by the failure of my sight and my want of a fitting coadjutor" (V, p. 54). That he has not been able to gather the threads of his knowledge into a coherent web, the metaphor in Eliot that always suggests the synthesis of meaningless fragments into a significant whole, tells us more than Bardo realizes. Like Casaubon in *Middlemarch,* whom he foreshadows, Bardo is always on the verge of insight, yet he is never able to cross that stubborn threshold. And as in Casaubon's case, the obstacles are not altogether external. It is the absence of neither his sight nor his son that ultimately hinders Bardo. His work lacks the same key that Casaubon's lacks. Bardo's knowledge, like Casaubon's, is incomplete, not in his case because he has been remiss in scholarship, but because he does not truly understand the past he so faithfully attempts to record. Collecting the data he gathers in the pigeonholes of his mind, Bardo cannot rise to vision. He has information, but he is unable to encompass knowledge, to find meaning. The past that Bardo resurrects, therefore, is a dead past.

It is for this reason that Bardo is, historically, doomed. It is perhaps appropriate that we should find Bardo working on Thucydides (XI, p. 126). The Eliot/Lewes library included a Greek copy of Thucydides (no. 2147), a French translation (no. 2148), and an English translation by Benjamin Jowett (no. 2149), whom Eliot was later to meet, published in 1879. Thucydides is only one of the many historians Eliot recalled in *Romola* in reminding us of her own historical purpose; and it was Thucydides, of course, who in *The Peloponnesian War,* described the event that was to be the end of the Golden Age of Athens and therefore the end of the great age of Greece. That end is implied in Bardo. For Romola, Bardo's world will later be replaced by Savonarola's, and in a very early letter Eliot explained precisely why this was historically inevitable. "The 'Romantiker' or Romanticist," Eliot wrote to Sara Hennell in July 1848, "is one who in literature, in the arts, in religion or politics endeavours to revive the dead past. Julian [the Apostate] was a romanticist in wishing to restore the Greek religion and its spirit when mankind had entered on the new development, the nearer approach to the imago state of Christianity." The letter continues with a quotation from David Friedrich Strauss's *Julian der Abtrünnige:* "Christian writers have disfigured the death scene of Julian. They have represented him as furious, blaspheming, despairing and in his despair exclaiming—*Thou* hast conquered, O Galilean. . . . This phrase, though false as history, has a truth in it.

It contains a prophecy—to us a consoling prophecy—and it is this: Every Julian i.e. every great and powerful man who would attempt to resuscitate a state of society which has died, will infallibly be vanquished by the Galilean—for the Galilean is nothing less than the genius of the future!" *(Letters,* I, 270-71).[3] Like Julian, Bardo attempts to rescue a dead past.

The pagan past is not, however, intrinsically dead in Eliot's view. Early in the book, Nello the barber, quoting Angelo Poliziano, had provided a touchstone against which we might measure at least one true function of paganism when he had spoken of the old "gods awaking from their long sleep and making the woods and streams vital once more" (III, p. 34). That vitality, however, Bardo cannot share, for it is not the living spirit of the gods Bardo worships but their dead forms. In his library, therefore, Bardo sits "among the parchments and marble, aloof from the life of the streets" (XI, p. 120)—aloof, that is, from the life of his contemporaries in whom flows the stream of history. It is for this reason that Eliot describes his library as a grim and sepulchral place, a dark room in which are scattered truncated torsos, severed limbs, and objects of pale and somber color. It is the home of "cold marble" that is "livid with long burial" (V, pp. 49-50), the tomb of "lifeless objects" (V, p. 55).

Bardo's library is, of course, the very symbol of the past, the repository of history. The fact that for Bardo it is nothing but a tomb suggests not only that he betrays the past but that he betrays the Renaissance as well, for the historical significance of the Renaissance is its rediscovery not of a dead but of a living past. How ironic, then, that Bardo should castigate Romola for not having sufficient strength to carry the heavy volume of Callimachus (V, p. 54), for it is not Romola but Bardo who falls short of that ancient model. Eliot had noted in the *Quarry* that in 1494 there had "appeared in Florence a magnificent edition in capitals of the Greek anthology and the poem of Apollonius Rhodius. And in the same style some tragedies of Euripides and the hymns of Callimachus." Although these hymns, written in the style of the Homeric hymns, make a further ironic comment on Bardo, who is unable to participate in the epic journey, it is not the poetry of Callimachus that Eliot recalls here but his connection with the library at Alexandria. Unlike Callimachus, who in the third century B.C. made an enormous contribution to that already remarkable library by cataloguing its holdings in literature with such ample annotations that he produced the first literary history, Bardo cannot put his own library, or his own mind, in order.

With wonderful economy, Eliot suggested in Bardo both the greatness of the revival of learning in the Renaissance and its failures; just as Bardo's aspirations imply the Renaissance ideal, so his inability to realize them implies its shortcomings. It is not the revival of learning itself that Eliot questions here. As the very genesis of a new age in history, as well as a reassimilation of the past, the revival of learning was of great interest to her, and she read considerably in this area in preparation for *Romola,* not only in the many histories of Renaissance literature, but in several other volumes. Through the spring and summer of 1861, for example, she studied Gibbon, whose *Miscellaneous Works* we find in the Eliot/Lewes library (no. 802), on the revival of learning (Yale MS 1). In her *Quarry* she entered in one of her bibliographies for *Romola* the *Delizie degli eruditi toscani,* assumedly Giovanni Lami's, as well as Christian Meiners's *Lebensbeschreibungen berühmter Männer aus den Zeiten der Wiederherstellung der Wissenschaften,* a book in the Eliot/Lewes library (no. 1435), and one of the many volumes marked only in Lewes's hand that Eliot used.

It is in such histories, of course, that Bardo himself hopes one day to be remembered, but in a delighfully satiric chapter called "A Learned Squabble" Eliot suggests the vanity of that dream. The chapter, which relates the correspondence between Bartolommeo Scala and Angelo Poliziano, caricatures the kind of work that engages Bardo's mind by reducing Renaissance scholarship to its most pedantic level. As always, Eliot chose her historical characters carefully. Like Bardo, with whom he is a virtual contemporary, Poliziano is a humanist, and in this sense therefore a true man of the Renaissance. Unlike Bardo, however, Poliziano did make an enormous contribution to the learning and literature of his age. Educated under the patronage of Lorenzo de' Medici, and later tutor to the young Medicis, Poliziano shared in most of the remarkable achievements of Lorenzo's circle. Like Lorenzo himself, for example, he was one of the leaders in the movement for the use of the Tuscan vernacular, a subject to which I will return in Chapter VI, in which he himself wrote some works of considerable merit. One of these was the *Orfeo,* a play that appears at several crucial moments in *Romola,* as we shall also see in Chapter VI. Eliot read the *Orfeo,* along with the *Stanze* (the copy that contains both is in the Eliot/Lewes library, no. 2358) in November 1862, and noted in her Diary that she thought the latter "wonderfully fine for a youth of 16. They contain a description of a Palace of Venus which seems the suggestion of Tennyson's Palace of Art in many points" (Yale MS 3). More than a year earlier, she had already begun Poliziano's *Epistolae,* which occupied her for many months, beginning her study perhaps in the 1622 edition that we find in the library, a copy well marked in Eliot's hand (no. 2356), but continuing surely in the Aldine edition (no. 2357), over whose arrival she rejoiced on December 19, 1861 (Yale MS 3). In addition to other works by Poliziano, one of which I will cite shortly, Eliot was prompted by her reading of Henry Hallam's *Introduction to the Literature of Europe, in the Fifteenth, Sixteenth and Seventeenth Centuries* (a copy of which, with copious notes and underlinings by Lewes, was included in the Eliot/Lewes library, no. 927) to read a book Hallam often mentioned, Christian Meiners's *Lives of Mirandola and Politian* (Yale MS 3). (Pico della Mirandola, if by report only, does appear later in the narrative.) Although less important than Poliziano, Scala too is a major historical figure who played a creditable role in the Florentine Renaissance, chiefly in a political capacity as the Segretario of the city, and Eliot went to the British Museum to look up Domenico Maria Manni's *Life of Bartolommeo Scala* in February 1862 *(Letters,* IV, 15), shortly before she began writing the chapter of his quarrel with Poliziano.

While in addition to her considerable reading in the literature of the Florentine Renaissance, Eliot consulted numerous secondary sources, the work that seems to have served as her chief general reference was Girolamo Tiraboschi's *Storia della letteratura italiana,* a long, ample history of Italian literature from the time of the Etruscans to 1700, thirty-one years before Tiraboschi's birth. Eliot read Tiraboschi continually through the summer and fall of 1861, sometimes for many hours a day, making notes and copying extracts (Yale MS 3). It is no surprise that this book should have pleased her better than all others, for Tiraboschi had, like Eliot, a mind quick to discern large historical movements and a profound interest in tracing their evolution. His work is a remarkable literary history and remains a standard source.

The quarrel between Scala and Poliziano suggests the ambivalence that makes these two figures glosses on Bardo. Eliot seems to have taken the background of the hostility between the two from William Roscoe's *Life of Lorenzo de' Medici.* In her *Quarry,* she summarized from Roscoe the quarrel the two had long been engaged in, a quarrel that began when Scala refused to allow his daughter Alessandra to marry Poliziano. With appropriate fictional embellishment, that summary appears in *Romola* at the opening of the chapter. In her *Quarry* too, and from the same source, Eliot commented on Poliziano's practice of attacking his enemies in outrageous epigrams, and it is in such epigrams that the learned squabble is carried on. Epigrammatically competing in the hope that each might discredit the other, Scala and Poliziano debase not only the literary form but, of course, themselves. Although they attempt to imitate the ancient epigrammatists, they succeed only in proving how degenerate the ancient tradition has become. The competition reaches its climax at last when Scala permanently disgraces his literary reputation by sending Poliziano a Latin epigram with a false gender. It is not of such pedantry that the great classicism of the Renaissance was made, but it is in such pedantry that Bardo himself is entangled, a pedantry whose pettiness corrupts not only the mind but, as Scala and Poliziano testify, the soul also. Although Bardo himself escapes that secondary corruption for the most part, how closely he risks it is suggested when Bardo recalls one of his teachers, Filelfo (V, pp. 53-54), a Renaissance scholar whom Eliot was studying in the second half of 1861 (Cross, II, 254), and whose works we find in the Eliot/Lewes library (nos. 1682, 1683). Although a brilliant writer and scholar, and in principle at least a great humanist, Filelfo was, unfortunately, a thoroughly unprincipled man who, like Poliziano, was passionate in his study of the ancients but even more passionate in his venomous attacks on those he considered his enemies.

Whatever their intellectual contribution, such men plant the seeds of their own destruction. That this world is, in fact, about to come to an end Eliot assures us in the first chapter in which the narrator announces the death of Lorenzo de' Medici. Lorenzo, the center of intellectual activity in Florence and the patron of many of the characters present and alluded to in *Romola,* defines the Renaissance in its pagan character. Indeed, when Bardo hears of Lorenzo's death, he remarks, prophetically, that "a new epoch has come to Florence," one that will be, from his pagan point of view, a "dark one" (VI, p. 77). Bardo does not understand that the only future possible for the pagan past is one that can be assimilated into the next historical stage, the Christian Florence about to be born under Savonarola. In that future, therefore, Bardo can have no share. He has already disowned it in disowning his son for becoming a Christian, and in that act he has disowned the present as well, the link that binds the past to the future, for Bardo has only contempt for his contemporaries, whose work he considers "superfluous and presumptuous attempts to imitate the inimitable." For Bardo, nothing can equal the "supreme productions of the past" (V, p. 55). He allows only one exception, the "divine Petrarca" (V, p. 57), but not only is Petrarch too long dead in Bardo's day, he is not altogether a good choice in this context. Eliot had read Petrarch's poetry very early, in a copy in the Eliot/Lewes library (Appendix I, no. 552; the library also contains another copy of Petrarch's poetry, perhaps Lewes's, no. 1672). But in preparing to write *Romola* she was more interested in Petrarch's letters, which she read in the second half of 1861 (Cross, II, 254). Perhaps the reason for Eliot's interest, and the basis of the connection she made between Bardo and Petrarch, can be found in a note she entered in her *Commonplace Book* commenting on Petrarch's contempt for women and indentifying him as a misogynist (Yale MS 6). He shares that distinction, of course, with Bardo himself, and it is a particularly misogynistic passage that Bardo quotes to Romola from Petrarch (V, p. 57). While the sentiment is not unusual in men of either Petrarch's or Bardo's day, it is a somewhat ironic one in the context of this book, since it is a woman, Romola, who carries, and even pioneers, civilization. The irony is compounded when Bardo remarks that Petrarch's words derive from Plautus's *Aulularia* (a French translation of Plautus was included in the Eliot/Lewes library, no. 1701), and when he adds that Plautus owed the passage to the Greek dramatics, for here again is a thread in history, a sequence of cultural inheritance that traces the evolution of Western civilization, although here not in its best aspect.

Bardo's misogyny, given the context, carries metaphorically the same significance as his remark that to him his now Christian son is in effect dead. And since Bardo repudiates the future, we are not surprised to hear that, by his own confession, he prefers to live with ghosts. "For me," he tells Romola proudly, "even when I could see it was with the great dead that I lived; while the living often seemed to me mere spectres—shadows dispossessed of true feeling and intelligence" (V, p. 53). It is because Bardo lives with the dead that he fails to understand history. He does not understand mythology either and misinterprets a crucial passage from Poliziano's *Miscellenea,* a passage that tells the story of the blind Teiresias, a figure with whom Bardo identifies, and not only because they share the same affliction. Commenting on that part of the story that speaks of Teiresias being blinded for having seen Minerva undressed but being granted, in exchange, the power of prophecy, Bardo remarks that it "is a pure conception of the poet; for what is that grosser, narrower light by which men behold merely the petty scene around them, compared with that far-stretching, lasting light which spreads over centuries of thought, and over the life of nations, and makes clear to us the minds of the immortals who have reaped the great harvest and left us to glean in their furrows" (V, p. 53). Clearly, for Bardo history has long ago come to an end. And while Bardo may be right in wishing, like Eliot herself, to grasp the larger movements of civilization, his understanding of those movements is entirely mistaken. The story Bardo misreads passes metaphoric judgment on him, for Teiresias exchanged sight for insight, not for blindness, a condition from which Bardo suffers on a more than literal level. By his own confession, that blindness sends "the streams of thought backward" in him, "along the already-traveled channels," and hinders the "course onward" (V, p. 54). The water imagery is significant, for it was always as a stream that Eliot envisioned the progress of civilization, and in using that imagery Bardo tells us no less than that through him progress is impossible. Venerating the dead forms of the past, all

Bardo can imagine is that we may retrieve the past to relive it. Bardo's view of history is, of course, a characteristically pagan one: a cyclical view, which contrasts sharply with the Christian concept, which sees time as a movement from creation to judgment, from a beginning toward an end, and which therefore allows for the possibility of progress.

As important as the water imagery is the imagery of sight, always a central metaphor in Eliot's fiction. It is also an extremely complex one. Generally in *Romola,* the pagan world is blind and the Christian world sees visions. But there is much paradox here, for although visions, as the narrator remarks at one point, are a mode of seeing (XXXI, p. 218), they come in many varieties, and they are not all a corrective to blindness. In this context, Piero di Cosimo is an important part of the book's argument.

While I do not agree with William J. Sullivan when he concludes, in "Piero di Cosimo and the Higher Primitivism in *Romola,*" that Piero is a moral touchstone in the book—for as we shall see in Chapter V Piero too has very serious limitations—I think Sullivan is right in saying that one of Piero's great virtues is his clear vision. Piero is a touchstone in two other, related areas. As Sullivan rightly observes, Piero is an empiricist.[4] Since Tito and Baldassarre are also empiricists—a subject I will return to later—it is clear that empiricism alone is by no means sufficient for moral vision. Eliot was to show in Savonarola and later in Romola that sight which passes beyond the empirical fact is indispensable to the world's moral progress. But sight that escapes the empirical fact is morally fatal, as we discover in Dino, who disappears into the invisible world and is forever lost to human experience. Thus, Piero's vision defines a middle ground. In its narrowest sense, the strictly empirical perspective is inadequate. Morally neutral, it is blind to the moral nature of human existence. At the same time, it is necessary as a tether to the rash impulses of imagination, and it is the range between blindness and imagination that Piero covers in the book. Although he never rises to a synthetic moral understanding, he never falls into the error of living, like Tito, on the level of strictly empirical, sensory stimuli.

We should not be surprised that it is not the artist of the book who is the moral touchstone. Eliot's artists never are. If Eliot mirrored herself in them, as in some sense perhaps she did, she did so only partially. To the degree that characters like Piero, or Adolf Naumann in *Middlemarch,* whom Piero most closely resembles, embody the aesthetic passion, they are necessarily dissociated from the moral one. That is the warning Eliot implied in her artists. When Eliot insisted on the moral responsibility of art, it was not because she did not understand the amoral nature of the aesthetic experience but because she understood it all too well. It is for this reason that Eliot always reminds us to place the aesthetic faculty at the service of a moral purpose, as in the Epilogue to *Romola* she brought Piero, among others, into the small circle of those who might survive the moral chaos of the world if they could accept the guidance of the moral vision Romola has achieved.

The range of Piero's vision defines another important center of perception for Eliot, one that again is in itself insufficient for the highest moral knowledge but without which moral knowledge cannot be attained. Piero was not one of the great painters of his time. It was not for his genius Eliot chose him as a character in her book but for several other reasons. Among these reasons is the fact that Piero was a painter in the tradition of Leonardo da Vinci. Eliot made sure we would know that. Nello reminds us that Leonardo is Piero's favorite painter (VIII, p. 94) and that he never ceases to "rave" about him (IV, p. 46). Perhaps it was in connection with *Romola* that Eliot read one particularly pertinent work on art in the Eliot/Lewes library (no. 1832), Alexis François Rio's *Leonardo da Vinci e la sua scuola.* There as elsewhere Eliot could have read what she undoubtedly knew already—that, although not alone in his view, Leonardo and his school were especially distinguished by the conviction that the conceptual center of art must be not God but man. Thus Leonardo and those of like persuasion were instrumental in bringing art out of the Middle Ages and into the Renaissance, and so in contributing to the progress of civilization. It is this humanism and this contribution to progress—a subject that very much concerned him, as we shall see—that Eliot valued in Piero; he reminds us that our vision must encompass the sweep of history, that it must keep to the human perspective, and that we must formulate our ideals in human terms.

Just where the limits of this human world are is made clear in the contrast between Bardo and Dino, both of whom have passed its proper boundaries. They are opposites who meet at the extremes. In them too we are introduced to the first direct confrontation between the pagan and Christian points of view. This confrontation is the first of many, since the book is a dialectical argument, which in the process of exploring the perspectives of the two dominant cultures defines the moral center through a series of antitheses.

In Bardo's Stoicism are contained both his virtues and his faults. The discipline that is the backbone of Stoicism is based on its equal indifference to joy and sorrow. Committed to reason and moderation, Stoicism repudiates the irrational passions on either side. This much had already been predicted in Piero's sketch in which the Stoic's mask had stood cold and unmoved between the laughing satyr and the sorrowing Magdalen—between the passionate worlds of Bacchus and Christ. Different as the competing gods of this epic are, they nevertheless have much in common, as students of mythology and religion have long observed. While Eliot stressed chiefly the moral differences between them, she acknowledged similarities as well. The similarities were in fact very important to Eliot; through them she identified the religious history of the West as a series of transformations in which we can see one aspect of the evolution of civilization. That this was Eliot's intention we can confirm no only in the text itself but in various notes and comments she jotted down while constructing the scheme for *Romola.* For example, in her *Commonplace Book* she remarked that the Roman church and the churches of the Western world generally might in a sense be considered "Greek religious colonies," and she cited as one of the many vestiges in Christianity of Greek ritual the "kyrie eleison" (Yale MS 6). That Eliot alluded to the introit to the mass was perhaps not accidental. As a celebration of the greatest of Christian mysteries, it was a subject that particularly engaged her thoughts. In her *Quarry,* for example, is a curious note in which she wondered whether the "Compagnia di San Marco" was "a company for the performance of mysteries." Although nothing more is heard of the matter, the question itself implies her focus. For Bacchus and Christ are alike in no respect more than in the fact that both are mystery gods, and it is this similarity that Eliot especially pointed to. The subject of mystery, in the religious sense, becomes increasingly important, and ironically perhaps most important when Romola enters her secular period. But Eliot wished us to remember from the beginning that the two gods are both gods of passion, however different their passions may be, and that as such they are in a totally different category from the rational gods of Bardo's world. It is against Bardo's rational, and therefore cold and passionless, world that Romola and Dino rebel, each escaping to one of the passionate mystery gods.

In a sense, this rebellion is a repudiation of Roman civilization. Although Eliot herself did not repudiate ancient Rome, in Romola's and Dino's rejection of their father's creed she did pass judgment on it. For although the moral discipline that was, in Eliot's view, one of the chief legacies of ancient Rome, is an essential foundation for human progress, as it is the foundation of Romola's moral vision, it is a limited virtue, a means rather than an end. In itself it is neither psychologically nor morally satisfactory; neither psychological need nor moral sensibility is ultimately rational. Although both require reason to temper enthusiasm, both are mysteries, as are the religions of the god who embody them.

Dino is the first to leave his father's house, and he leaves because, although he perverts it, he has, early in life, made a very important discovery, He has discovered that there is sorrow in the world. In the sense in which Eliot means it, Dino's is no trivial insight. It is not only his own personal experience of sorrow that Dino has recognized but the principle rather that pain and suffering are the inevitable lot of man, that the human condition is neither happy nor perfectible, and that the creed we hold is only as true as its acknowledgment of that central fact. Dino's repudiation of his father's philosophy is a repudiation, therefore, of the Stoic's indifference to the unalterable agony of human life.

It is because Dino has accepted that agony as unalterable that he has become a Christian. Eliot's exploration of Christianity in *Romola,* in which we find her most extensive study and her clearest assessment of religion, provides an answer to a question that has long troubled us. For over a century Eliot's religion, her relationship to Christianity, has been the subject of much discussion and disagreement. We have long known, of course, that throughout her adult life Eliot was an atheist, but we have known also that her early Christian passions somehow found their way into her fiction. Because Eliot was not generally given to inconsistency, this has disturbed us. Our usual explanation has been biographical or historical, but I believe that neither should satisfy us. If Eliot's work is in any sense Christian or religious—and in some sense it is—it is not because the fervent evangelicalism of her youth left a deep, if incongruous, mark on her work; nor is it because, like others in her century, she replaced God with a social good whose divine origins remained all too discernible. The religion of Eliot's fiction is neither vestigial nor cultural. What it is Eliot defined for us in *Romola,* and not only for us perhaps but possibly for herself. In Eliot's letters one can trace a distinct progression in her attitude and understanding of religion, from the militant atheism that followed her apostasy, to the inevitable mellowing of her maturity, and to a substantial reassessment in the light of continuous reinterpretation. But the letters mark only the milestones of her thought. The journey itself is chronicled in her fiction, and especially in the spiritual odyssey that Romola experiences. In this respect too *Romola* is the pivotal book in Eliot's fiction, the bridge that took her from *Adam Bede,* her most secular novel, to the visionary mysticism of *Daniel Deronda.* While Eliot's other novels trace various stages of her evolution, *Romola* records the transformation itself. In this sense, *Romola* is essentially autobiographical. It is perhaps autobiographical in other ways too, as fiction in general tends to be to some point. Perhaps in Romola's relationship to her brother Dino, for example, we may infer something of Mary Anne Evans's relationship to her brother Isaac. But it seems to me far more significant to recognize, not factual correspondences between Eliot and her characters, but the spiritual and intellectual autobiography projected in the book as a whole. For *Romola* records the most important moment in the development of Eliot's thought. It was possibly for this reason as much as for any other that Eliot singled it out to John Walter Cross as the book she had begun a young woman and finished an old one.

Thus, although the more significant portion of the argument is mirrored in Romola herself, in Dino, Eliot began to reflect the basis of her own religious history. Eliot had read zealously in every aspect of religion in her own Christian years. In an early letter to her teacher Maria Lewis, Eliot wrote that she had not the time or inclination to read anything that was not religious. Indeed, she condemned the reading of fiction particularly, for the "weapons of the Christian warfare," she wrote, "were never sharpened at the forge of romance" *(Letters,* I, 23). Although happily Eliot soon after revised her youthful view of fiction, her subsequent loss of faith in no way diminished Eliot's reading in religion. In fact, it extended it. With unabated although altered interest, Eliot began to read not only devotional and theological books but works she would have, in her earlier period, dismissed as trivial or heretical. The history of religion engaged her especially, for in ceasing to be a body of revealed truth, religion became for her a far more important record of the human effort to envision and achieve its own perfection. It was in this light that Eliot considered religion in *Romola,* and in July 1861, while preparing to write the book, she studied, and read aloud to Lewes, Ernest Renan's *Etudes d'Histoire Religieuse,* a book in whose sympathies Eliot must have concurred completely, for like herself Renan had begun his life as a believing Christian—he had in fact been ordained a priest—only to discover that his faith, like Eliot's, was not in Christian doctrine but in its historical and metaphoric meaning. The copy Eliot used was in the Eliot/Lewes library (no. 1795), where the subject of religion and religious history was extensively represented. In addition to the histories of monastic orders and other works we shall have reason to mention in chapter VII, we find, for example, general histories such as Johann Carl Ludwig Gieseler's *Compendium of Ecclesiastical History* (no. 803); the *Allgemeine Kritische Geschichte der Religionen* by Christian Meiners (no. 1431), whom Eliot had also read on the revival of learning; Johann Lorenz von Mosheim's *Institutes of Ecclesiastical History* (no. 1519); and James White's *The Eighteen Christian Centuries* (no. 2280). We find also such items of interest as Gieseler's account of modern religious history, the *Kirchengeschichte der neuesten Zeit. Von 1814 bis auf die Gegenwart* (no. 804); a copy of *Early Christian Anticipation of an Approaching End of the World, and its bearing upon the character of Christianity as a Divine Revelation . . . and an examination of the argument of the Fifteenth Chapter of Gibbon* by Eliot's friend, Sara Sophia Hennell (no. 998); as well as many entries published or acquired after *Romola's* completion, since Eliot never considered that subject closed.

Although Dino has found in Christ precisely what Eliot found, the symbol that acknowledges the eternal human agony, Dino has learned his lesson too well. Not surprisinly, given his antecedents, Dino has fled to the furthest limits of his new faith, to the monastic life, and even further, to self-imposed exile and privation. Among the many sources Eliot consulted on religious orders was Pierre Helyot's *Histoire des Ordres Monastique,* and most of the notes Eliot entered in her *Commonplace Book* from Helyot concern the austerity and self-abasement that was characteristic of the Dominicans (Yale MS 6). It is to such unnecessary austerity and self-abasement that the Dominican Savonarola has converted Dino. And it is this that is the very substance of Dino's perversion. Indeed, in his misunderstanding of Christ, Dino's Christian world is little better than the pagan world he left behind, and in some ways it is worse. If Bardo did not recognize sorrow, at least he did not court it. Dino does, for he has become enamored of pain. In one sense, therefore, Dino is after all very much like his father; he too has mistaken the means for the end. It was not such fanatical idolatry of suffering that Eliot considered the gift of Christianity.

George Bernard Shaw would have called Dino a Crosstian rather than a Christian, a worshiper not of the spirit that gives life but of the letter that kills. If Shaw was not thinking of Dino when he made that distinction in the Preface to *Major Barbara,* it was *Romola* he remembered when he wrote the play, and more favorably than he cared to confess. Shaw, of course, enjoyed a lifelong love-hate relationship with George Eliot. To satirize Roebuck Ramsden in *Man and Superman* as the prototypical Victorian moralist, for example, Shaw hung on the wall of Ramsden's study, among other portraits, an enlarged photograph of George Eliot. Apparently with the same intention Shaw wrote the following dialogue in *Major Barbara* between Snobby Price and Rummy Mitchens:

> PRICE: Wot does Rummy stand for? Pet name praps?
> RUMMY: Short for Romola.
> PRICE: For wot?

RUMMY: Romola. It was out of a new book. Somebody me mother wanted me to grow up like.

Yet Shaw remembered *Romola* in *Major Barbara,* not I think only to condemn the character he took as the ideal of Victorian morality, but more likely because he recognized in that work a pattern for his own. To resurrect in Barbara the spirit of a new, a modern Christianity, Shaw had to rescue her from the ashes of the old—the Crosstian—faith, just as to embody in Romola the modern legacy of Christianity Eliot had to free her from the calcified form it assumes in Dino.[5]

Form indeed is all that Dino's religion is. Despite his ardent faith, Dino's Christianity is nothing more than dogma. Here we have the first of many antitheses between form and substance Eliot explored in this book. While substance is always preferable, and while form without substance often becomes a betrayal of substance, the relationship between the two is seldom a simple one. As we shall see in Chapter VII, form too has its necessary function, although Dino's case does not illustrate it. Tito, who by his nature is unable to understand Christianity in any sense other than dogma, is in a good position to characterize this dogmatic form of Dino's religion, and to Tito it is nothing but vain superstition (XXXII, p. 249). Essentially it was that for Eliot as well. Ironically, Dino has entirely misunderstood the meaning of the cross for which he left his pagan father. "What is this religion of yours," Romola asks her brother, "that places visions before natural duties?" To Dino, the answer seems obvious. To "live in the life of God as the Unseen Perfectness," he replies in characteristically vague and therefore suspicious language, he has had to "forsake the world," to hold to "no affection, no hope, that wedded me to that which passeth away" (XV, pp. 162-64). Ravished by the spiritual life, Dino is lost to the concrete human world.

This disjunction between the divine and the human is precisely the heart of Dino's error. It is the error to which, according to Ludwig Feuerbach, religion itself must inevitably lead. The influence of Feuerbach on Eliot's views, especially on her religious views, is too well known to need substantiation here. "With the ideas of Feuerbach," Eliot once wrote, "I everywhere agree" *(Let-*

ters, II, 153). The "fellowship with suffering" Romola comes to understand as the meaning of Christianity is possible only, in Feuerbach's and Eliot's view, in the symbolic, not the literal interpretation of religion. To worship the cross as the "*image* of a Supreme Offering, made by Supreme Love, because the need of man was great," as Savonarola suggests (XL, p. 373; my italics), is to look to it, although Savonarola himself does not always succeed in doing so, as a symbol, and therefore as a reminder, of a human ideal whose end is the brotherhood of man and whose dictates are the mutually supportive acts of human fellowship. But for Dino, Christ, God, has become an objective, not a symbolic, reality. The moment we no longer believe that in God we have only idealized human aspirations, Feuerbach argues in *The Essence of Christianity* (Eliot's translation of which had appeared in 1854), but accept him as an independent being, we force on ourselves a choice between two mutually exclusive objects of allegiance, the perfect creator or his rebellious, imperfect, and consequently sinful creation. One is reminded here of that memorable and chilling passage in Dante's *Inferno* in which Virgil, guiding Dante through unspeakable suffering in hell, warns him that to feel compassion for those tormented souls is to question the justice of the God who condemned them to that agony. "Here pity, or here piety, must die," Virgil concludes. It is that choice that Feuerbach and Eliot wished to avoid.

In this as in so many other areas, Feuerbach was in complete agreement with Auguste Comte. There has been much discussion and much controversy about the influence of Comte on Eliot.[6] It is not my intention to enter that debate here, but the question has some bearing on my reading of *Romola,* and I will state at the outset what my own view is. Although I do not think that we can consider Eliot a disciple, it seems to me obvious that she owed Comte a profound, if eclectic, debt. Eliot made her position fairly clear on this point. In July 1861, while she was studying for *Romola,* she reported reading Comte's account of the Middle Ages (Yale MS 3). Comte's was not Eliot's only source for her estimate of this period. Undoubtedly she was familiar with Christian Meiners's compendious *Historische Vergleichung der Sitten und Verfassungen der Gesetze und Gewerbe des Handels und der Religion der Wissenschaften und Lehranstalten des Mittelalters,* contained in the Eliot/Lewes library (no. 1434);

with the more general but more compendious accounts in Anton von Tillier's *Geschichte der Europäischen Menschheit im Mittelarter* (no. 2158) and in Wilhelm August Gottlieb Assmann's *Geschichte des Mittelalters von 375-1492* (no. 76), the latter bringing the historical narrative up to the year in which *Romola* opens; with the more specialized *Economie Politique du Moyen Age* (sic) by Giovanni Antonio Luigi Cibrario (no. 435); and with Chrysanthe Ovide Des Michels's general outline, the *Manual of the History of the Middle Ages* (no. 578). Needless to say, chapters on the Middle Ages were included in most of the many histories Eliot read both before and for *Romola.* But of Comte's discussion Eliot wrote that few studies "can be fuller of luminous ideas. I am thankful to learn from it." At the same time, however, she remarked that while "Comte was a great thinker," his philosophy was "one sided" *(Letters,* III, 438-39), a point she made in *Romola* as she developed Tito's story. In a letter to Frederic Harrison, who was one of the leading Positivists in England and who had urged her to write the great Positivist novel, Eliot, while explaining the impossibility of such a task on aesthetic grounds—that dogma was incompatible with art—made a specific reference to *Romola* as a work in which this had not been her purpose *(Letters,* IV, 300-301). Thus, while we certainly cannot read *Romola* as an exposition of Positivism, it is often enlightening, and sometimes indispensable to our understanding of the book, to recognize sources and parallels in Comte's thought.

Whether or not Eliot's portrait of Dino was inspired directly by Comte, as well as by Feuerbach, therefore, Dino does in fact become exactly what Comte had predicted would follow a complete commitment to God. "Love of God," Comte wrote in *A General View of Positivism,* "was essentially a self-regarding principle. . . . Not only did it encourage monastic isolation, but if developed to the full extent, it became inconsistent with love for our fellow men." [7] For Dino, the divine world replaces rather than inspires the human. He worships abstract love but feels none for his father and sister. He idealizes abstract brotherhood but withdraws to the isolation of a monastic cell. And although he speaks for universal charity, it is only self-righteous judgment he offers Bardo and Romola. As he practices it, Christianity has indeed become exclusively self-regarding. Eliot stresses this point in many ways, and nowhere more tellingly than in the fact that Dino and Tito are ultimately guilty of parallel betrayals—of Bardo, of Romola, and of the human community in general as it is represented in the book by the city of Florence. Fidelity is a major theme in this work, and ironically it is Dino's betrayal that leaves all three vulnerable to Tito's corruption.

Betrayal is one of Bardo's severest charges against his son. Although his own perspective is distorted, Bardo holds, in theory at least, to the criterion of a human good. That is one of the virtues of his paganism. Dino, he tells Tito, was "a scholar like you but more fervid and impatient . . . showing a disposition from the very first to turn away his eyes from the clear lights of reason and philosophy, and to prostrate himself under the influence of a dim mysticism which *eludes all rules of human duty* as it eludes all argument" (XII, p. 134; my italics). In eluding all human duty, religion has lost its only moral purpose. This is made evident in the last meeting between Romola and her brother. Close to death, Dino summons Romola to deliver to her an urgent message. The scene takes place in the monastery of San Marco, but what might have been one of the striking pictorial moments in the book is not, for, as Eliot recorded in the text—surely not without a touch of bitterness—no woman was allowed beyond the chapter-house in the outer cloister (XV, p. 160). Eliot did have access to some information, however, for she had sent Lewes to inspect San Marco for her, and he had returned with ample notes.[8] Too, Eliot certainly found some useful material in Vincenzo Marchese's *Storia di San Marco,* which she had read in the fall of 1861 (Yale MS 3). That information could not, however, be used in this scene, since like Eliot, Romola herself is not permitted to enter San Marco, and it is in the outer cloister that the meeting takes place.

Although repelled by his "monkish aspect," by memories of the acute pain he has caused their father, Romola nevertheless feels drawn to Dino by sisterly affection, which is quickly rekindled even after so long and unhappy a separation. But Dino does not return that affection. It is only as an "unearthly brother" (XV, p. 163) that Dino addresses her, looking at her "with the far-off gaze of a revisiting spirit," and speaking to her "in a low passionless tone, as if his voice were that of some spirit not human" (XV, p. 161).

Confident of divine inspiration, but indifferent to Romola's actual daily life, Dino feels he has been sent to her "not to renew the bonds of earthly affection, but to deliver the heavenly warning conveyed in a vision" (XV, p. 164)

As it happens, Dino's vision is entirely prophetic. He sees Romola marrying a man who is "the Great Tempter," in a ceremony performed by a priest who has "the face of death." Tito will indeed be the satanic force that attempts to subvert the moral vision of the book; and Romola's marriage to him threatens the death of her soul. "I believe," Dino concludes, "it is a revelation meant for thee: to warn thee against marriage as a temptation of the enemy; it calls upon thee to dedicate thyself . . . to renounce the vain philosophy and corrupt thoughts of the heathens; for in the hour of sorrow and death their pride will turn to mockery, and the unclean gods will . . ." (XV, pp. 166-7). With these words, Dino dies. Although subsequently this encounter comes to have a profound influence on Romola, the dying message falls far short of the help Dino might have given his sister. For entirely by chance Dino has knowledge of the facts that assure the reader that this vision will come to pass. It is Dino, as Fra Luca, the name he assumes when he becomes a Christian and a monk, who happens to carry to Florence the letter in which Tito's father, Baldassarre, announces that he has been sold into slavery and asks to be ransomed, a letter Dino delivers to Tito and whose contents he accurately guesses (X, pp. 118-19). Only one link is missing for Dino to understand Romola's place in these events, and that is for him to learn that this is also the man Romola intends to marry. Tito cannot conceive of Dino's failing to make this last connection. "He foresaw the impulse that would prompt Romola to dwell" on the prospect of their marriage and "what would follow on the mention of the future husband's name. Fra Luca would tell all he knew and conjectured, and Tito saw no possible falsity by which he could now ward off the worst consequences of his former dissimulation. It was all over with his prospects in Florence."

Tito should have been right. The meeting between Dino and Romola should have been as Tito imagined it. Had Dino been an earthly brother rather than an unearthly one, he would undoubtedly have received Romola's confidences and so been led to relate what he had learned of Tito. But the "prevision that Fra Luca's words had imparted to Romola," the narrator remarks in concluding the scene, "had been such as comes from the shadowy region where human souls seek wisdom apart from *the human sympathies which are the very life and substance of our wisdom;* the revelation that might have come from the simple questions of filial and brotherly affection had been carried into irrevocable silence" (XV, p. 169; my italics). In Dino, Christianity has cultivated isolation and indifference rather than the generous human impulses through which it was meant to ease the inescapable suffering of human existence.

Ironically, it is that same isolation and indifference, engendered though it is by a very different concept of life, that characterizes Bardo. As we shall see throughout, the pagan and Christian worlds reflect one another, in different contexts, but through a complete circle of connected points. The image of the circle is a dominant metaphor in *Romola*. There is much geometric imagery in this book, as in all of Eliot's fiction, and here it is generally the geometry of circles. Eliot was a good mathematician and confessed to a particular preference for geometry, a study in which she believed she might have achieved considerable excellence had she pursued it further (Cross, III, 342).[9] In her fiction, geometry assumes a moral dimension. We are first introduced to the circle in the arc that describes the life of the night-student of the Proem, and in the circle of light and glory he hopes will extend the arc of experience into meaning. This image, quite properly placed at the opening of the book, is the archetypal pattern for the geometric imagery and identifies the circle with perfection itself. For that Eliot had ample historical warrant, in that since antiquity the circle has been the perfect form, the only geometric form that can turn on its center in its own space. It is the circle of the Proem that Romola follows in the course of the narrative, although that circle becomes at last a spiral. The pagan and Christian worlds are circles also, each revolving around a different center—symbolized in the different gods—but always in one another's shadow.

It is in this sense that Bardo and Dino are contiguous points of the pagan and Christian circles. Each mirrors the faults of the other. As Dino is misled by religious dogma, so Bardo is misled by its parallel, scholarly pedantry. As Dino withdraws from the human world by retreating to the spiritual life, so Bardo retreats to the past. Dino's monastic cell echoes Bardo's library. Both commune only as, and with, ghosts. Both have chosen to live their solitary lives in the land of the dead.

Eliot contrasted the worlds of both to Tito and the passions that impel Romola to choose him. Like Dino, Romola had found life in Bardo's house unsatisfying. Unlike her brother, however, Romola does not embrace self-negation. She has no desire to repudiate the flesh—quite the contrary. Whereas Dino regretted Bardo's blindness to sorrow, Romola had felt numbed by his blindness to joy. The contrast between Romola's "healthy human passion" and Dino's "sickly fancies" (XV, p. 167) is a contrast between life and death. It is not for the mortification but the gratification of desire, therefore, that Romola yearns, and it is the answer to her passion for life that Romola recognizes in Tito, who seems to her the "deep draught of joy" for which, as Romola later tells Tito, she had long been thirsting (XVII, p. 191).

In short, Romola has been awaiting the arrival of Dionysus, of Bacchus, and it is as Bacchus that Eliot identifies Tito from the very beginning. The identification is indeed one of the many implications of the title of the opening chapter, "The Shipwrecked Stranger," for "the stranger," as Eliot often calls Tito in the book, is one of the traditional, and one of the most important, epithets of Bacchus. "Shipwrecked" too suggests Bacchus, as well as Odysseus; it reminds us that Tito, like Bacchus, arrives by the sea, and arrives appropriately enough, on April 9, in the spring, the season of the vegetation god. These are only the first few hints of the subtle Bacchic imagery that saturates the book. That Eliot intended to do no less we can infer not only from the text itself, which always remains the best source, but from countless notes, some of which I will cite later, in her Diaries, her *Quarry,* and her *Commonplace Book.* One of the least significant of these notes, and for that reason perhaps the most convincing, may be found in Eliot's *Quarry,* in which she wrote that the "culture of the mulberry tree" had been "introduced into Tuscany at the beginning of the XVth C." That information has nothing whatever to do with the action or even the scenery of *Romola,* and Eliot would not have considered it important enough to copy into her notes had she not known that the mulberry, like all varieties of the fig, is a symbol of fertility and therefore a symbol of Bacchus. It is indeed as an analogy to his own ancestry that Tito mentions that tree in the book (III, p. 31).

The same intention is confirmed in many of Eliot's readings. I will postpone for Chapter IV a discussion of Ovid, in whose *Metamorphoses* Tito instructs Piero di Cosimo to find the Bacchic legend he wants painted on the triptych, although it is pertinent here to mention that many of the images through which Eliot defines Tito as Bacchus are included in Ovid's description in the passage Tito cites, and therefore in Piero's painting of the legend. Ovid was not, however, Eliot's only ancient source. In the summer of 1861, Eliot was reading Virgil's *Eclogues* (Yale MS 3), in which she would have found a good deal of information on the rituals of Dionysus, rituals that structure part of Tito's story. From the text, we know that Eliot had read Nonnus's *Dionysiaca,* a book that describes the triumphal progress of Dionysus to India, and one to which Bardo refers for his mythological information (V, p. 51). It is very likely that Eliot had read the copy in the Eliot/Lewes library of the *Opuscoli Morali* of Plutarch (no. 1706), who is often concerned with Dionysus, and it is certain that she had read the volume of Apollodorus the Athenian's study of Greek heroic mythology, the *Bibliotheca* (No. 44), in which there are both English and Greek annotations in her hand. One suspects that Eliot had also consulted three general accounts of ancient myths contained in the Eliot/Lewes library: Thomas Keightley's *The Mythology of Ancient Greece and Italy* (no. 1151), L. F. Alfred Maury's *Croyance et légendes del'antiquité* (no. 1412), and the encyclopedic *Dictionary of Greek and Roman Biography and Mythology* by Sir William Smith (no. 2036). Needless to say Eliot would have found more scattered but no less important information in nearly all of her vast reading in ancient literature.

Eliot approached the Graeco-Roman myths in the same way she approached the Christian, and in her understanding of both she took up the argument of the avant-garde in one of the great controversies of the nineteenth century, one that may be described as the controversy between myth and religion. The line that distinguishes the two is, of course, belief, and although it is difficult to say whether it was more the loss of faith that was responsible for the reinterpretation of religion as myth or whether it was more that reinterpretation, growing out of historical and anthropological research, that undermined faith, it is clear that both, each encouraging the other, had a common origin in the Renaissance, whose humanism, in its broadest sense, implied the ultimate repudiation of faith, for Western culture if not for individuals. It was that transition that Eliot experienced in her own life and that she mirrored in Romola's evolution.

Eliot was intimately acquainted with the vast literature devoted to these questions, and several works are especially relevant to this discussion. From an allusion in a letter written in August 1849, it is evident that Eliot was familiar with the work of Johann Gottfried von Herder *(Letters,* I, 293), several of whose works are in the Eliot/Lewes library. In his most massive and comprehensive work, the *Ideen zur Philosophie der Geschichte der Menschheit* (no. 1007), Herder argued for a historical view of all aspects of culture and for an understanding of all religion, Christian and especially pagan, as an expression of the collective vision of a people. Herder was, in fact, concerned with language in its historical aspect, and he looked on the mythology of the ancients as a poetic expression of experience—very much as Eliot did. Although there is no evidence to suggest a direct debt, Herder was clearly the eighteenth-century heir to the work of the first modern intepreter of mythology, Giovanni Battista Vico. Eliot and Lewes owned a number of Vico's works, including his important *Principi di una Scienza Nuova,* which we find in both the original Italian (no. 2220) and in a French translation (no. 2219) which is heavily marked and annotated by both Eliot and Lewes. Although Vico died in 1744, the year in which Herder was born, he was in some respects more modern than Herder in his more disinterested, more "scientific," historical assessment of the evolution of succeeding cultures; but he arrives in essence at the same conclusion: myths were not to be considered superstitions—false religions, that is—but rather the communal language of the peoples that invented them.

The work pioneered by Vico and Herder, although still radical, became increasingly the direction of nineteenth-century studies. Perhaps no one did as much to popularize as well as to further such views in the middle of the century as Max Müller, the German philologist whose chief interest was to provide a philological interpretation of mythology. We do not know whether or not Eliot read Müller's *Comparative Mythology,* published in 1856, but we do know that in January 1862 she was intently studying his lectures on the "Science of Language" (Yale MS 3), several reviews of which are included in the Eliot/Lewes library (nos. 1523, 1524). In these lectures Müller reiterated his earlier findings in proposing a philological theory of mythology in which all myths are seen as variations on the primal solar myth. It may have been from Müller that Eliot derived the elaborate sun imagery with which she identifies the Bacchic myth.

Although those who attempted to interpret Christianity, the established faith, in a similar manner met with more resistance and were not themselves as inclined as students of ancient and folk myths to arrive at or state as radical a conclusion, it was inevitable that sooner or later even Christianity would be claimed by the study of comparative religions. Eliot was herself instrumental in that movement. To its earlier stage, in which belief moved to the halfway house of pantheism, Eliot contributed her translation of Spinoza's *Tractatus Theologico-Politicus,* which, however, she did not finish, although later she did finish a translation of Spinoza's *Ethics.* She had read Charles Christian Hennell's pantheistic *Inquiry Concerning the Origin of Christianity* as well as his bolder *Christian Theism,* her copies of which she marked and annotated (nos. 994, 995 in the Eliot/Lewes library). A far more important contribution were Eliot's translations of David Friedrich Strauss's *The Life of Jesus Critically Examined,* which was published in 1846, and of Ludwig Feuerbach's *The Essence of Christianity*, which was published in 1854. Although inspired by different ends, and although by no means in total agreement on other points, Strauss and Feuerbach shared essentially the same view of Christianity and of religion in general. Strauss had begun his work in an attempt to distinguish the historical Jesus from subsequent accretions, but in concluding that there was no historical authority for assuming a divine truth in Jesus or in the Gospels, he had pronounced Christianity a myth that, like other myths, allowed us to understand not the divine but the human world that had created it. It is with this thesis that

Feuerbach began. Moved, however, by a profound desire to see the birth of a new humanistic philosophy, Feuerbach pursued his argument further, holding not only that belief was impossible but pernicious, that religion was not only a myth but that only as a myth did it express the vision of perfection that had first engendered it.

To return to Tito. Tito's paganism is clearly very different from Bardo's. With Tito we move from the rational to the chthonic deities, the mysterious forces of nature, the vital principles of life. This is paganism in its most enthusiastic form, fulfilling the prophecy of Angelo Poliziano that the ancient gods would awaken and make vital once more the woods and the streams. But these dark, mysterious forces of the earth, among whom Bacchus is numbered, who hold the secret to life hold also the secret to death. The young Bacchus appears in *Romola,* as he does in mythology, as the god who can both nurture and destroy: one aspect is implied in the other. In one form, Tito is the rejuvenating fertility god, the gentle giver of new life. In this guise, Tito's is a truer paganism than Bardo's pedantic veneration of the past, for the Bacchic ritual is a perennial celebration of life. As a Roman, Bardo is, after all, once removed from the springs of ancient civilization, but Tito is the spirit of Greece reincarnated. He is, as Bardo is not, a Greek and is frequently called "the Greek" ("el Greco"), a term that becomes one of his epic epithets. It is significant that on first meeting Tito, Bardo's interest in this stranger is aroused because he has traveled to the places described by Pausanias and Pliny, surely an allusion to the mythic travels of Bacchus. Yet Bardo does not recognize Tito as Bacchus (V, pp. 70, 74). Somehow, the principle of life escapes him. It does not escape Romola. When Tito first enters Bardo's library, Romola is like one awakened from death. From the moment she first sees him, "the stranger" is as astonishing to her in his beauty as though, the narrator observes, he had worn "a panther-skin and carried a thyrsus" (VI, p. 61). The imagery of the fertility god here is unmistakable. Tito is a "warm stream of hope and gladness" (XVII, p. 185), the "wreath of spring" in Romola's "wintry life" (VI, p. 62).

This aspect of Bacchus is darkened by no fearful premonitions. At the beginning of the book, partly because we do not yet know what Tito is, partly because we do not yet suspect what corruption may lie hidden in Bacchic worship, and partly because, on the novelistic level of the narrative, Tito has yet a chance to fulfill a happier fate, Tito is associated, in rapid succession, with all divine beings, pagan and Christian. Nello, who recognizes him as Bacchus at once, is equally inclined to think him a young Apollo (IV, p. 43) and continues to call him "my Apollino" (VIII, p. 97, for example), for Tito seems certainly a "youth that might be taken to have come straight from Olympus" (II, p. 28). Or, for Nello is not partial, Tito might be a St. Sebastian (IV, p. 43). To Bratti he has the face of San Michele (I, p. 11), a comparison that occurs to Tessa as well (XIV, p. 154), who also thinks Tito as beautiful as something that belongs in paradise (X, pp. 112, 113). Each in his own idiom sees in Tito the fulfillment of his own passion for beauty and joy. No one except Piero di Cosimo and Bernardo del Nero fails to delight in his presence; his very existence seems to brighten the lives it touches. "That bright face, that easy smile, that liquid voice, seemed to give life a holiday aspect," the narrator remarks, "just as a strain of gay music and the hoisting of colours make the work-worn and the sad rather ashamed of showing themselves" (IX, p. 102)

But even in this last remark, we begin to suspect the ambivalence of the god. Joy nurtures life and beguiles sorrow, but it may also make us forget that there is sorrow. As the narrator observes at a later point, the "light can be a curtain as well as the darkness" (XXXIX, p. 354). It is the very gift of the god that is also his curse. Damning the whole tribe of monks, Bardo had called them "*besotted* fanatics" (VI, p. 70; my italics). In turn, Dino had spoken of the atmosphere of sin in Bardo's house as one that had "threatened to steal over my senses like *besotting* wine" (XV, p. 162; my italics). The flaw each had seen in the other but not in himself, and that each had expressed in a Bacchic metaphor, is finally embodied in Bacchus himself.

Bardo's and Dino's metaphor recalls the drunken satyr of Piero's sketch. But Bacchus was no mere drunken god for Eliot, and indeed there is not the slightest hint of dissipation in Tito. The corruption of Bacchus is far subtler, to be found not in the excesses of revelry but in the very nature of joy. The vine that brings relief also brings oblivion. Eliot once wrote in a letter that we must learn "to do without opium" (*Letters,* III, 366). But Bacchus is the god of the poppy. Eliot's remark suggests not only that we must see things as they really are but that we must accept them as well, without illusions. How hard that reality is on our expectations and desires Eliot knew, and she knew too how tempting it is too look for escape. But it is precisely because reality is inescapable that Eliot urged us to confront it. To live in the land of the Lotos Eaters is merely to allow oneself to be victimized by the lawlessness of the suitors and to abandon the *polis* to their moral chaos. That is why Homer, who knew all too well how sweet is the land of forgetfulness, brought Odysseus home again, to the hardships but the satisfactions as well of civilization. That epic theme is as central to Eliot's fiction as it was to the Greek mind, and Eliot often explored the subject in Homer's own metaphors; the novels abound with characters who taste the lotos, in one form or another, and Tito is the prototype of this group. As it turns out, Tito is no more a true representative of the best paganism than Bardo—he is somewhat worse, in fact—although different. We discover that he is, after all, not a Greek but a Graeculus, as he himself acknowledges, and although he has traveled widely in the Hellenic world with his father, Baldassarre, it is not Greece but Bari, Italy (III, p. 31) that is his birthplace. We can only conjecture why Eliot chose Bari as the site of Tito's birth. Perhaps the explanation can be found in the account Eliot copied into her *Commonplace Book* of the life of St. Nicholas of Myra. The account is taken from Anna Brownell Jameson's *Sacred and Legendary Art,* a book Eliot read during August and September 1861 (Yale MS 3) and from which she entered copious notes into her *Commonplace Book.* A delightful record of travels, readings, reflections, and observations, *Sacred and Legendary Art* suited Eliot's purpose ideally, not only because it gathered information on the lives of saints, martyrs, evangelists, and many others, nor even because it provided a treasure store of details on Italian art, but most of all because Mrs. Jameson, like Eliot, had an acute perception of the symbolic. In the story of St. Nicholas, Mrs. Jameson included two pertinent items. Eliot noted in her *Commonplace Book* that St. Nicholas was sometimes called St. Nicholas of Bari because his relics were stolen and deposited there, and that he was the patron saint of children (Yale MS 6). In a sense, then, Tito owes St. Nicholas a great debt, since it was assumedly through his patronage that as a street urchin he was found, in Bari in fact, and adopted by Baldassarre. Here Eliot not only suggests that as an orphan Tito is dissociated from his past, from the history he will later betray, but alludes as well to the mysterious origins of Bacchus himself, who like Tito is said in some accounts to have had both an adopted, earthly, father as well as an unknown, or in any case unnamed, one. Baldassarre's reward for taking in the abandoned child was, however, to be betrayed by him, and as the city known for housing the stolen relics of St. Nicholas, Bari is the most suitable birthplace of the child who grew up to become a man untouched by moral awe.

To some degree, Tito is a symbol of the disintegration of Greece in the late Middle Ages and Renaissance. Tito's description to Bardo of his travels in Greece (VI, pp. 68-75) shows a country that has long lost not only its greatness but also its moral and political coherence. The subject interested Eliot a good deal, for in a sense in the condition of Greece at this time we might see, on the one hand, the flaws of the ancient world brought in time to light and, on the other, a prophecy of the future Tito's Hellenism would shape. In March 1862, just before she wrote Tito's account to Bardo of his travels, Eliot noted in her Diary that she had "been lately reading some books on the medieval condition of Greece"; and in an earlier entry, in January 1862, she identified at least one, George Finlay's *History of Medieval Greece* (Yale MS 3). In this connection, Eliot provided a gloss on Tito in the poet Marullo. The husband of Alessandra Scala (who is the daughter of Bartolommeo Scala), Marullo, one of the book's historical figures, appears in the chapter called "A Learned Squabble," and not to great advantage. A Greek who migrated to Florence, Marullo reveals his true nature in his hymns and epigrams, a copy of which was contained in the Eliot/Lewes library (no. 1405), perhaps the same copy Lewes brought Eliot on August 24, 1861, when she had nearly despaired of being able to read Marullo anywhere but in the British Museum, a place she avoided whenever she could (Yale MS 3). Eliot seems to have studied Marullo at some length, and his life as well in Humphrey Hody's *De Graecis Illustribus* (Yale MS 3), not with admiration, but because Marullo suggested to her the moral and cultural confusion of his day. It is that point that Eliot made in the *Quarry* when she summarized her view by noting that the "three Books of Hymns of Marullo are addressed to the pagan deities."

In his historical as well as mythological role, therefore, Tito is at best an ambivalent figure. The former, indeed, merely reinforces the latter. Which of the two aspects of Bacchus come into focus depends entirely on point of view. In a natural context, in which all moral values are neutralized, we see him always as the benevolent god of joy. But the moment we place him in moral perspective, Bacchus seems transformed. Romola calls Tito "My joy!" when she turns to him for comfort from the thoughts evoked by Dino's crucifix, but it is the crucifix that raises the moral question of the book, and seen in its light Tito brings not joy but sorrow.

3.

The Clashing Deities

Bacchus and Christ enter Romola's life nearly at the same time. She meets Tito in April 1492. That September, she witnesses Dino's death and receives the crucifix from him. Just as Piero's sketch had foretold, joy and sorrow stand on either side of the world she had inherited from Bardo. And both appeal to something very deep in her own nature. As Bacchus appeals to her passion for joy, so Christ finds in her a latent capacity for the moral imagination that was, in Eliot's view, the unique legacy of Christianity.

Romola's epic journey through the book stresses that man's moral history is an evolution. From the dawn of consciousness, mankind has won, age by age, that truer and subtler light that he has yearned for and faintly imagined, like the night-student, even in his infancy. Thus, the Christian sensibility that is about to be awakened in Romola by the crucifix has a pagan precedent, a glimmer of the same light in fainter tones. We find it, before either Bacchus or Christ enters her experiences, in her strong fidelity to Bardo.

It is on this fidelity that Romola's moral evolution is founded.

Here, Eliot seems to have followed Comte very closely. Romola's progress into moral consciousness traces the three stages Comte outlined in his survey of man's development from egotism to moral responsibility, for in Comte's rudimentary and excessively schematized psychology Eliot recognized a skeletal truth. Comte's scheme was based on the model of the family, and the family was sufficiently important to Eliot's design in *Romola* to make her devote some time to its study. In December 1861, Eliot noted in her Diary that she had been reading Pompeo Litta's *Famiglie* (Yale MS 3). More influential than Litta, however, was a book Eliot did not read for *Romola,* but one that undoubtedly left a lasting imprint on her views of the subject—Wilhelm Heinrich von Riehl's *Die Familie.* Eliot had begun *Die Familie* in December 1858, undoubtedly in the well-marked copy in the Eliot/Lewes library (no. 1827), and on finishing it she pronounced it a "delightful book" (Yale MS 1). *Die Familie* was the third in a series that had started with *Die burgerliche Gesellschaft* and continued with *Land und Leute,* both of which Eliot had reviewed for the *Westminster Review* in July 1856 in one of her most important essays, "The Natural History of German Life," an essay that not only records much of her thought on various subjects but that also testifies to Riehl's influence on it. We do not know whether Eliot had read Leon Battista Alberti's *Della Famiglia.* Alberti is cited in *Romola* in such a way that one is tempted to believe that Eliot was acquainted with his work (XXXIX, p. 351) but Alberti's thesis—that the family is the paradigm of the state—is not unique. Among others, Comte shared it, and his psychological analysis of familial relationships had for him, as for Eliot, historical and political extension.

For Comte, filial love is the first step on the moral ladder to altruism. The love a child feels for a parent, Comte argued, is the first step away from the natural egotism of the human heart, and it is the easiest step since the parent is in some way a shadow of the child's self, although at the same time a being distinctly different. We are weaned, as it were, from self-love in stages, each stage taking us a little further from our own selves. It is clear that in part at least Eliot agreed. So important does filial love and loyalty become in *Romola* that it is symbolically projected in the image of Antigone, one of the chief images of the book.

Antigone was a figure Eliot had long admired, not only in mythology, but in Sophocles' representations of her. Eliot knew no Greek playwright better. In September 1856 she began reading *Ajax.* In August 1857 she read *Electra,* and in October *Philoctetes,* possibly in the copy in the Eliot/Lewes library (no. 2051). Earlier that year, between February and April, she had read *Oedipus Tyrannos* and *Oedipus Coloneus,* and she apparently returned to both in June when she read the two plays aloud to Lewes. Both were favorites. "I rush on the slightest pretext to Sophocles," she wrote to Sara Hennell in April 1857, "and am as excited about blind old Oedipus as any young lady can be about the latest hero with magnificent eyes" *(Letters,* II, 319). But above all, she was moved most deeply by *Antigone,* which she had first read in December 1855 and to which she returned many times (Yale MS 1). There are two copies of *Antigone* in the Eliot/Lewes library (no. 2048 and Appendix I, no. 566), the second marked in Eliot's hand. The only work by Sophocles Eliot did not mention reading is the only remaining play of those that survive, *Trachiniai,* although there is no reason to assume that she had not read this play as well, perhaps in the English translation of the complete plays of Sophocles in the library (no. 2052), an event she would not have been as likely to mention in her Diary as her reading of the Greek texts. Indeed, she had very likely read many or perhaps all of Sophocles' plays in English long before she attempted them in Greek. Her interest in Greek drama is evident at least ten years before she began what seems a systematic study of Sophocles. Early in 1844, for example, Eliot had read Carl Eduard Geppert's *Die altgriechische Bühne,* which she had marginally lined throughout (no. 794 in the Eliot/Lewes library), and while three other books on Greek drama in their library—George Heinrich Bode's *Geschichte der dramatischen Dichtkunst der Hellenen bis auf Alexandros den Grossen* (no. 252), Otto Friedrich Gruppe's *Ariadne. Die tragische Kunst der Griechen in ihrer Entwickelung und in ihrem Zusammenhange mit der Volkspoesie* (no. 897), and Henri-Joseph-Guillaume Patin's *Etudes sur les tragiques grecs ou Examen critique d'Eschyle, de Sophocle et d'Euripide, précédé d'un histoire générale de la tragédie Grecque* (no. 1649),—belonged to Lewes, one suspects that they found their way into Eliot's hands as well.

No one can better explain Eliot's view of the figure of Antigone than Eliot herself. In her essay. "The Antigone and its Moral," ostensibly a review of a new edition of Sophocles's play, published in the *Leader* in March 1856, Eliot made clear that for her Antigone was a mythic embodiment of the visionary and that it was the visionary who extended man's moral frontier. In some sense, Eliot's reading of Sophocles' play was loosely Hegelian. Later in *Romola,* the Hegelian reading is of particular importance to an understanding of Romola's disagreement with Savonarola over the case of Bernardo del Nero. Eliot did not see Creon as a wicked or unprincipled man. There are no villains in her reading of the play. Creon's position in the confrontation is rational, intelligent, and even benevolent. To some degree at least, the conflict between Antigone and Creon is a contest between two rights. But not entirely. For the right Creon represents is the right of the world as it is and however sincere his moral passion is, Creon's can only therefore be a present right. As such, it is inevitably less desirable than the future right for which Antigone speaks, the right, that is, the visionary imagines and that has yet to be achieved. If history is progress, then future is better than past and present. It is not because Creon is blind, then, that Eliot finds him wanting, but because he sees only in his time, while Antigone sees horizons of greater possibilities. The hope of civilization lies with her.[1]

It is not only *Antigone* that provides the context for this image but *Oedipus Coloneus* as well, for both plays are reenacted in the course of the narrative. It is the Antigone of *Oedipus,* in fact, that we meet first. The picture of the blind Bardo, isolated, neglected, nurturing a sense of injury, haunted by the memory of a faithless son and attended only by a faithful daughter, suggests the exiled Oedipus even before Piero sees in Bardo and Romola the natural models for his painting of that portion of the myth (XVIII, p. 196). As for Piero, the important feature of the relationship between Oedipus and Antigone was for Eliot the daughter's fidelity. In this image, therefore, Eliot once more showed an important point at which the pagan and Christian worlds touch; as Dino's Christianity had come close to Tito's egotistic paganism and Bardo's human sterility, so Romola's pagan sense of fidelity is the foundation of her Christian sympathy.

Here the two points are contrasted. In her loyalty to Bardo,

Romola is a foil for both Tito and Dino, both betrayers in different ways. What has kept Romola with Bardo is precisely what the other two lack. Romola, the narrator remarks, seemed an "image"—a recurrence of that common word which points here directly to Romola's mythic identity—"of that loving, pitying devotedness, that patient endurance of irksome tasks, from which [Tito] had shrunk and excused himself" (XII, p. 123). We recognize that "patient endurance" as part of Romola's Stoical education. It has nurtured in her a "habitual" self-discipline (V, p. 52), an important concept to which I will return in Chapter VII. But the love and pity to which the passage also refers are not Stoical virtues. Indeed, although Romola does not yet know it, they are the germ of her Christian sensibility. The key word, of course, is "pity," which Eliot used, in *Romola* as elsewhere, interchangeably with "sympathy." As Romola ministers to the irritable demands of her father, it is pity that fills her hazel eyes, the only outlet, in her young secluded life, for her "deepest fount of feeling" (V, p. 52).

The period of Romola's initiation into Christianity is one of great confusion. Having accepted, unlike Dino, her father's contempt for religion, Romola recoils in horror from Dino's dogma, his superstition, his visions (XV, p. 165). Yet the crucifix, repugnant as it is to her at first, begins to haunt her imagination. Dino's diatribe against her father's philosophy of life angers her. What moves her is not theory or argument or prophecy but the direct empirical confrontation with her brother's suffering and death. At this moment the symbolic significance of the crucifix that Dino will give her is concretely before her. Until now, Romola's life "had been sombre, but she had known nothing of the utmost human needs; no acute suffering—no heart-cutting sorrow; and this brother, come back to her in her hour of supreme agony, was like a sudden awful apparition from an invisible world" (XV, p. 168). The language here associates Dino's death with the crucifixion ("agony"), not as a parallel event, but as the relation in Romola's mind between symbol and meaning.

The language also elaborates another aspect of the vision metaphor. The "invisible world" from which Dino seems to come as an "awful apparition" marks the beginning of a new vision in

Romola. Romola had been as blind as Bardo to the world to which she is here introduced. That blindness, moreover, had, ironically enough, been the consequence of their confinement to the strictly visible world. For the invisible world does exist. Dino, to compound the irony, had been equally blind to it in believing it to be something supernatural. It is Romola alone who has perceived it rightly, as the world beyond the reason and analysis to which Bardo limits himself but on this side of the supernatural to which Dino has fled. The invisible world is nothing more than the world that lies beyond our own senses, the world that is inaccessible except to the imagination.

I earlier suggested that one of the chief considerations that made it necessary for Eliot to express herself symbolically was the fact that the sensibilities that concerned her, the deepest sensibilities, are and must remain by their very nature inarticulate. This philosophic problem has a psychological parallel; what is inarticulate to language is equally inarticulate to perception. In itself, experience is not enough. That is precisely why the empiricists of the book can never achieve moral vision. Man requires more than experience; he requires symbols that order and synthesize his experiences and render them meaningful to his own consciousness. Here, as so often, the form and substance of *Romola* are one. It is not only art but life that demands the poetry of myth. It is as such a symbol that Dino's crucifix suddenly reveals to Romola the significance of all her disordered experience. That crucifix comes to her as a "new *image* of death" (XVII, p. 185; my italics), an image through which reality becomes coherent. Death is real, literally and as a symbol of all that is sorrowful and futile in human existence. In one moment, her meeting with Dino has shown her this truth on both the literal and the figurative level. Fixed immutably in the metaphor of the crucifixion, this knowledge transcends the empirical reality and becomes for her a permanent center of perception. From that day, the image of the crucifix will make her a perennial witness in imagination to that moment of supreme suffering with which is identified all the pain of earthly life. Later, Romola remarks that the memory of Dino's eyes raised to the crucifix in his dying moment "will come between me and everything I shall look at" (XVII, p. 186). It is not that Romola will see something different. It is only that she will see it in a different light. For the first time, Romola has seen the invisible.

Tito, to whom Romola attempts to escape from this agonizing encounter with Dino, is only too willing to coax her away from the thoughts the crucifix has suggested. Such thoughts, he tells her, "are fit for sickly nuns, not for my golden-tressed Aurora" (XVII, p. 188) While Tito foreshadows here the habit Romola will eventually assume when she leaves him, the habit of the nun, he inadvertently characterizes Romola's meeting with Dino in his reference to Aurora, the goddess of the dawn. The cycle of the day—another circle in the geometric pattern—is a recurrent metaphor that outlines the whole progress of the book, as well as its smaller analogues. In the Proem, for example, we are introduced to the angel of the dawn who symbolically marks the beginning of moral consciousness. The chapter in which Tito is first brought into Bardo's house echoes that image in its title, "Dawning Hopes." And that same image returns here in Tito's allusion, for the scene with Dino has been for Romola the dawn of a new awareness, an initation into sorrow that has driven the first wedge of moral reflection into Romola's spontaneous passion for joy.

Romola's meeting with Dino takes place on September 7, 1492. Among the many remarkable things that have never been noticed in *Romola* is the fact that the events of the book follow a very strict symbolic calendar. Calendars always fascinated Eliot. In a letter she wrote to her teacher Maria Lewis in March 1840, when she was twenty, Eliot announced with great enthusiasm that she had just purchased John Keble's *The Christian Year (Letters,* I, 46), "a little volume of poems adapted to the Sundays and Holy Days according to our Prayer Book arrangement," which she recommended with equal enthusiasm the following month to her friend Martha Jackson *(Letters,* I, 48). That this book remained one of Eliot's favorites is evident in the fact that she quoted from it in *The Mill on the Floss* (book VI, chap. IX) some twenty years later and that in *Middlemarch* she made it one of Dorothea Brooke's favorite works, one of the few to which Dorothea turns for comfort in sorrow (chapter XLVII). Eliot's response to Keble was not unique. By the time she acquired the book the Tractarians had succeeded in stirring an immense revival of interest in the Christian calendar, a revival to which Keble's volume, published in 1827, had materially contributed. But nowhere did that movement find as fertile a soil as in Eliot's mind. For someone who sought meaning in every particle of existence, a calendar that informed every day of the year with symbolic significance distinguished every moment of life as both unique and universal.

Keble's is not the only book of its kind Eliot read. We do not have Eliot's bibliography on the subject, but three works at least in the Eliot/Lewes library must have been of particular interest for her, and very likely of some use in *Romola.* One is S.J., Le Pedro de Ribadénéyra's *Les Vies des Saints et fêtes de toute l'Année* (no. 1819), possibly useful to Eliot in her coordination of events with the feast days of John the Baptist, an important figure in *Romola.* John James Bond's *Handy-Book of Rules and Tables for Verifying Dates with the Christian Era: giving an account of the chief eras, and systems used by various nations; with easy methods for determining the corresponding dates* (no. 262) probably had some historical as well as calendaric interest for Eliot. And John Brady's *Clavis Calendaris; or a Compendious Analysis of the Calendar, Illustrated with Ecclesiastical, Historical and Classical Anecdotes* (no. 282) would certainly have been a fruitful study in that it provides the pagan, Christian, and historical significance of individual days of the year.

It was possibly to the calendar of *Romola* that Eliot referred when she told Lewes her idea for the "backbone" of her work on August 15, 1861 (Yale MS 3), or perhaps it was the "scheme" she conceived on December 11, 1861 (Yale MS 3), that finally made it possible for her to begin the book the following January. That she had been thinking quite early in terms of a symbolic calendar, perhaps even before she herself realized what use she would make of it, we can infer from her Journals of her trips to Italy in which, instead of or in addition to a date, she sometimes identified days by their place in the cycle of the Christian year. Nowhere, more than in Italy would Eliot have been reminded of Keble and others, and nowhere would she have been more conscious of the rituals of the Christian cycle. Although calendaric symbols are important in all of Eliot's fiction and are always a clue to the poetic structure of the narratives, it may have been the Italian setting of *Romola* that inspired, not the more conventional use Eliot made elsewhere of the calendar—of seasons, for example, in *Adam Bede,* or of Christmas Day in *Silas Marner*—but a complete annual calendar in which every event assumes symbolic significance.

Although we can only speculate about the origins and the history of the idea, it is certain that the symbolic calendar was part of Eliot's design. For one thing, Eliot's notes for *Romola* leave no room for doubt. Nor is there any doubt what purpose the calendar was meant to serve. Eliot not only jotted down general information, such as that the old Florentine and Siennese years began on March 25 *(Quarry),* but alluded, and far more often, to the mythological significance of the events. Here indeed we see the outlines of Eliot's epic intention to explore the historical confrontation, and to trace the influence on Western civilization, of the pagan and Christian cultures in their mythological forms. In the *Quarry,* for example, she noted that in Florence prisoners were set at liberty on St. John the Baptist's Day; some pages later, she described a brutal children's game as "a sort of Saturnalia." Again, early in 1862, just after she had begun the final writing of *Romola,* she recorded in her Diary that she had been delayed from continuing because she was unsure of the exact dates of Corpus Christi Day and Easter in 1492 and had to suspend her work to look them up (Yale MS 3). And in what is surely a final and incontrovertible confirmation of her plan, in her *Commonplace Book* she copied an entire page of the Attic calendar, each month entered by its Greek name, identified by the corresponding period of our calendar, and, most importantly, characterized by its appropriate gods and festivals (Yale MS 6) (see frontispiece).

As satisfying as such preliminary assurances may be, we do not need anything more than the text to discover and understand Eliot's design. Once we are prepared to see the book's poetic implications, we immediately recognize the calendar as one of the book's most obvious and striking features. It is in itself a complete symbolic structure, reflecting and shaping the thematic movement throughout. For that reason, it is at the same time a wonderful example of how Eliot transformed the novel into the epic. On the surface, *Romola* appears to give a very ordinary chronology of events. Sometimes Eliot mentions a precise date; more often she seems only to be suggesting, in conventional ways, that time has passed. But every allusion to time, however casual, is precise, and one realizes very quickly that even the unspecified dates can be computed, and are meant to be. For every event in *Romola* takes place on a date whose mythological significance transforms temporal order into poetic syntax. Once more, the novel and the epic are one.

September 7 is a typical example of the rich symbolic imagery suggested in the calendar. This day, on which Romola has taken her first step in her conscious moral development; on which she has been initiated into Dino's vision; on which she has met Savonarola for the first time; and on which she has accepted, however unwillingly, the crucifix whose meaning she has yet to discover, is the Eve of the Nativity of the Virgin, the figure with whom Romola is to be associated in her moral maturity.

It is somewhat ironic, then, that on the next day, the Day of the Nativity, Romola reeinforces her commitment to Tito, the antithesis of the vision of the crucifix. But this is Romola's last, desperate effort to obliterate the haunting knowledge she had glimpsed with Dino; to escape the burden of knowing the invisible; and to return to the bright, simple, sunshine of the Bacchic life. Romola's ambivalence is all too human: it is the heart of the conflict between our natural and our moral inclinations, a conflict Romola will never escape nor entirely resolve. The contrast is also thematically and formally enlightening. It is only in the context of the other that each vision is revealed. Neither Bacchus nor Christ is fully intelligible except as the contrast to the other, and from the moment Tito is seen in the shadow of the crucifix the flattering Christian allusions at the beginning of the book take on satanic overtones.

Tito had himself introduced this symbolic line on his first arrival in Florence when he had emphatically repudiated all Hebraic associations. Answering a question put to him by Bratti about his origins, Tito had, with some spirit, declared that he was "no Hebrew" (I, p. 14). Tito's assertion is confirmed when he comes to the Piazza del Duomo where the Cathedral of Santa Maria del Fiore identifies the Christian center of the city. Tito has nothing but contempt for that magnificent cathedral. As his eyes follow upward the lines of the campanile, which points symbolically to the sky, there is a "slight touch of scorn on his lip," for such buildings, Tito observes, "smack too much of Christian barbarism" (III, pp. 33-34). These hints are fully realized when Tito next turns to the bronze gates of the Baptistery by Lorenzo Ghiberti. Although these interest him to the degree that they seem to be conceived by a "human mind" rather than by a religious one, Tito does not examine them long because his "appetite for contemplation" is "soon satisfied" (III, p. 34). Ghiberti's gates, one of the glories of Renaissance Florence, are central to Eliot's purpose, for in them Ghiberti traced the biblical history of man from the Garden of Eden to Solomon. In a sense, therefore, they chronicle a portion of history, just that portion that precedes Eliot's starting point in *Romola.* Thus, they are a pictorial extension of time, one more of the rivers that contributed to the stream of civilization, a record of another aspect of human progress. In turning away from them, then, Tito prophetically rejects both history and progress. Ghiberti's gates are called the Gates of Paradise, and in rejecting history and progress Tito will lose his opportunity to enter through them. From this point on, Eliot develops Tito, with increasing clarity, as an Antichrist. The crucial test enacted in the Piazza del Duomo is reenacted when Tito first confronts Dino's crucifix shortly after Romola has returned with it from her meeting with her brother. Such echoes, in which private symbols shadow public ones, are common in *Romola,* and are formal patterns of substantive points; as we shall see in Chapter V the relationship between the individual and the collective life is a central subject in the book. Although, when Romola returns with the crucifix, she denies that she will always suspect Tito of being the Great Tempter of Dino's vision (XVII, p. 89), an involuntary quiver passes across her face as Tito's hand touches the crucifix (XX, p. 209); the war between the gods has begun.

It is at this moment, when Romola wavers between them, that Eliot chooses to identify some of the major images that are to characterize each of the gods. Romola has just received Dino's crucifix. Shortly, she will be given the other gift, Tito's triptych. In the relationship between the two, the major question of the book is raised. In the important, magnificent, passage that follows in which Tito recalls Romola from her memory of her last conversation with Dino, Eliot defines the contrasting worlds of Bacchus and Christ:

> and now in the *warm sunlight* she saw that *rich dark beauty* which seemed to gather round it all *images of joy—purple vines* festooned between the elms, the *strong corn perfecting itself* under *the vibrating heat,* bright winged creatures hurrying and resting among the *flowers, round limbs beating the earth in gladness with cymbals held aloft, light melodies chanted* to the *thrilling rhythms of strings*—all objects and all sounds that tell of *Nature revelling in her force.* Strange, bewildering transition from those *pale images of sorrow and death* to this *bright youthfulness,* as of a *sungod who knew nothing of night!* What thought could reconcile that *worn anguish* on her brother's face—that *straining after something invisible*—with this *satisfied strength and beauty,* and make it intelligible that they belonged to the same world? Or was there never any reconciliation of them, but only a *blind worship of clashing deities,* first in *mad joy* and then in *wailing?* (XVII, p. 188; my italics)

The imagery, especially the Bacchic imagery, describes the rituals of the gods, rituals fully enacted in the stories of the two figures in whom the gods are embodied, for Tito's end will be a frenzied celebration of the omophagous Bacchic rite and Savonarola's a crucifixion. These indeed are the only possible ends to which Bacchus and Christ lead. When Romola asks, therefore, as she does here, whether the gods can be reconciled, and how, she asks no idle question, for herself or for Eliot. It is only in their reconciliation that human life can be saved.

This has not been the common view of Eliot's moral perspective, which has, I believe been too much identified with the general Victorian principle of self-sacrifice. Self-sacrifice however is not what Eliot urged, here or elsewhere. Far from asking us to repudiate Bacchus, Eliot insisted that we must, like Romola, accept the gifts of both gods, for only together do they shape our Western heritage. Indeed, what Bacchus offers is very precious. "Precious gift," or more strictly, "precious object," is what Tito's name, Melema, means in Greek. Eliot knew as well as Euripides that we deny Bacchus only at our peril, for he is always, as the Greeks said, the stranger within us. As Bacchus himself tells Pentheus in Euripides' *Bacchae,* to accept or deny the god is not a choice man is given. All we can choose is whether we will accept Bacchus willingly or unwillingly; one way or another, accept him we must. It is not in man's power to rescind the laws of nature, not even the laws of his own nature.

However, the laws of nature cannot be accepted as the model of moral law. Eliot once wrote to John Morley that it was the business of morality to "lighten the pressure of hard non-moral outward conditions" *(Letters,* IV, 365). Between nature, which is indifferent to human welfare, and morality, whose end is to promote it, there are some conflicts that are irreconcilable. That is the tragedy of the human condition. If the human condition were not tragic, we would have no need of morality and we would never need to understand the invisible world of Christ. In doing what was natural, we would happily do what was right. But that is not the world Eliot saw. Rectitude and desire are not always one. Our task, like Romola's, is to find that path that is narrower than the razor's edge that will trace a journey somewhere between the folly and futility of attempting to deny nature on the one hand and the immorality of accepting nature as a valid criterion for action on the other.

At this early point in her life, that path eludes Romola. She fears that no compromise is possible between the gods, and in fact no compromise can come out of the extremes to which Romola has so far been introduced. As they are embodied in Tito and Dino, Bacchus and Christ, in overstepping some unspecified boundary, deny not only their opposites but themselves. If the religious, as contrasted with the symbolic, figure of Christ, represents the ultimate in the negation of the self, as it does in the crucifixion, it also represents the negation of all selves and therefore of humanism. That is implicit in Dino's repudiation of the Renaissance spirit. Similarly, and ironically, Bacchus too negates humanism. The Bacchic cultivation of the self has no extension. It begins and ends in a narrow egotism that has its conclusion in a self-destruction, which although unintended is nevertheless inevitable. Tito's path is the road to annihilation as surely as Dino's, not because Eliot subscribed to the simple formula that evil is punished—she knew all too well that often it is not—but because human suffering, the recognition of which is the whole and entire concern of Christianity, is real, no less real than the natural instincts we call Bacchus, and one way or another we must yield to it. That is the lesson Romola will learn.

4.

Bacchus and Ariadne Betrothed

Ironically, Romola enters her discipline in sorrow when she marries the god of joy. The marriage, although Romola does not learn it in time, is completely foreshadowed in the triptych, Tito's betrothal gift to her.

It requires no speculation to understand why and how Eliot chose the crucifix as the symbol of the Christian tradition, but we can only guess how she came to devise the symbol of the triptych. That the symbol was to be a concrete object, like the crucifix, was undoubtedly part of Eliot's plan in *Romola* to root the transcendent in the particular. The details came perhaps from many sources. The form of the triptych—the gift could have been a locket, for example—may have been inspired by a triptych painted by Fra Angelico which Eliot had seen at the Uffizi Gallery during her first trip to Italy. Although Fra Angelico painted a Christian subject, a Madonna and Child surrounded by angels with saints on the side panels, Eliot was so immensely struck by the work (Cross, II, 173), that she might have recalled its form when she came to decide on the design of Tito's gift.

The source for the painting on the triptych is Ovid. It is in Ovid that Tito tells Piero to look for the "necessary hints" of what he has in mind. "I want a very delicate miniature device taken from certain fables of the poets which you will know how to combine for me," Tito says.

> It must be painted on a wooden case—I will show you the size—in the form of a triptych. The inside may be simple gilding: it is on the outside I want the device. It is a favourite subject with you Florentines—the triumph of Bacchus and Ariadne; but I want it treated in a new way. A story in Ovid will give you the necessary hints. The young Bacchus must be seated in a ship, his head bound with clusters of grapes, and a spear entwined with vine leaves in his hand: dark-berried ivy must wind about the masts and sails, the oars must be thyrsi, and flowers must wreathe themselves about the poop; leopards and tigers must be crouching before him, and dolphins must be sporting round. But I want to have the fair-haired Ariadne with him, made immortal with her golden crown—that is not in Ovid's story, but no matter, you will conceive it all—and above there must be young Loves, such as you know how to paint, shooting, with roses at the points of their arrows— (XVIII, p. 194)

Although Ovid gave a number of accounts of the myths of Bacchus, Tito's description to Piero suggests a passage in the *Metamorphoses* in the story of Pentheus and Bacchus. Two volumes of Ovid, one of the *Metamorphoses* with an interlinear translation and another of that and other works entirely in translation, were contained in the Elliot/Lewes library (nos. 1591, 1592); whether or not it was from these or other volumes, it is obvious in *Romola* and elsewhere in her fiction that Eliot knew Ovid well.[1] But it may not have been only of Ovid's picture of Bacchus that Eliot was thinking. In the list of the chief remains of Greek sculpture Eliot entered in her *Commonplace Book* among her notes for *Romola* are included the *Vatican Bacchus*, the *Vatican Torso of Bacchus*, the *Bacchus* in the Louvre, the *Silenus with the Infant Bacchus* in the Louvre, and numerous other representations of Bacchus (Yale MS 6), many of which Eliot had seen and on which she had commented in earlier

Journals. She may have recalled them all in forming the picture of Bacchus she had in mind.

And it is indeed not precisely Ovid's account that Tito wants translated into the triptych. He wants not only Bacchus but Ariadne depicted as well. That request would not have surprised Piero. As Tito rightly observes, "the triumph of Bacchus and Ariadne" is a "favourite subject with you Florentines." It appears in many accounts, both literary and pictorial. Among the songs of Lorenzo de' Medici, to which I will return shortly, Eliot had undoubtedly read "The Triumph of Bacchus," which, despite its title, describes the triumph of both mythological figures. We know that she owned and had read (no. 1778 in the Eliot/Lewes library) Francesco Redi's *Bacco in Toscano, Ditirambo, con Note brevi scelti dell' Autore.* A seventeenth-century scientist, engaged in creditable biological research, as well as a poet, Redi envisioned a characteristically Bacchanalian scene in which Bacchus and Ariadne arrive in the Tuscan hills with a full retinue of satyrs and maenads. From a note in the *Quarry,* it seems that Eliot especially enjoyed Redi's rhapsody on wines, a rhapsody in which, with the delight of a fine connoisseur, Redi surveys the finest vintages through a large portion of the poem.

As far as we know, Piero himself never painted a work such as the triptych describes. He did, however, paint a Bacchus and Ariadne whose general conception derives from Ovid. I think it was this painting that Eliot chiefly had in mind. The work would have appealed to Eliot in any case, since in it Piero argues, characteristically, for the view that civilization is indebted largely to uncelebrated acts, a view Eliot expressed most movingly in the last words of *Middlemarch.* But it no doubt appealed to her even more as a study of human progress. *The Discovery of Honey,* as the painting is called, was one of the Bacchanalian scenes Piero painted for the Vespucci Palace in Florence. Piero mentions a commission from Giovanni Vespucci in the text, although he is referring to a commission to paint the portrait of Oedipus and Antigone, the portrait for which he uses Bardo and Romola as his models (XVIII, p. 196). Vespucci, of course, reminds us of another discovery—the discovery of America—a subject important to Eliot's purpose, as we shall see in Chapter VI.

Like Ghiberti, who traced the history of the Old Testament in the Gates of Paradise, and so echoed Eliot's larger survey, in *The Discovery of Honey* Piero traces the history of mankind, from a humanistic perspective, from its primitive beginnings to the more civilized present of his own age. The temporal sequence is translated into spatial divisions, from the dawn of time in the lower right quadrant to a more developed form of life in the upper left. Like Eliot, Piero places Bacchus in the primitive world. Here it is the gentle, life-giving Bacchus Piero envisions. As the discoverer of honey, an immemorial attribution recorded by Ovid in *Fasti* III, Bacchus appears in his most benevolent form. This is not, however, the only Bacchus Piero imagined. Piero was indeed as alert as Eliot was to the potential corruption of the god. In the other Bacchanalian scene he painted for the Vespucci Palace, *The Discovery of Wine,* a more intemperate, uncivilized Bacchic force is revealed. This more sinister perception is also hinted at in *The Discovery of Honey.* Just beside the figures of Bacchus and Ariadne we find Silenus on a mule, in a state of obvious intoxication. The debauchery expressed on his face suggests nothing so much as the laughing, drunken satyr of the sketch Eliot introduced early in the book.

In choosing the myth he commissions Piero to paint on the triptych, Tito wishes to express his vision of himself, of Romola, and of their relationship. The gift, he tells Romola, is meant to display "pretty *symbols* of our life together" (XX, p. 210; my italics), and these words prove to be truer than Tito intends. From its very conception, the triptych is tainted. Tito presents it to Romola as a gift of love, but it was not love that prompted Tito to commission it. The thought had never occurred to him until he had been forced to find a way of explaining the absence of a ring he had claimed to wear for the sake of his lost father (XVI, p. 170; XVIII, p. 191). This ring, which had been given to Tito by Baldassarre, and the wedding ring Tito gives Romola—two more circles in the geometric pattern—are central images in the book and together form part of Eliot's historical and epical argument. As external symbols of deeper bonds, the rings represent a relationship to two of the three closest possible ties, to parent and spouse, and therefore, as the family is the paradigm of the whole, a relationship to the past and to the present human community. Tito betrays both of these relationships.

The ring is only one of many valuables Baldassarre had left in

Tito's keeping, and Eliot used both the ring and the various gems Tito brings to Florence in a symbolic way. Eliot's readings and elaborate notes in her *Commonplace Book,* much of which did not finally find a place in *Romola,* suggest that she must have long contemplated these images, and perhaps experimented with a number of possibilities. One source, Camillo Leonardi's *Speculum Lapidum,* an account of the state of knowledge on the subject of gems in the fifteenth century, is cited in the text (VI, p. 74). In her *Commonplace Book,* Eliot also mentioned Johann Joachim Winckelmann's *Catalogue of Stosch's Gems;* Gotthold Lessing's *Antiquarische Briefe;* Pliny, a copy of which was included in the Eliot/Lewis library (no. 1704); and above all Thomas Joseph Pettigrew's *On Superstitions Connected with the History and Practice of Medicine and Surgery,* a well-marked copy of which was also included in the library (no. 1673). The idea to use gems in the book may have been a visual recollection, for on her first trip to Italy Eliot had seen, at the Uffizi—at the same time she had seen Fra Angelico's triptych—a "cabinet of gems, quite alone in its fantastic, elaborate minuteness and workmanship in rarest materials" (Cross, II, 173).

Gems have been mysterious objects since antiquity and have been endowed by all peoples with strange and wonderful powers, often with specific medicinal or other effects. Although Eliot based her symbolic use of the gems on this long tradition, she selected and shaped their history for her own purposes; each reveals another aspect of Tito in his Bacchic form. When Tito first looks for someone to purchase his gems, Romola suggests Bartolommeo Scala, since his daughter Alessandra "delights in gems" and calls them her "winter flowers" (VI, p. 74). And so they are in their symbolic aspect. Alessandra's description is ironic and ambiguous. Like all flowers, winter flowers are the special province of the vegetation god, and in one sense these are all the more precious for their scarcity. But winter flowers are no flowers at all, and the gems might be thought of as petrified life, as symbols of death. It is these gems Baldassarre asks Tito to use in his ransom, and these that Tito chooses to sell for his own profit instead. When Bardo hears what the estimated worth of the gems is, he exclaims "Ah, more than a man's ransom" (VI, p. 74), words that later echo in Tito's memory when he receives Baldassarre's letter, although he has, characteristically, forgotten their origin (IX, p. 103). When Tito refuses, then, to use the gems in Baldassarre's rescue, it is death, not life, that Bacchus chooses for Baldassarre and, in the inevitable consequences of that act, for himself as well.

In the many notes on rings and gems she entered in her *Commonplace Book,* Eliot traces the history of insignia from Egypt, which she called "the fountainhead of European civilization," to Greece, to Rome, and finally to Renaissance Florence (Yale MS 6). Here, in a sense, is one more thread in the history of civilization, another small analogue to Eliot's own design. In one note, Eliot commented that Christianity acted more and more as a check on the pagan practice of designing on the stones set in rings representations of mythological subjects and so inadvertently encouraged the substitution of self-portraiture. But symbolically Tito's ring is both. The intaglio of a fish with a crested serpent above it on Tito's ring (IV, p. 44) suggests Bacchus, the epiphanic god of the sea who numbers among his special creatures the serpent. One another gem, the Jew's stone—so called, Eliot explained in her *Commonplace Book,* because when the art had expired the gnostic amulets were ascribed to the ancient Hebrews (Yale MS 6)—we find a serpent again, this time with the head of a lion, another creature of Bacchus. In another configuration, the lion appears again on the agate, this time bearing a wonderful semblance of Cupid (VII, p. 84). The animal imagery on these gems, especially the image of the serpent, enters the poetic narrative again when Baldassarre reaches Florence and begins the long revenge that ends in Tito's death, for Baldassarre himself becomes the serpent of the gems, even as he becomes the tiger of the triptych, as we shall see in Chapter VI. There is considerable irony, then, in the fact that the agate is traditionally held to counteract the venom of serpents, a venom against which, in selling the gem, Tito leaves himself defenseless.

This agate is intimately connected to Tito's ring; it is not only the intaglio of the serpent that is significant in the ring but the stone itself. The stone is onyx, of the same family, Eliot noted in her *Commonplace Book,* as the agate (Yale MS 6), and of all stones the most appropriate, since it is held to have the peculiar power of inciting quarrels, an effect antithetical to the symbolic meaning of the ring as a bond, but one characteristic of Bacchus. Yet it is

Eliot's point that such bonds cannot be broken with impunity. Entirely innocent of implications, Tito explains that the ring as a whole is "of virtue to make the wearer fortunate, especially at sea, and also to restore to him whatever he may have lost" (IV, p. 44). What Tito has lost is the past, represented in Baldassarre—and that past will be brought back to him with a vengeance.

It is with the profit made from the sale of this ring that Tito plans to pay Piero for the triptych, although Piero, who does not know the events but has an intuitive understanding of Tito, refuses to accept payment. To keep the ring for Baldassarre's sake, Tito had concluded when Bratti had spoken of the good price he could get for it, was nothing more than "mere sentiment" (XIV, p. 148). Indeed, Tito needed very little persuasion to part with it, since it had been that very ring that had identified Tito to Dino when, as Fra Luca, Dino had carried Baldassarre's letter to Florence. There was no telling when another inconvenient message might find Tito in the same way (XIV, p. 148), and in that reflection the last vestige of sentiment died. Thus, the gift that is offered as a token of Tito's love for Romola is, prophetically, a subterfuge of deceit and purchased with the profit of betrayal.

The legend Tito asks Piero to paint on the triptych is mythologically appropriate. The marriage of Bacchus and Ariadne, a tale that became as popular in Renaissance Florence as it had been in antiquity, expressed a significant moment in the vegetation ritual. When Dionysus finds Ariadne abandoned and dying on the island of Naxos and brings her back to life, he enacts the promise that is the heart of the vegetation myth: the promise of immortality, of life in death. It is in this form, as Romola's savior, that Tito envisions himself. But this myth has an alternate and quite different version. In another account, Ariadne is not rescued by Bacchus but dies on Naxos where Theseus had, somehow, forgotten her. Eliot was not concerned in *Romola* with one aspect of Ariadne in the Theseus myth, the erotic Ariadne. Eliot's Ariadne is not the daughter of Pasiphaë, who became enamored of the Cretan bull and bore him the Minotaur, or the sister of Phaedra, whose lust for her stepson Hippolytus brought about both his death and hers, or who, herself fired by passion, conspired with Theseus against her own people. However, Eliot was concerned with another aspect of the Theseus myth, with the Ariadne who gave Theseus the thread that led him safely out of the Cretan labyrinth, an important image to which I will return in Chapter V. In this version of the myth, it is Ariadne who is the savior, a reversal of roles that lurks with prophetic irony behind Tito's instructions to Piero.[2]

Ultimately, it will not be in Tito's power to save anyone, least of all Romola. This much is already implicit in the physical form of the triptych, which, like the well-known variation on the myth, contradicts the painting on it. In fact, it is not exactly a triptych that Tito wishes to give Romola, but a box of which the triptych is the cover. And lovely and seductive as its adornment is, we cannot fail to notice that when Tito brings Romola his gift, the box is empty. On first meeting Tito, Romola's godfather, Bernardo del Nero, had remarked that Tito's mind seemed to him "a little too nimble to be weighted with all the stuff we men carry about in our hearts" (XIX, p. 202). The triptych, concealing under its Bacchic legend an inner vacuum, is a full graphic translation of this remarkable insight.

Ironically, although he does not realize the meaning of his action and intends the exact opposite, it is Tito who first reveals what it is that the hollow triptych should enclose (X, p. less 117). When Romola had earlier placed Dino's crucifix on top of a cabinet in the newly decorated apartment of Bardo's house in which she and Tito would spend their married life, she had symbolically announced that she would attempt to base their marriage on a moral foundation. Tito, however, had rejected that emblem. Once again there is satanic overtone in Tito's reaction to the crucifix and in his hurry to remove it from the prominent place Romola had given it. But it is with Romola's consent—for she "wished to subdue certain importunate memories and questionings which still flitted like unexplained shadows across her happier thought"—that Tito, looking for someplace to hide the crucifix out of sight, locks it within the hollow space of the triptych. "It is a little shrine," he says, "which is to hide away from you for ever that remembrancer of sadness. You have done with sadness now; and we will *bury* all *images* of it—*bury* them in a *tomb of joy*" (XX, pp. 208-9; my italics).

Tito's words are rich in irony. Reversing the religious associations of the triptych and the crucifix, Tito has accidentally hit on the truth. If the triptych is a shrine, it is a shrine, not to Bacchus, as Tito would have it, but to Christ, to the crucifix it now contains. In the course of the narrative, the triptych is often called a tabernacle—with all the biblical and ecclesiastical allusions of that word—and in this gesture Tito has in fact transformed it into one, for the triptych is now the hallowed receptacle of the crucifix. Thus, if the triptych becomes a "tomb of joy," a deliberately ambiguous term, it does so not because it buries the crucifix, as Tito thinks, but because the knowledge that crucifix confers must forever subdue the spontaneous passion for joy Bacchus represents. The term is also ambiguous in another sense. Tito's action is a symbolic reenactment of the Easter ritual. In burying the crucifix, Tito recalls Christ's burial, and it is Christ's tomb rather than Tito's that will prove to be a "tomb of joy," for through it mankind symbolically passes to salvation.

Just as the hollow triptych is a visual translation of Bernardo del Nero's description of Tito, so the juxtaposition of the two images—of the crucifix locked inside the triptych—is a visual translation of one of the chief moral metaphors in the book. Eliot took this metaphor from Aeschylus's trilogy, *The Oresteia,* which, in tracing the evolving sense of justice in Greek civiliation, parallels Eliot's purpose in at least one respect. Although he was not her favorite Greek writer, Eliot knew Aeschylus very well, as her use of *The Oresteia* shows. She read Aeschylus in Greek in 1857 and 1858 (Yale MS 1), perhaps in the Aeschylus volumes contained in the Eliot/Lewes library. Many of these belonged to Lewes who seems to have acquired them quite early. Although the French and English translations of Aeschylus (nos. 12, 13) are unsigned and unmarked, the Greek text with a Latin translation carries Lewes's signature and marginal linings (no. 14), and his signature or his linings, or both, are also in the Greek text with a German translation (no. 39), and a Greek and German text of the *Prometheus Bound* (no. 11). We do not know, however, who acquired W. Linwood's *Lexicon to Aeschylus Containing a Critical Explanation of the More Difficult Passages in the Seven Tragedies* (no. 6), an extremely useful book, as every reader who has confronted the mysteries of an Aeschylean ode knows; Heinrich Blumner's *Uber die Idee des Schicksals in den Tragö-*

dien des Aischylos (no. 250), and the *Dissertations on the Eumenides,* an English translation of C.O. Müller's German work (no. 10).

The last must have especially interested Eliot for it was *The Eumenides,* surely one of the most remarkable plays ever written, that particularly fired Eliot's imagination. It is from *The Eumenides* that Eliot takes the lines that provide the central moral metaphor in *Romola.* The passage Eliot quotes is the one in which the Eumenides claim that a sense of moral awe is necessary to inspire men to do what is right. And therefore, the passage continues, "it is good that men should carry a threatening shadow in their hearts under the full sunshine" (XI, p. 122). These lines, like the union of the two major symbols, is the point around which all the arguments of Eliot's book turn. Here is the reconciliation Romola had looked for, the balanced compromise between nature and morality. Under the full sunshine of the Bacchic worship must be concealed the threatening shadow of the crucifix: within joy there is pain; amid the celebration of life there is death. No vision of human existence can ignore the ambivalence of human experience.

It is especially significant that Tito presents Romola with this gift, conceived in deceit, on the day of their betrothal, a ritual on which Eliot places considerable stress, since, as the word "betrothal" suggests, it involves the pledge of fidelity and forms, thus, another link in that major theme. It is in fact the betrothal that Eliot includes in the narrative, leaving the wedding to be sketched in in retrospect, in part perhaps because it is not in Bacchus but in Christ that Romola finds her true marriage. However, the two events are described together, in succession, since here the temporal sequence is broken by a hiatus of eighteen months. And they do indeed belong together, for both are controlled by the same imagery, precisely the imagery suggested in the relationship between the triptych and the crucifix. The imagery, like the narrative, seems to focus on the triptych, for the union appears to be the one depicted on its legend. But within this Bacchic framework we perceive hidden Christian images that reveal, with persistent irony, the moral character of the events.

The betrothal is one of the most pictorial scenes in the book. Here, Eliot virtually paints the imagery that is implied chiefly through color. From the beginning, color had distinguished Romola's and Tito's natures. In Romola's fair skin and blond hair we infer, through conventional associations of light and dark, a capacity for the life of the spirit, while in Tito's swarthy complexion, in the sensuality of his dark brown curls (I, p. 11), smooth olive cheek (I, p. 13), and long dark eyes (II, p. 26), we sense only the soft, pleasure-loving creature of the earth. Although we can with certainty identify neither with a specific figure in a Renaissance painting, Romola reminds us of countless Renaissance representations of the Virgin, whose role she later assumes, while Tito, in his peculiar form of beauty, recalls ancient images of Dionysus, even, indeed, in his maidenlike appearance (III, p. 38), a characteristic description of Dionysus among the Greeks.

That distinction is fully elaborated in the dress of the two figures on the day of their betrothal. Eliot spent considerable time and energy gathering information on costumes. In March 1861 she wrote to Joseph Munt Langford that she was grateful to him for looking up old-fashioned costumes for her. "You would oblige and help me very much," she added, "if you would keep your eyes open for all books or fragments that will serve as memoranda of costume either mediaeval or modern. In the London Library they have nothing better than Fairholt's scanty book, and unhappily, with my temperament, I fear it would be next to impossible for me to go to the British Museum. I would go to some expense for a good book on mediaeval costumes" *(Letters,* III, 393-94). Despite her disinclination, Eliot did, however, go to the British Museum at last on November 14, 1861 (Cross, II, 250), although Langford had not ignored her request. In July 1861 he had, as Lewes recorded in his Journal, brought Eliot "a magnificent book," *Le Moyen Age Illustré (Letters,* III, 435). The less important of the two books by Jean Charles Sismondi Eliot studied for *Romola,* and useful to her chiefly in its account of popular superstitions (Yale MS 3), *Le Moyen Age Illustré* did provide her with considerable information, both descriptive and pictorial, on the medieval costumes she wanted to know about. These are not exactly the costumes of *Romola.* Eliot's interest in medieval dress was epical, for again she wished to know not only how her Florentine characters might have looked in the period of her book but how the Renaissance dress of the Florentine had evolved. The more immediate models for the costumes of the book are found elsewhere.

We can identify several sources from Eliot's correspondence with Frederic Leighton, who illustrated *Romola* and to whom Eliot made a number of suggestions for specific items. Eliot's perennial concern with historical authenticity, in this as in all matters, is witnessed by her final instructions to Leighton. "Approximate truth," she wrote, "is the only truth attainable, but at least one must strive for that, and not wade off into arbitrary falsehood." To that end, she sent Leighton, in the same letter, to consult Varchi on male costumes of dignified Florentines in the period *(Letters,* IV, 43), specifically to a passage she had had marked in her copy of Benedetto Varchi's *Storia Fiorentina* (no. 2206) in the Eliot/Lewes library). Again in the same letter, Eliot asked Leighton to check whether the women in Ghirlandajo's frescoes wore "that plain piece of opaque drapery over the head which haunts my memory." It was more than the drapery of those frescoes, however, that haunted Eliot's memory. Although, as she told Leighton, she had been prevented by repairs then going on from seeing the frescoes the second time she visited Florence, Ghirlandajo's work left a deep impression on her. Eliot's admiration was inspired not so much by the quality of Ghirlandajo's work as by its philosophic bias, as Eliot explained in *Romola* itself, in the first chapter in which the narrator remarks that Ghirlandajo had made "the walls of the churches reflect the life of Florence . . . translating pale aerial traditions into the deep colour and strong lines of the faces he knew" (p. 21). As the subordinate clause suggests, Ghirlandajo, like Piero di Cosimo, was one of the first painters to break with the Middle Ages and to enter the Renaissance. Not only was he, again like Piero, a realist who painted what he saw—in their way medieval painters, too, painted what they saw—he saw differently, as a Renaissance humanist did, and he proclaimed his vision as a challenge on the very walls of medieval churches. His frescoes "reflect" the life of the city in the same way in which Eliot had promised to "mirror" life in the seventeenth chapter of *Adam Bede.*

Ghirlandajo was important to Eliot for another reason. On first seeing some of his frescoes, she was reminded that Ghirlandajo had been the master of Michelangelo (Cross, II, 171). If by report only,

Michelangelo too has a place in the narrative (III, p. 32). Eliot seems to have been reluctant to introduce the great painters still living in Florence at the time as actors in the book, perhaps because she felt it inappropriate to use artists of such stature in functional roles only. But their presence is felt neverthless. Piero, the disciple of Leonardo, also still living, although not at this time in Florence, and Ghirlandajo, the teacher of Michelangelo, are in a sense their voices in the book. Through the lesser we perceive the greater figures, figures that towered over their contemporaries not only in their art but, endowed with all gifts, as epitomes of the Renaissance man. We know in fact that it was not only Michelangelo's art that interested Eliot. In her *Quarry,* Eliot noted that in preparing to write *Romola* she had studied Harford's *Life of Michaelangelo,* and it may have been for the same purpose that she acquired for her library Richard Duppe's *Lives and Works of Michael Angelo* (no. 637 in the Eliot/Lewes library). It was probably not in Duppe's book, however, but in her Italian volume of Michelangelo's plays (no. 338) that in November 1861 she read *La Tancia* (Yale MS 3), useful in part, like other Florentine comedies, for the familiarity it gave her with the idiom of the vernacular, but undoubtedly of equal significance in Eliot's thorough research on a symbolically central allusion.

To Frederic Leighton also Eliot identified as a source for the feminine dress in Renaissance Florence Ginevra's trousseau described in the Ricordi of the Rinuccini family *(Letters,* IV, 43) The trousseau is copied in full in Eliot's *Quarry,* in which she recorded also that she had read the Ricordi while in Florence. In the *Quarry* too we find many pages of entries on the costume of the Renaissance Italian, entries taken from Ademollo's *Marietta de' Ricci,* from Ludovico Muratori's *Antichità* (a book to which I will return in Chapter V), and from many other assorted sources. We find similar entries in her *Commonplace Book,* in which, in addition, Eliot copied several pages of notes on ecclesiastical vestments from Rock's *Hierurgia* (Yale MS 6), a book she had been reading in August and September 1861 (Yale MS 3) and from which she took as well, as she reminded herself in the *Quarry,* hints on various aspects of church ceremony.

One more item in Eliot's letter to Leighton seems significant.

Eliot was quite concerned to have a precise image of the headdress of the Florentine woman, at first perhaps only for the sake of being able to imagine a complete costume. In her copy of Donato Velluti's *Cronica di Firenze dall' anno MCCC, in arca sino al MCCCLXX,* a book edited by Manni, whose *Lives* of Bartolommeo Scala and of Savonarola she read as well, Eliot had, for example, marked a passage that contained a description of a characteristic headdress (no. 2210 in the Eliot/Lewes library). Similarly, in recommending to Leighton Ginevra's trousseau for his study, Eliot suggested that although incomplete and belonging to a somewhat earlier period, it was the best authority she knew, for it illustrated even the then prevalent rage for pearls in women's caps. It is that rage that characterizes the *berretta* she described to Leighton, a close-fitting velvet cap, square at the ears, and embroidered everywhere with pearls. Not by accident perhaps, we find such a pearled headdress in Piero di Cosimo's painting of Simonetta Vespuccia, whose face, coloring, stature, and general appearance present just the picture we form of Romola from the descriptions in the book. The painting was commissioned by Giovanni Vespucci, who in *Romola* commissions the painting for which Piero wants Romola to sit, and was displayed in the Vespucci Palace, where Piero had also painted the two Bacchanalian scenes. It may well have been Simonetta Vespuccia's face that Eliot carried away from Florence as the image of Romola's. If Eliot herself did not make that attribution, it may be because Vasari, on the basis of the asp coiled around the figure's neck, identified the painting as a portrait of Cleopatra, with whom Eliot would not have wished to associate Romola.

Those same pearls, not on a *berretta* but on a veil, reappear in the betrothal scene (XX, p. 208). As symbols of purity, the pearls dissociate Romola from the man with whom she is about to be joined. Indeed, the contrast of light and dark that had distinguished Romola and Tito in their appearance is stressed again in the colors of the betrothal. Romola is "all lily-white and golden," while Tito, "with his dark glowing beauty," wears a "purple red-bordered tunic" (XX, p. 209). This color imagery is doubly suggestive. In one sense, the colors dissociate Tito and Romola by placing them in entirely different moral worlds; purple and red, the colors in which we almost always find Tito, are the colors of Bacchus, whereas white and gold are the colors of Christian purity and heavenly glory. Here we are reminded again of the similarities in the two mystery gods. Tito's purple tunic recalls not only Bacchus but Christ's purple robe at the crucifixion, and the reason for that color is in both cases the same, the grape with which Bacchus is associated, and the vine with which Christ identifies himself (see John 10:5). In this sense, Romola's betrothal to Tito foreshadows her later "marriage" to Christ.

The moral distinction between the two figures is elaborated still more in the reference to the lily. Early in the book, Nello, intending no more than to praise her beauty, had given Romola an epic epithet, one that appears many times in the course of the narrative, when he had called her "the Florentine lily" (III, p. 41). As a literal flower, the lily is the proper province of the vegetation god, and in this sense the allusion binds Romola to the pagan savior. Indeed, Tito has had a rejuvenating effect on Romola, which is pursued in terms of this metaphor. In his presence, the narrator remarks, Romola "seemed to unfold like a strong white lily" (XIX, pp. 199-200). But the lily is also a central Christian symbol. It is, first, like the white to which it is here hyphenated, and like the pearls of Romola's white veil, a symbol of purity. Second, it is the flower of the Virgin, a symbol of the Annunciation. When Romola had received the triptych, she had at first acquiesced in its apparent meaning. "I am Ariadne," she had said to Tito, "and you are crowning me" (XX, p. 209). Romola alludes to the crown of stars which in some versions of the myth Dionysus is reported to have given to Ariadne. But even this allusion is ambiguous. Eliot was an excellent astronomer. She had, Cross reports, "a passion for the stars," and "in later days, the map of the heavens lay constantly on her table at Witley" (Cross, III, 342-43). Her astronomical allusions are never vague. The crown of stars supposed to have been Ariadne's is actually the corona borealis, a manifestation of the aurora borealis. Thus, even this Bacchic crown is assimilated into a Christian image, for it echoes Romola's identification with Aurora, an identification Tito had appropriately made but one that, ironically, had marked the beginning of Romola's moral consciousness. Ironically, too, the triptych Romola had at first accepted as a

Bacchic gift and on which Tito had asked Piero to paint a "crowned" Ariadne, had been commissioned on September 8, 1492, the Day of the Nativity of the Virgin—the image that in the middle of the book, transforms the Bacchic Ariadne into the Christian Madonna. In the allusion to the lily, that transformation is foreshadowed here. Finally, the lily is the flower of the Christian resurrection. It is clear that this union with Bacchus is superseded by a metaphoric union with the other savior, who, in fact, dominates the entire ceremony: the three colors together—white, red, and gold—are the colors of Easter.

Thus, in the very moment in which she is joined to Tito, Romola begins the metamorphosis that will lead her from the triptych to the crucifix. That transition is implied here in another aspect of the color symbolism, for here the contrast of light and dark takes on another dimension. In the passage in which Romola had defined for herself the world of Bacchus and Christ, Christ had appeared as a *pale* image and Bacchus as a *sungod* who knew nothing of night. When Romola had allowed Tito to remove the crucifix from the cabinet in their apartment, it was because she wished to avoid the *shadows* that the crucifix cast over her happier thoughts. And the passage Eliot quotes from Aeschylus speaks of moral awe as a threatening *shadow* in man's heart under the full *sunshine.* In the sunlight in which Bacchus stands, there is always vibrant color. But in the invisible, dark world where the Christian pilgrimage is made, color becomes indistinguishable; and the white Romola wears on the day of her betrothal to Bacchus is, ironically, her first step out of color. Although Tito continues to wear the Bacchic red and purple, from the day of her betrothal Romola wears no colors, but assumes the colorless uniforms of sorrow, moving from the white of her betrothal gown to the gray of the nun's habit and finally to the black mantle of the Dominican Piagnoni. Ironically again, Tito also on occasion wears a black mantle over his red and purple clothing, and while that black is not Dominican but Bacchic and satanic, it is for him as for Romola a mantle of sorrow that reminds us, as Tito will at last discover, that whether we accept it willingly or not, sorrow is inescapable.

The two worlds revealed in the betrothal are reflected in the calendar, which, like the symbolic structure everywhere, alludes to both the pagan and the Christian saviors, Characteristically, Eliot here collapsed time to make a historical and universal point. By making the pagan and the Christian eras not sequential as they were in history, but contemporaneous, Eliot not only suggests the parallels between the rituals of Bacchus and Christ—parallels that allow us to see every event in both its Bacchic and its Christian aspect—but permits us to make a comparative assessment of the two gods that is a symbolic equivalent of a philosophic dialectic. Thus, the epic form not only reenacts the historical evolution but enables us to examine in the modern era the coexisting historical legacies of the past.

The betrothal takes place in the last week of the pre-Lenten carnival, which came in 1493 in the last days of January and the first of February. It is precisely the time of the Lenaean festival, a partially obscure celebration of Dionysus in which the cult statue of the Lenaion (the temple of Dionysus in which the god's birthday was commemorated) was worshiped as the "mask god," an image that recalls the representation of Bacchus in Piero's sketch of the three masks. It is an appropriate time for the betrothal, for the Lenaea falls in the month of Gamelion, which, as Eliot had noted in her *Commonplace Book* under her entry on the Attic calendar, was so named because it was the favorite month for weddings (Yale MS 6), chiefly because of the Bacchic rite.

But in remembering that these are also the last few days before Lent, we realize that we must look at this event in shadow as well as in sunshine. Eliot did in fact place the Bacchic rite in a Christian perspective, and as Christ's antithesis Tito assumes once more a satanic role. Dino's vision that Romola would marry the Great Tempter recurs now at the betrothal when Romola fears that her brother's prophecy has been half fulfilled. As she and Tito leave the church, the betrothal procession becomes entangled in the wild pre-Lenten carnival the Florentines are celebrating, and images as though of the "sheeted dead" seem to glide past the couple, images chanting "a wailing strain," a "strange dreary chant, as of a *Miserere*" (XX, pp. 211-12). This is a fitting chant for both Romola and Tito at this moment, for like all those who commit themselves to the Bacchic life, they will have great need of the divine mercy for which the words of David's penitential psalm plead.

The scene of the betrothal is a striking one and calls up memories of Dante's *Inferno* as well as Book XI of the *Odyssey*, the Book of the Dead, on which Dante drew indirectly, although this is not yet Romola's traditional descent into Hades. Eliot may have been thinking of Dante and Homer when she wrote this scene, but I think we can identify several more immediate sources. The staging of carnivals had become a popular enterprise in Renaissance Florence and, greatly encouraged by Lorenzo de' Medici, himself responsible for staging many, had acquired the character of a sporting competition, something reminiscent of the Roman circus. Eliot had read a good deal on these carnivals in the *Tutti i Trionfi, Carri, Mascherate o Canti Carnascia leschi* [sic], *andati per Firenze, dal tempo del magnifico Lorenzo de Medici, fino all' anno 1559* by Antonio Francesco Grazzini, the sixteenth-century Florentine apothecary known as Il Lasca (no. 879 in the Eliot/Lewes library). Eliot must have added to this general background the account given by Vasari, in his life of Piero di Cosimo, of a carnival procession devised by Piero, an account that suggests the scene at the betrothal, not only in several details, but also in its strange, ominous mood. The prominent place of the Miserere is not Piero's device, however, but Eliot's. When she wrote this scene, she may have recalled the Miserere she had heard, and by which she had been deeply moved, at St. Peter's in Rome on Good Friday of 1860 (Yale MS 2). Certainly she was thinking of Savonarola's reflections on Psalm 51 in his *Expositione sopra il Psalmo Miserere mei Deus,* one of the many works of Savonarola Eliot had studied, and a copy of which she had very likely acquired for her library while preparing to write *Romola* (no. 1928).

To Romola the strange events that surround her betrothal seem prophetic. Ironically, as Tito attempts to allay Romola's fears, he alludes to the symbolic current that will prove them true. "My Ariadne," Tito says, "must never look backward now—only forward to Easter, when she will triumph with her Care-dispeller" (XX, p. 212), words that move the action, literally and symbolically, forward to the wedding.

Metaphorically, the wedding evolves inevitably from the betrothal. The time set for the ceremony suggest that there are in fact two weddings, as in a sense there had been two betrothals. On the pagan calendar, it is now the month of Anthesterion, the "feast of flowers," as Eliot described it, etymologically, in her Attic calendar, and the season of the three days' feast of Dionysus at Athens (Yale MS 6). This is indeed the height of the celebration of the fertility god, and it was, in fact, at this time that the marriage of Bacchus and Ariadne was said to have taken place. In the wedding that is celebrated according to this calendar, therefore, Ariadne does marry the "Care-dispeller," a traditional epithet of Bacchus, who is known, in one of his many names, as "Lyaeus," the "loosener" of care. The persistent emphasis on the fertility cult stresses the sexual union, the resurrection—the awakening—of the flesh. In contrast, the marriage that is celebrated according to the Christian calendar, at Easter, is a spiritual union in which the "Florentine lily" chooses the right date but the wrong husband. Yet, precisely because Tito is the wrong husband, the marriage serves as Romola's personal baptism in sorrow and thus fulfills not only Dino's prophecy but the meaning of the crucifix she had inherited from him. In this sense, Romola's marriage to Tito foreshadows her later "marriage" to Christ and, ironically, marks the beginning of her spiritual life.

Like Romola, Tito too marries twice in the course of the narrative. It may be, as Gordon Haight suggests, that Eliot was indebted for Tessa to the naive young heroine of T.A. Trollope's *Beata (Letters,* III, 435, n. 3), but Tessa is far less important in Eliot's book as a character than in her symbolic relationship to Tito. Tessa in fact plays two symbolic roles that are intimately connected. Tito identifies one of her functions when he remarks to himself about Tessa: "Here is a little contadina who might inspire a better idyl than Lorenzo de' Medici's *Nencia da Barberino,* that Nello's friends rave about; if I were only a Theocritus!" (X, p. 112). Here Eliot alluded to the "Nencia" *strambotti,* rustic love songs, which became the rage of Florence around 1475. Everyone seemed to be composing them, even Bartolommeo Scala, who, however, jealous of his reputation as a classicist, wrote not a *strambotto* but, undoubtedly in imitation of Virgil, an eclogue on the subject.

Although there is some controversy today as to whether or not it was Lorenzo who composed the longest of the "Nencia" *strambotti*, until recently he was believed to be its author, and Eliot attributed to Lorenzo the portion of it that she copied into her *Commonplace Book* (Yale MS 6). In reminding us of Theocritus, Eliot suggests that we have here one more of those historical threads, which in this case traces the literary tradition of the idyl from pagan times to the Renaissance. Through November and December 1861, Eliot was "peeping into Theocritus" (Yale MS 3), whose *Idylls* she owned in both a French (no. 2132) and an English (no. 2134)) translation, but which she must have read in the original Greek, for it is that volume in her library that contains her notes and marginal linings (no. 2133).

In imagining Tessa the heroine of an idyl, Tito identifies her with the pastoral life that surrounds the city of Florence, and at the same time therefore distinguishes her from Romola, who is wholly identified with the city. Indeed, when Tessa asks Tito to join her in a rustic feast, she invites him to sit with her under a tree *outside the gate* of the city (X, p. 113; my italics), and it is outside the city's gates that Tito later sets up his home with Tessa. As we shall see again in the conversion scene (chapter VII) in *Romola* Eliot symbolically thought of "civilization" in its etymological sense, as the history of cities, and it is with the life of the city of Florence that civilization is identified here. The pastoral life of the idyl is, therefore, life outside civilization, life lived according not to the laws of man but to the laws of nature. Thus, Tessa is Tito's "natural" bride, just as Romola is his "civilized" bride.

In a sense, therefore, Tito's "marriage" to Tessa is analogous to Romola's "marriage" to Christ, for in each case the partners belong to the same historical and moral sphere. As Romola belongs more truly to the spiritual world of Christ, so Tito belongs more truly to Tessa, who, as a child of nature, is like himself both pagan and amoral. This brings us to Tessa's second symbolic role. In all these ways a reflection of Tito himself, Tessa becomes his counterpart, a fertility goddess. Appropriately it is the vegetation god who initiates her into that role when he selects from among his many gems a red coral to give her (X, p. 117) for the red coral has traditionally the talismanic power to end sterility. It is Tito, too, who keeps bringing Tessa the nuts to which she is so addicted, and through which Eliot ingeniously identifies Tessa with fertility rites, for nuts are the conventional symbol of fertility in medieval and Renaissance art. It is for this reason, of course, that it is Tessa rather than Romola who bears Tito's children.

Romola's two marriages (I will return later to the second) are central both to her individual and to her epic life. In mirroring the two major symbols, they represent to Romola both an individual moral choice and a historically cultural one. Marriage, the narrator observes at one point, is a relationship either of sympathy or of conquest (XLVIII, p. 427). Since nothing is morally neutral in Eliot's universe, every moment of life asks us to make that same choice. Marriage is not, therefore, merely a literal union here but far more a symbolic one, a metaphor for every other social relationship. Once more, it is the model of the family that is the image of the community, of the political structure, of society at large, and finally of the entire race of man. Thus, as Tito and Savonarola represent to Romola her own individual choices, so in their mythic manifestations as Bacchus and Christ they represent her historical and epic alternatives.

There is another and related significance to the crucial place marriage is given in *Romola,* as in fact in all of Eliot's fiction. In tracing the three stages through which the individual's capacity for love and sympathy grows into social and moral consciousness, Comte suggested that marriage is the second step beyond the love of self. The expansion of self that begins in the filial relationship is extended in marriage, he argued, to a stranger, through whom the individual passes to a sense of fellowship with a wider group, a fellowship that includes in the end all his contemporaries and so society as a whole. But if Eliot was following Comte here, as she seems to have been, she followed him only so far. Comte's argument rested on the supposition that the love for another individual that is expressed in marriage strengthens sympathetic over egotistic inclinations and thus makes one capable of even greater, more comprehensive love. We learn to love, as it were, by loving But this is not the point of Romola's marriage to Tito. Eliot's conclusion was not that we learn love by loving but, rather, that we learn compassion for pain by feeling pain ourselves. Sympathy, that is, is a leap of the imagination through which we enter the experiences of others and feel them as our own.

In choosing whether it will be sympathy or conquest that will characterize our relationships with others, we choose implicitly to follow either Bacchus or Christ. As the very symbol of a fellowship in suffering, Christ is the choice of sympathy. Bacchus, in contrast, had announced which of the two he preferred when he had asked Piero di Cosimo to paint the god on the triptych in an attitude of triumph. Originally, Tito had envisioned the painting on the triptych as the triumph of both Bacchus and Ariadne. But that had been only one more of the many illusions by which Tito's vision of life is warped; not even lovers are in such perfect harmony. If the end is triumph, conquest, as for Bacchus it is, it can fall to only one of them. And in their marriage, Tito never yields.

Love, the narrator remarks of Romola's feeling toward Tito, "does not aim simply at the conscious good of the beloved object"—and "beloved object" is surely a translation of the Greek meaning of Tito's surname—"it is not satisfied without perfect loyalty of the heart; it aims at its own completeness" (XXVII, p. 263). To this Christian principle is contrasted the Bacchic. Self-love too aims at its own completeness. In its perfect loyalty to itself, it is invariably false to others with whose interests and wishes it comes into conflict. It is here, therefore, where the symbolic significannce of marriage and the theme of fidelity meet, that Eliot makes clear why Tito's and Romola's marriage fails, both morally and psychologically.

Piero, who had seen the unlikelihood of the union from the beginning, had remarked that "Bacco trionfante" had "married the fair Antigone in contradiction to all history and fitness" (XXV, p. 241). His choice of metaphors is entirely appropriate, since it is with Antigone that the triumphant Bacchus clashes in the first and most important conflict of their marriage. Although Romola had needed no encouragement to marry Tito, she had felt justified in choosing him because it had seemed to her that Tito was the very man to replace for Bardo the son he had lost. A scholar but not a monk, Tito had seemed to possess all of Dino's virtues but none of his faults. It had been with great pain, therefore, that Romola had discovered, from the beginning of their married life, that Tito was no better a son to Bardo than Dino had been and that, in fact, Tito had asked her as well to choose between Bardo and himself. Upon Bardo's death, she had, not without some guilt, expected their relationship to improve, but it is precisely at this moment that the conflict between Bacchus and Antigone reaches its climax.

The persistent model of fidelity, Romola had entered her marriage with the same sense of loyalty to Tito that she had felt for her father. In her relationship to Tito, she had assumed, as an extension and a parallel to her role as Antigone, the identity of Alcestis (XIII, p. 139), the faithful wife of Admetus. Although Eliot's knowledge of Euripides is no less certain than her knowledge of the other Greek dramatists, it seems to have been less extensive. The Eliot/Lewes library contained an individual copy of *Alcestis* (no. 677); a copy of the second volume of Zimmermann's edition of the complete plays (no. 676); and a Greek text with a Latin translation of the complete plays (no. 679), a smaller collection than we find under Sophocles or Aeschylus. Similarly, Eliot did not quote from Euripides as readily, or allude to him as often. The most interesting question, therefore, for *Romola* is one to which we have, unfortunately, no answer. No reference appears anywhere in Eliot's Diaries, Journals, or elsewhere to Euripides' *Bacchae,* the play that is most pertinent to her own book. Yet it is difficult to believe that Eliot had not read it, that this would be an exception in Eliot's extensive knowledge of Greek drama. Whether or not she had read it, however, she did know at least Ovid's narrative of the play, a narrative that appears in the section of the *Metamorphoses* from which Tito instructs Piero to take his details for the triptych.

The two mythological figures, Antigone and Alcestis, have a natural kinship in their deep capacity for love and loyalty, but it is the peculiar nature of Bacchus to bring them into conflict. In expecting perfect loyalty to himself, Tito implicitly demands Romola's disloyalty to others. Thus, although Romola, as Antigone, had wished to execute faithfully her father's request to have his library set up as his memorial in Florence, as Bacchus, Tito had instead chosen to sell it for his own profit. In that act Tito repudiates the heritage of the past, all history, all culture. His quarrel with Romola over the library is therefore not only a quarrel with his wife but with all of Western civilization, appropriately with the Christian era, but, ironically, also with his own pagan civilization, which was what Bardo's scholarship had, however poorly, attempted to resurrect.

It is in this conflict between her roles as Antigone and Alcestis that Romola begins to discover what a complete commitment to Bacchus entails. At their wedding, Tito and Romola had "had a rainbow-tinted shower of comfits thrown over them, after the ancient Greek fashion, in token that the heavens would shower sweets on them through all their double life" (XXI, p. 213). But a year and a half later, the narrator observes, it is clear that the "rainbow-tinted shower of sweets, to have been perfectly typical, should have had some invisible seeds of bitterness mingled with them" (XXVII, p. 251). The transition from the visible sweets to the invisible seeds of bitterness is a graphic parallel to the transition from the external beauty to the internal vacuum of the triptych, the vacuum in which the moral end of the Bacchic life is revealed. It forms as well the transition from the Bacchic to the Christian life, to the crucifix that represents the "invisible" and "bitter" world, and thus prepares for the image of the nun into which Antigone is about to be transformed.

5.

Tito and Florence—A Prophecy

That transformation, and the reasons for it, is described in one of the most important sentences in the book. The "crowned Ariadne, under the snowing roses," the narrator remarks, "had felt more and more the presence of unexpected thorns" (XXVII, p. 251).[1] The Bacchic wreath Tito had asked Piero to paint on the triptych had proved to be not the crown of stars but the crown of thorns. The two marriages Romola had undertaken, the joyful and the moral, had resisted fusion, on one level because, although Romola might have been able to balance joy and sorrow, Tito could not, for, on a still more symbolic level, Tito represents Romola's discovery that pure joy is morally and psychologically impossible—psychologically, in fact, because morally.

Romola had once remarked that the memory of Dino raising his eyes in his dying moment to the crucifix would forever stand between her and everything else she would ever look at. It was this thought that Tito had tried to obliterate when he had locked the crucifix inside the triptych and called it a "tomb of joy." But Romola had explained the true meaning of Tito's action and, ironically, of his words. The key is in Romola's reference to memory, central in all of Eliot's fiction, and nowhere more fully explored than here. Memory is intimately connected to imagination, and both expand the metaphoric theme of vision.

The three faculties describe both a moral and a psychological progression. Memory, the basis of imagination, is the faculty that brings the past into the present. In its absence we suffer not only an interruption in the continuum of self that results in a confusion of identity—as in Baldassarre's case—but a moral lapse as well. "The feelings that gather fervour from novelty," the narrator observes in connection with Tito, "will be of little help towards making the world a home for dimmed and faded human beings; and if there is any love of which they are not widowed, it must be the love that is rooted in memories and distils perpetually the sweet balms of fidelity and forbearing tenderness" (IX, p, 105). Without memory, we live only in the present moment and respond only to its temptations. Without memory, we can feel no ties of affection whose roots are in the past and that might check a present inclination to make an egotistic choice. Without memory there can be no bonds of any kind, for to lose the past is to be condemned to meet even those we know each time as though it were the first.

The egotists of Eliot's fiction are characteristically beings without memory. Although unlike Baldassarre they have not been afflicted with amnesia, they lack what Baldassarre's amnesia symbolizes, the ability to recall the past vividly, to feel it as though it were sensorily present. In that failure, they have lost the only bridge, in Eliot's view, to imagination. In a sense, imagination is memory projected. As memory recalls our own past, so imagination recalls not only the past of our own experience but the past, present, and future as well, of all experience which is analogous to our own. As in memory we carry with us the whole of our own lives, so in imagination we bring into our own consciousness the life of mankind and possess it as concretely as if we had lived it ourselves.

It is memory and imagination that cast the moral shadow across the Bacchic life of joy. The marriage to Bacchus described on the triptych would be possible only in a world in which there is no pain and is possible, as long as it lasts, only for those who are troubled by neither memory nor imagination. Romola is not such a character, but Tito is. When Romola first meets Tito, she wonders whether he, like herself, ever forgets a scholarly reference (VI, p. 67). He does not, but he does forget what is far more important; in fact, Tito is a very forgetful man and finds it very difficult to remember anyone who does not happen to be with him at the moment. Even those he remembers only partially. Thus, from the day he arrives in Florence, Baldassarre, who is not only his father but his symbolic past, becomes immediately remote to his imagination.

Here we begin to understand why Eliot named Tito's adopted father after one of the Magi. The idea for the connection may have been implanted when, on her first trip to Italy, Eliot saw the *Adoration of the Magi* by Gentile de Fabriano, which very much impressed her (Cross, II, 176). But Eliot's decision to identify Tito's father with Balthazar rather than one of the other two serves a symbolic purpose. It was Balthazar who brought the gift of myrrh, the gift in which the crucifixion was presumably prophesied because it was the symbol of life's bitterness. That is the same bitterness whose absence the narrator had noted at the time of Tito's and Romola's wedding. It is appropriate, therefore, that it should be Baldassarre, whose ring Tito had sold to buy the myth of joy represented on the triptych, and who would have been present in the enactment of that myth at the wedding had Tito not refused to ransom him, in whom Tito should find his own seed of bitterness. "Bitter" and "bitterness" are two of Baldassarre's favorite words. Ironically, it is as his seed of bitterness that Baldassarre describes Tito. "I saved you," he tells Tito when they meet at Tessa's home, "I nurtured you—I loved you. You forsook me—you robbed me—you denied me. . . . You have made the world bitterness to me" (XXXIV, p. 321). Ironically again, the god of joy, who can be the god of joy only because he acknowledges neither memory nor imagination in his vision, must also, for that reason, become the god of sorrow.

In his amnesia, therefore, as in other ways, Baldassarre is a gloss on Tito. When Eliot tells us that Baldassarre's power "of imagining facts needed to be reinforced continually by the senses" (L, p. 447), it is Tito she characterizes as well. Eliot's words, which she chooses very carefully, take us to the very heart of the issue. In binding imagination to the senses for Baldassarre and Tito, Eliot describes a strictly empiricist psychology. Yet in her psychology Eliot was herself an empiricist. For her, no less than for Tito and Baldassarre, imagination was rooted in experience, experience that had its ultimate origin in the senses. It is those experiences that memory recalls as it engenders imagination. Echoes of Hume, Locke, and Hartley are evident here, of course, for in this as in other ways heir to the tradition of British empiricism, Eliot believed as firmly as they in the chain of associations that begins in the senses and shapes the contents of our consciousness.

But surely we see here as well the influence of another heir of the empiricist tradition, Wordsworth, whose profound influence on Eliot remains yet to be fully assessed. Wordsworth points to the essential difference between Tito's and Eliot's empiricism. Once again, the difference is memory, the nonempirical bridge from one bundle of perceptions to another. All of us are creatures of the senses, and all of us are capable, without effort, of feeling our own pleasures and pains. Moral imagination, however, requires us to feel, to imagine as though they were our own, the pleasures and pains of others, and to achieve that level of imagination we store in memory our knowledge of pleasure and pain so that, recalled, it may become the basis of our sympathy for another. As Eliot remarks of Will Ladislaw in *Middlemarch,* "pain must enter into its glorified life of memory before it can turn into compassion" (Chap. LXXVIII). Although in some sense empirical, the abyss memory spans is nonempirical, for we cannot, except through memory, experience one another's pain. That abyss is therefore part of the invisible world, a world to which Tito is, like the other pagans of the book, like Bardo, blind. Though not literally blind, Tito is nevertheless a sleeper and a dreamer. Our first glimpse of him is Bratti's, who finds him sleeping on the pavement in a posture that distinctly recalls the reclining figure of Dionysus—thought by some to be Theseus—on the east pediment of the Parthenon. Eliot had very likely seen that figure, since the relief, which is one of the infamous Elgin Marbles, had been displayed since 1816 at the British Museum, where Eliot did some of her research for *Romola.*

Although to a lesser extent, the pagan world, especially Greece, was like the world of Renaissance Italy, a predominantly visual world in which art—in Greece, chiefly sculpture—flourished as an expression of the culture. The epic possibilities are obvious, and Eliot did not fail to seize them, in *Romola* or elsewhere. She had long been interested in the art of the Greeks, and to some degree of the Romans. She had written two brief pieces on the subject, "The Art of the Ancients," published in March 1855 in the *Leader,* and "The Art and Artists of Greece," published in May 1856 in the *Saturday Review.* On all her travels, in which museums were at the head of her itinerary, rivaled only by musical events, in addition to native work, Eliot always looked especially for German, Italian, and Greek collections, the last rapidly growing in bulk everywhere as Europe plundered the treasures of its past. Usually, after haunting museums by day, she took advantage of free evenings to read various studies of the works she had seen. For example, on a trip to Germany in 1858 she read Johann Friedrich Overbeck's *Geschichte der Griechischen Plastik für Kunstler and Kunstfreunde* (Yale MS 2), a copy of which (perhaps the same copy) is in the Eliot/Lewes library (no. 1590). On an earlier trip to Germany, in 1854, when she was seeing a considerable number of Greek originals for the first time, Eliot spent long hours with Lessing's *Laocoön,* a book she pronounced "acute and pregnant" (Yale MS 1), to which she returned many times in later years, and from which she copied a good deal of information into her *Commonplace Book* among her notes for *Romola* (Yale MS 6).

When Tito awakens from his sleep in that initial scene, he looks up with the "startled gaze of a . . . dreamer" (I, p. 10). There is considerable irony in the contrast Eliot suggests here between the visionary and the dreamer, terms one might find used interchangeably elsewhere but that for Eliot stand in complete opposition. Vision is an extension of imagination, although it can pass into dreaming—as it does in Dino, in Camilla Rucellai, and later in Savonarola—if it crosses the line that binds it to human sympathy. The dreamer, however, is not a seer in any sense of that word; he is a sleeper, one in whom the eyes are closed to the world outside the self and are turned, even as they had been in Bardo's blindness, inward. Nello rightly calls Tito Endymion (VIII, p. 98), the mythological symbol of the eternal sleeper. There is further irony in the fact that Endymion should act as an explication of Bacchus.

The savior—he whose function it is to resurrect the dead—is himself sleeping. In this, the apparent similarities between the mysteries of Bacchus and Christ resolve, in their implications, into one more antithesis.

Tito's moral failure, then, is a psychological, even a natural deficiency. He is an egotist by default, for he acts on the only basis he understands, and therefore in one sense at least it is not Tito but nature that is morally culpable. Thus, although Tito's story moves through a series of betrayals, it is not betrayal Tito intends, but indeed only loyalty to himself. Since that self is the only object in the world that is real to his imagination, Tito does not think of his actions as betrayals but, as we shall see in Chapter VI, as thoroughly rational and sensible choices, to which there can be no intelligent alternatives.

In one way or another, all of Tito's betrayals concern Romola; and it is Romola whom Tito betrays first. Romola's role as Alcestis in their marriage had inevitably defined Tito as Admetus, the egotistic husband of that exemplary wife. Like Admetus, in turning to Tessa, Tito betrays his wife because he seeks to avoid death, or at least one form of death. Although his mock marriage to Tessa is the result of a misunderstanding—one he is unwilling to correct, however—Tito feels increasingly closer to Tessa as Romola's harsh criticism and their constant quarrels alienate him from her. Indeed, never reluctant to see paradox, Eliot suggests that in time it is Tessa's unquestioning love rather than Romola's cold judgment that nurtures whatever good is left in Tito. But here the epic contradicts the novel. Although in their literal relationship Tessa proves to be a better wife for Tito than Romola, she is symbolically identified as the "siren" (XII, p. 131, XIII, p. 139) who calls Tito to his death, for however happy the amoral union may be for Tito, in betraying the moral union he betrays Romola in her widest epic role, as the growing moral consciousness of civilization.

The allusion to the siren identifies Tito with Odysseus, with whom Tito himself claims kinship when he remarks, recalling Athena's false directions to Odysseus, that he has been misdirected to Florence by a "fallacious Minerva" (III, p. 31). The image of Odysseus is implied in the first metaphor of the book, in the title of the opening chapter, "The Shipwrecked Stranger." While on one level that title introduces Tito as Bacchus, "the stranger," and makes it appropriate for the chapter to dwell on the beauty and charm of the young traveler, the allusion to Odysseus foreshadows the betrayals of which Tito's nature is capable. It is not, of course, the heroic Odysseus Eliot is thinking of here, but the wily one, as subsequent elaborations of this image make clear. And it is not by accident therefore that a few lines below the title we are reminded of Dante, who reserved a special place for traitors in his *Inferno.*

Early in the book, Nello remarks that he can "never look at such an outside" as Tito's "without taking it as a sign of a lovable nature" (IV, pp. 45-46). But the less superficial Piero recognizes that in its very beauty Tito's face is the perfect model for a traitor's; it is a face, Piero explains, "which vice can write no marks on" and which will "keep its color without much help of virtue" (IV, p. 44). Thus, Tito's beauty is itself a betrayal, lovely as the legend on the triptych and, like that legend, hollow within.

Although not usually so perceptive, Nello had remarked when he had first met Tito that "it is said of the Greeks that their honesty begins at what is the hanging-point with us, and that since the old Furies went to sleep, your Christian Greek is of so easy a conscience that he would make a stepping-stone of his father's corpse" (III, p. 39). Nello proves to be entirely right. In addition to Romola, Tito betrays Baldassarre, his adopted father and Romola's father-in-law. He betrays Bardo, who accepts him not only as a son-in-law but as a surrogate son as well. There is some irony in the fact that Bardo had thought he had recaptured in Tito the Greek son he had lost when Dino betrayed him. Tito also betrays Bernardo del Nero, Romola's godfather. He betrays Savonarola, Romola's spiritual father. And he betrays, finally, the city of Florence, which adopts him as Baldassarre once had. In his public career, the image of Odysseus returns, as though to close the circle, when Giannozzo Pucci, commissioning Tito as a spy against the city's government, comments that Tito "can help us better than" if he were "Ulysses himself" (XXXIX, p. 358). Pucci refers to Odysseus's work in devising the scheme of the Trojan Horse, a sly plot that finally succeeded in the Greeks' capture of Troy. That image fulfills the insight Piero had had long before when he had first met Tito and asked him to sit for a portrait of Sinon, partner to Odysseus in designing the Trojan Horse, betraying Priam (IV, p. 43).

These betrayals have both a universal significance and a historical one, since in betraying the fathers of the book Tito symbolically betrays the past, and therefore the progress of history, as is evident in his betrayal of Romola, in whom that progress is embodied. But it is not only the past up to the Renaissance Tito betrays, nor even the Renaissance itself. It is, rather, all history, past and future. In a remarkable perception of historical parallels, Eliot saw in Tito not only the corrupting element of the pagan world but the danger threatening the modern world as well.

Here we must take note of a significant point of disagreement between Eliot and Comte, for Eliot's vision was a warning against the purely scientific and secular world Comte urged. Eliot did agree with Comte that mankind must extricate itself from the first two stages of its evolution—from the superstition, as he would call it, of religion and from the empirically unfounded sytems of metaphysics—the latter a halfway house at best, enjoying neither the "truth" of empiricism nor the comfort of religion. She also agreed with Comte that mankind must enter, and in some ways had entered already, the last stage of his evolution, the Positive stage of science and scientific, secular philosophy. But she nevertheless insisted that we must not entirely repudiate our heritage, for if we did we would open ourselves to the moral corruption that lies concealed in a world stripped of wonder and dread.

Thus, although there can be no doubt that the moral vision to which Romola finally arrives at the end of the book is in some part the Positive vision, there is no doubt too that Eliot saw in science and empiricism sinister possibilities that Comte never imagined. Whether we go in one direction or the other depends on whether or not we reach the modern era on the currents of history—whether, that is, we assimilate, like Romola, the whole moral evolution of civilization, or choose, like Tito, to live, in a sense anachronistically, outside the historical stream, inspired not by the evolving communal mythology of the race but in the worship of our private gods. Indeed, Eliot believed that the modern world, like Tito, may already have chosen the latter. In putting an end to the Christian religion, science and secularism may have repudiated

Christian mythology as well, and like Tito returned to the pagan gods. It is as a pagan god that Tito embodies the danger of which Eliot warns us. Divested of mystery, Bacchus proves to be the most thoroughly modern of men, philosophically, ethically modern, entirely freed from the religious and metaphysical past, not only from its supernatural and doctrinal content but from its moral vision as well. Tito is all that science and secularism imply, a complete empiricist, the total philosophic materialist, and he embraces, in fifteenth-century Florence, the ethical systems that secularism and science engendered in the nineteenth century and that have become the essential premises of the twentieth.

Tito, in short, is a utilitarian, as we shall have many occasions to observe in the utilitarian language he always echoes. Although it required no preparation for Eliot to examine in *Romola* the complex philosophic heritage of Western civilization, she read or reread many volumes, some of which shed particular light on her purpose. Perhaps at this time Eliot looked through two pertinent volumes in the Eliot/Lewes library: Charles-Joseph de Mayer's *Galerie philosophique du seizième siècle* (no. 1420), apparently a volume, however, which no one found especially useful, since some of its pages remain uncut; and Xavier Rousselot's *Etudes sur la philosophie dans le moyen age* (sic) (no. 1888). We know that in July 1861 Eliot read Wilhelm Gottlieb Tennemann's *A Manual of the History of Philosophy* (Yale MS 3), a copy of which is in the Eliot/Lewes library (no. 2131), perhaps because she wished to review the entire philosophic tradition. But it was not only the general history of philosophy, or the philosophy of the Middle Ages and the Renaissance, that interested Eliot at this time. As she noted in her *Quarry,* she was reading at the same time Johann Gottlieb Gerhart Buhle's *Geschichte der neuern Philosophie seit der Epoche der Widerherstellung* [sic] *der Wissenschaften,* also a book in the Eliot/Lewes library (no. 332). Unlike Tennemann's, Buhle's volume reviews, not the entire philosophic history of Western civilization, but philosophy from the period of the revival of learning to the end of the eighteenth century, a span that is almost wholly beyond the terminal date of action in *Romola,* and one in which Eliot would have had little interest had she not intended to extend the period of the epic far beyond the period of the novel.

Unfortunately, we know very little of Eliot's readings in Jeremy Bentham, James Mill, or John Stuart Mill, at this time or earlier. We do know that both James Mill and John Stuart Mill were well represented in the Eliot/Lewes library, and that Lewes had read in and written about utilitarianism. It is difficult not to suspect that from Lewes, if from no other source, Eliot had gained considerable familiarity with the utilitarian principles of Bentham and the Mills. But perhaps Eliot's utilitarianism was, in part at least, not theirs as much as Comte's, and to a lesser extent Feuerbach's. Comte's philosophy so far embodies the fundamental premises of utilitarianism that John Stuart Mill himself acknowledged the kinship and, with his usual generosity, was chiefly responsible for introducing Positivism to English readers.

Utilitarianism was, of course, merely the infant child of a far older philosophic tradition, and it was in this tradition that Eliot wished to place her own examination of the philosophy. In her bibliography for "Historical Studies" for *Romola,* Eliot entered into her *Commonplace Book* a note that she had been reading a history of materialism (Yale MS 6). That history, which covers the same period as Eliot's epic, begins with Leucippus and Democritus in Hellenic Greece, passes through Epicurus and Lucretius, submerges as an undercurrent in the Christian era up to the Renaissance, and is born again in all its ancient vigor in empiricism. It is of utilitarianism seen in the context of this long historical tradition that Tito is, in his modern dress, the complete incarnation. In a remarkable leap of the imagination, Eliot recognized that the eternal amoral principle embodied mythologically in Bacchus finds its expression in the modern world in the pleasure-pain calculus, a calculus that does indeed seem to be the logical and inevitable extension of the worship of the god of joy.

It was not utilitarianism as such that Eliot objected to. Eliot was something of a utilitarian herself, if only to the degree that she was a Positivist, and she shared many of the premises and conclusions of the utilitarian point of view. If Eliot condemned Tito, it was not for the same reasons that Dickens condemns Gradgrind and Bounderby in *Hard Times.* In the great and ever ongoing Victorian controversy between the utilitarians and their critics, Eliot took, if anything, the side of those who argued for human happiness as the only moral end. What troubled her was not the calculus itself, although she found it simple and shallow, but rather that the modern world might, in its frenzied pursuit of happiness, so completely repudiate the moral heritage of its past that it would reject the truth of the past along with its falsehood, as Tito does when he betrays the fathers of the book, and that it would disengage itself from the restraints of reason the Greeks taught us and from the moral imagination we learned through Christianity. If we did that, Eliot warned us, we would commit historical suicide, just as Tito commits moral suicide in the end, for the choice of pleasure that Bacchus promises, lovely and desirable though it is, leads, in this hard and indifferent universe, paradoxically, only to pain. That is what Romola discovers for us, and what Eliot traces in the remainder of Tito's story.

The nature of the age—the social, cultural, and political context—is of great importance here, as it is in all of Eliot's fiction. Just as "in the tree that bears a myriad of blossoms," the narrator remarks in a characteristic epic simile, "each single bud with its fruit is dependent on the primary circulation of the sap, so the fortunes of Tito and Romola were dependent on certain grand political and social conditions which made an epoch in the history of Italy" (XXI, p. 213). It is not only their fortunes that the historical context shapes but their characters as well. In his inner life, each member of society mirrors the structure that contains him and, in turn, helps to shape that structure. Tito's case is a parable.[2]

Eliot studied the epoch of her book with what Lewes considered an encyclopedic and therefore an excessive thoroughness, as we have seen; but Eliot's research, which would not have been excessive had it served only to make her familiar with the details of her setting, had a far larger purpose. It is in this research that we can identify the nature of Eliot's realism and its relationship to her poetic imagination. If Eliot found the verisimilitude of formal realism entirely inadequate for her needs, and if both the scope and the nature of her vision required poetic expression, the truth she wished to convey remained a realistic truth, the "faithful account," in the famous phrase from *Adam Bede,* "of men and things." She had at no time the slightest intention of recording in her book a factual narrative of the history of civilization, or even of the Florentine Renaissance. The historical narrative enters *Romola* only after it has been translated into the symbolic language of poetry. But it was the exact historical narrative that Eliot wished to translate, the objective historical truth, as far as possible, understood in all its minute and subtle detail, that Eliot took as the proper subject of her epic.

Among its many historical notes, the *Quarry* contains a chronology of Florentine history that begins in the eleventh century. A true historian, Eliot characteristically could not rest in knowing merely the effect; she had to trace it back to its cause, and that cause again to an earlier cause, until the events of the last decade of fifteenth-century Florence were not only known but could become intelligible in the long historical perspective. Thus, to return to Eliot's image in the Proem, the novel, which encompasses only six years of Florentine history, is only one arc of the implied circumference that is the history of Western civilization.

For her historical material, Eliot turned as often as she could to the great Italian historians, and in many cases to the historians of the Florentine Renaissance; for even as she compiled the historical narrative for herself, she was tracing yet another aspect of the intellectual history of Europe. Indeed, in this respect the Renaissance was once more a turning point and a beginning. The writing of history was of course not new. Eliot herself acknowledged its ancient origins in her allusions to Herodotus and Thucydides, as we have seen. In many cases, it was the rediscovery of the ancients that inspired the Renaissance historians to write their own narratives. But, although influenced by the ancients, and sometimes imitative, history in the Renaissance not only assumed a new and different significance but became one of the most important, perhaps the most important intellectual development of fifteenth-century Florence. It was in the humanism of the Renaissance, in which attention became increasingly directed to the actions, not of God but of man, and in its secularism, in which human life became increasingly examined, not as a manifestation of the divine plan, but as a sequence of events determined by a causal order, that history began to replace the atemporal frameworks of logic and allegory as the conceptual means of bringing coherence to the chaos of experience. In this sense, the Renaissance is precisely the moment in the evolution of Western civilization in which myth and history meet, just as they meet in *Romola* in the relationship between the novel and the epic. And it is the moment too in which the universal, which is embodied in logic and allegory, becomes, in history, particularized, again just as the mythic epic becomes in *Romola* particularized in the historical novel. Here, then, is one more historical transition that brings us not only into the modern world but, for that reason, to the need for a different kind of epic, an epic that, unlike Dante's, can no longer be the imagined journey of a dream allegory but, if it is to speak in the idiom of the modern world that began in the Renaissance, must order its universal implications in a concrete historical narrative.

In her historical studies, Eliot came to the period of her novel through an ever narrowing spiral. The largest framework, and one that mirrors her own epic outlines, was provided by Giovanni Villani, from whom, we recall, she had taken much of her knowledge of the history of the Bardi family. Villani's *Histoire universali de suoi tempe* looks for the beginnings of Florentine history in ancient times—before Florence existed—and having, like Virgil in the *Aeneid*, found a spiritual heritage in Troy and Greece (as well as in the Bible), continues through Roman times and the Middle Ages up to April 1348, nearly to the moment of his death in the pestilence that beset the city in that year, the pestilence that is the setting of Boccaccio's *Decamerone*. A work of similar scope was undertaken by another fourteenth-century Florentine, Marchionne Stefani, whom Eliot cited in the *Quarry* as one of her sources. Beginning with the origins of the world, Stefani borrowed freely from Villani for his account of Florentine history up to the fourteenth century, and there would have been little here to interest Eliot. But for the period of his own time, Stefani's *Storia fiorentina* provides an original study based on original observation, and it was undoubtedly for her research in the fourteenth century that Eliot used him.

Of smaller scope but one of the most important histories of the Renaissance was Leonardo Aretino Bruni's *Historia universale de suoi tempi*. Although Eliot did not cite Bruni as a source in the *Quarry*, the Eliot/Lewes library contained a copy of his history (no. 322), and it is difficult to believe that Eliot would not have consulted so remarkable and significant a volume. With Bruni, in a sense history entered its modern form. Abandoning the myth and legend that was often incorporated into earlier historical narratives, and true in every respect to the new vision of the Renaissance, Bruni took as his subject men and their deeds, attempting not only to trace events as a causal sequence but introducing, for the first time in Renaissance historical writing, a thematic point of view that binds the narrative into a coherent whole. Such a unified perspective would undoubtedly have appealed to Eliot, since it was just what she attempted; and Bruni's thesis, that the history of Florence, to which he limited his work, was throughout characterized by the long struggle of the Florentines for liberty, would certainly have claimed her sympathies.

The dates covered in Eliot's chronology of Florentine history in her *Quarry* are the subject of two other important histories she used in her research, Lodovico Muratori's *Antiquitates italicae medii aevi* and Jean Charles Léonard Simonde de Sismondi's *Histoire des républiques italiennes du moyen âge.* The copy of Muratori contained in the Eliot/Lewes library (no. 1534) is marked by both Eliot and Lewes, and perhaps this was one of the many projects on which Eliot engaged Lewes's time. We know from her Diary that she was reading Muratori in the fall of 1861 (Yale MS 3), and from the *Quarry,* in which a considerable number of entries are attributed to him, that he was one of her major sources. Muratori, born toward the end of the seventeenth century, became one of the great scholars of the eighteenth; and his history, which covers the period between the years 1000 and 1500, is a comprehensive study of the Middle Ages in Italy, including discussions of everything from ecclesiastical law to coinage and costume. Although in no sense biased, Muratori, an ordained priest, wrote clearly as a Roman Catholic and offered a perspective very different from Sismondi's. Like Muratori, Sismondi too was one of Eliot's major sources. From his compendious work, of which she owned all ten volumes and marked heavily the first seven (no. 2025), Eliot entered many notes into her *Quarry.* Through July 1861, she seemed to be reading Sismondi nearly every day, sometimes apparently at the rate of a volume a day, and in October of that year she read portions of his history again (Yale MS 3), perhaps to compare his account with

Muratori's, which she was also reading at the time. A fierce Calvinist, Sismondi, who lived well into the nineteenth century, was as much concerned with the role of the Roman Catholic church in the Middle Ages as Muratori, but only because he considered it the chief enemy of Italian liberty, and therefore responsible for the decline of the Italian republic. It was in part from Sismondi's study that Eliot drew her own examination of Savonarola's role in the political affairs of Florence, as we shall see in Chapter VIII.

For the history of the fourteenth century, Eliot read additionally two accounts that touched on both public and private life. In Donato Velluti's history of the first seventy years of the fourteenth century, the *Cronica di Firenze dall' anno MCCC, in arca sino al MCCCLXX,* Eliot discovered a particularly fine record, in an autobiographical spirit, of the domestic life of Florence, a life Velluti set down, almost in diary form, to the day of his death. Not always particular about historical accuracy, Velluti was often, however, a minute observer of the details of daily life, and for that reason he must have been of special delight to Eliot. Similarly, in Buonaccorso Pitti's *Cronaca,* which she examined in September 1862 (Yale MS 3), Eliot found not only a history of the last years of the fourteenth century but, interspersed with it, an autobiographical narrative of Pitti's own adventurous and colorful career.

As she came closer to the precise dates of her book, Eliot also consulted, for the general character of the fifteenth century, Amans-Alexis Monteil's *Histoire des Français dans divers états, ou histoire de France aux cinq derniers siècles,* a book she owned (no. 1500) and one she was reading early in November 1862. Although primarily a history of the French, it also concerned Italy, whose fortunes were much involved with France at that time, as Eliot recorded in *Romola,* and provided in any case an excellent survey of the period. On completing it, Eliot pronounced Monteil's volume "marvellous," "crammed with erudition, yet not dull and tiresome" (Yale MS 3).

An especially important aspect of Florentine history was covered by Felippo de' Nerli's *Commentari de' Fatti civili occorso dentro la Citta Di Firenze dall' Anno 1215 al 1537.* Here she found an ample discussion of the civil conflicts that seemed always to characterize Florentine history, and certainly she would have been particularly interested in Nerli's study of the civil strife in Florence during the last decade of the fifteenth century. From Eliot's Diary we learn that she read Nerli in October 1861 (Yale MS 3), and from her own copy of the book (no. 1550) we discover that what especially interested her in it were questions concerning Savonarola, who was one of the leading participants in the conflicts of that decade.

One of the great historians of Florence appears, very briefly, as a character in *Romola.* Born in 1476, and in his youth a follower of Savonarola, Jacopo Nardi recorded, in his *Istorie della Citta di Firenze,* a minute account of Florence between 1494 and 1538. Eliot studied Nardi intensely from August through October 1861 (Yale MS 3), certainly in her own volume, which she marked heavily for her use (no. 1541). It is Jacopo Nardi who, at the burning of Savonarola, tells Romola to cover her eyes as others precede Fra Girolamo to the stake (LXXII, p. 595). A very different eyewitness account of fifteenth-century Florence was provided in Vespasiano da Bisticci's *Vite d'uomini illustri del sec. XV,* a work Eliot read in October 1861 (Yale MS 3). Vespasiano, who died just when the action of *Romola* ends but who does not appear in the book, had been a close friend of the first Cosimo de' Medici and had come to know all the illustrious men of his age. His biography of their lives, one of the first biographical volumes in Italy, recalls Plutarch in many ways, especially in the relationship it suggests between public and private life.

Although Savonarola's death, on May 23, 1498, closes the action of *Romola,* Eliot's historical readings did not stop with that date. She studied the period that followed immediately, between 1498 and 1512, in Biagio Buonaccorsi's *Diario de' successi piu importanti seguiti in Italia e particolarmente in Fiorenzio dall' anno 1498 in sino all' anno 1512.* Her copy of this book (no. 337) also contained N. V. Patrizio's biography of Lorenzo de' Medici, which she must have read.

On December 8, 1861, Eliot noted in her Diary that she had just begun the ninth chapter of Varchi, "in which he gives an accurate account of Florence" (Cross, II, 253). A remarkable, if controversial, historian, Benedetto Varchi provided one of the most incisive accounts of Florence between 1527 and 1538. Eliot entered many notes in her *Quarry* from Varchi's *Storia Fiorentina* and marked a number of passages in her copy of the book (no. 2206). Varchi offered Eliot far more than historical knowledge, however. It was to Varchi, we recall, as well as to other sources, that Eliot sent her illustrator Frederic Leighton for information on various items of Florentine dress. And, far more significantly, it was, although not alone, to Varchi that she herself turned for information on the subtler points of the Florentine vernacular. Author of literary as well as historical works, Varchi was a linguistic pioneer, a man committed to the use of the living language of the day, a fierce supporter of the vernacular against those who still considered it inferior to the ancient Latin tongue. That linguistic thesis is the subject of one of Varchi's chief nonhistorical works, *L'Ercolano,* a book Eliot owned (no. 2205) and that she included in one of the bibliographies in the *Quarry.* It was Varchi Eliot cited to T. A. Trollope as her authority in conceding a point on an Italian colloquialism on which they had disagreed *(Letters,* III, 431).

Also included in one of the *Quarry* bibliographies is another sixteenth-century Florentine historian, Scipione Ammirato. As we have seen, she had consulted Ammirato's *Trattato delle famiglie nobili fiorentine* in her research on the Bardi family, but his *Istorie fiorentine* must have been especially interesting to her for another reason. As I will discuss shortly, in her study of Tito and of the political turmoil of which he is a part, Eliot suggested the influence of a new philosophic perspective, of which Machiavelli is the chief exponent. It was essentially Machiavelli's philosophy of history that Ammirato followed in his study of Florence, which differed, therefore, in its point of view from many of the other histories Eliot examined, and in which she could trace the historical implications of Machiavelli's thesis.

Although this list of works by no means exhausts Eliot's historical readings, nor the volumes on Italian history in her library, it is sufficient to suggest that Eliot was not only careful to arm herself with full and precise historical knowledge but that in her historical research she attempted to distinguish the idiosyncratic features that uniquely characterized this period as well as to grasp the historical currents that placed the period in the context of the history of civilization. Such historical research was not unusual for Eliot, even when she wrote of a time and place more familiar to her. She prepared, in a similar way for *Middlemarch,* in which the period of the Reform Bill of 1832 was placed in the same epic context of the history of civilization; and *Middlemarch* is a particularly pertinent analogue in this respect, for, different as the periods of the two novels are, they share one important and encompassing feature.

The overall impression Eliot wished to give in *Romola* was that in the fifteenth-century Florence was a place of turbulence and transition. Philosophically confused, morally uncertain, and culturally uprooted, the city was a prototype of the upheaval of nineteenth-century England. In neither, to use Eliot's phrase from the Prelude of *Middlemarch,* is there "a coherent social faith and order." The two periods are more alike than either is to the ages that divide them, and there can be no doubt that Eliot saw the early nineteenth century not only as a final flowering of the modern temper that had been born in the Renaissance but also as a reenactment, at a later historical stage, of the Renaissance itself. Like the Renaissance, and like no period between them, the nineteenth century was, in one sense at least, a historically orphaned child, disinherited of the social coherence, of the faith, of the eighteenth century, as the Renaissance had been disinherited of the coherence and faith of the Middle Ages. Like an orphaned child, it seemed condemned, as the Renaissance had been, to shape a future with no memory of a valid past. It was indeed to salvage, as Carlyle had attempted to salvage, a spiritual heritage from the ashes of a dead past that Eliot traced her epic story of the progress of Western civilization, and embodied in Romola the living heritage in which the salvation of the West lay.

It is of that heritage of which Tito is bereft, by his own choice, in his betrayal of those many fathers, and in whom therefore we see the dangers that threaten modern man with annihilation. Disinherited, Tito can recapture neither faith nor coherence in the confusion and uncertainty of fifteenth-century Florence. For Tito, Florence is like the universe that is unintelligible, and as he glibly remarks at one point, that "astonishes us by the impossibility of seeing what was the plan of it" (XIII, p. 139). Without a plan, both the city and the universe are a maze, and it is in that central image that Eliot gives us our first glimpse of Florence. The city, Eliot tells us in the first sentence of the first chapter, was a "labyrinth" (p. 10). The image, of course, returns us immediately to the myth of Ariadne, and here one of the implications Tito had not envisioned of the legend he had asked Piero to paint on the triptych proves, ironically, to be the most important fact in that legend, for it is once more Adriadne who is the savior. Ariadne's thread, which guided Theseus out of the Cretan labyrinth, is the moral path we must choose to actualize in the labyrinth of possibilities, a labyrinth from which, however, although Romola offers to guide him, Tito will never escape.

In this argument, the mythic implications of the two dominant cultures of Western civilization assume political importance; I use the word "political" here in the largest possible sense, as the Greeks used all terms derived from the concept of the *polis,* to include the entire life of the community. The death of Lorenzo de' Medici, the event that opens the action of the book, had launched Florence on a new age. The conflict that was to mark Florence in that new age is prophetically alluded to in the superstitious rumors that Lorenzo's death ignites. There is talk that the lantern of the Duomo has been struck by the sword of St. Michael (I, p. 17), an incident Eliot had recorded in her *Quarry* in the chronology of Florentine history where she had entered Savonarola's vision, in 1492, of the *Gladius Domini,* the sword of God. That rumor is countered by another report in which a woman is said to have seen a "big bull with fiery horns coming down on the church to crush it" (I, p. 17). The conflict for which Florence will now be the battleground is indeed a conflict between the bull, an animal sometimes associated with Zeus and Poseidon, but equally and more anciently identified with Bacchus, and the *Gladius Domini.*

In the last decades of the fifteenth century, Florence is torn between two renaissances, a classical and a religious. In each there is much confusion. For many, the Christian heritage has been reduced to vague and grim superstition. For a few, it has been revitalized in the rebirth of religious movements of which the Dominican movement of Savonarola is one. The classical heritage too, newly reborn, is a maze of information that only occasionally rises to knowledge. In the general climate, there is a sense of something stirring, but both paganism and Christianity are obscure forces, dimly understood, and often badly translated.

The Florentine citizen feels in harmony with the ancients but holds to Christian ritual with uninspired dread. Sometimes, indeed, he cannot quite distinguish between the two. The hymns of Marullo, which, as we recall, had been addressed to the pagan deities, suggest the confusion. The *Laude* of Marullo are not the only humns Eliot examined. Her library contained C. A. Bjorn's *Hymni Veterum Poetarum Christianorum Ecclesiasi Latinae selecti* (no. 230) and Matteo Coferati's *Colletta di laudi spirituali di piu devoti autori sopra l'arie correnti fatta da Matteo Coferati Capellano nella Metropolituna Fiorentina* (no. 542); and several other volumes of hymns are cited in the *Quarry*. The current airs composed by Matteo Coferati might not fall under the general condemnation, but on the subject of hymns in Renaissance Florence, Eliot copied into her *Quarry* a note from Roscoe's biography of Lorenzo de' Medici that the *Laude* were sometimes sung, ostensibly for the sake of stirring by association the piety of the languid, to profane and even obscene tunes, some of which Lorenzo had himself composed.

This chaotic state of affairs is especially evident in the endless festivals celebrated in every city in Italy but nowhere as much and with such enthusiasm as in Florence. In these festivals, Christian rites are once more entangled beyond extrication with pagan rituals. On occasions of public events, such as the departure of the French invader, the Florentines seem, as Romola says, like a "Bacchante possessed by a divine rage." But Bacchus himself disowns them. The people are joyful, Tito acknowledges, but only "after a sour and pious fashion" (XXXI, p. 292). The Peasants' Fair is a case in point. Created to celebrate the birth of the Virgin Mary on September 8, the fair, Eliot noted in her *Quarry*, "è singolare una specie di bacchanale," and it is indeed in Bacchic terms that Eliot describes it in Chapter XIV. It is at this fair, appropriately therefore and inappropriately, that Tessa and Tito, the fertility gods, are "married," and married by Maestro Vaiano, a magician who plays at the role of priest, performing mock marriages at a mock altar (p. 151). Perhaps Tessa innocently hits on the truth when she childishly imagines Vaiano to be the devil

(X, p. 110), for the cultural confusion, failing to reach a synthesis, becomes a moral confusion.

The moral ambivalence is concentrated in two focal points in the city; time here is translated, as Piero had translated it in his paintings for the Vespucci Palace, into space. Each of the rival traditions claims its own territory. In preparing to write *Romola,* Eliot studied the topography of Florence and discovered in it a rich quarry for her symbolic purpose. The records she kept of her many travels suggest that she had a keen eye and a fine sensibility for physical place. Not only in monuments and landmarks, but in ordinary streets and buildings, she always recognized subtle expressions of the characters and histories of the people who had walked and inhabited them. On her second trip to Florence, in the spring of 1861, when she was beginning to suspect what question she would ask in *Romola* if not just how she would answer it, sightseeing was one of her main occupations. Lewes reported to John Blackwood that she was " 'drinking in' Florence" *(Letters,* III, 420). The city Eliot wanted to know in this physical sense had existed more than three centuries before her time, and while much of Renaissance Florence stood unaltered, as it does today, Eliot's intentions required some research as well. In addition to her readings in the history and literature of Florence, in which the city is always a physical presence, and in which therefore she learned much of its topography, Eliot looked into other volumes. In one of the bibliographies in her *Quarry,* Eliot entered Flavio Biono's *Italia Illustrata,* a work in which the cultural heritage of Italy is traced largely through its monuments. For a general geographic survey of the Tuscan countryside, with historical annotations, Eliot consulted Attilio Zuccagni-Orlandini's *Atlante Geografico, Fisico e Storico Del Granducato Di Toscana* (no. 2343 in the Eliot/Lewes library). And for Florence itself, she turned chiefly to Marco Lastri's splendid guide to all the historical monuments of the city, the *Osservatore fiorentine.* From Lastri Eliot made many notes in her *Quarry,* including one on the extent of Florence and its mileage from gate to gate, information that must have been extremely useful at several points in the book, especially when Eliot takes Romola from Bardo's house to the Porta San Gallo where Savonarola meets her, a scene to which I will return in Chapter VII. The *Quarry* is filled with topographical details: notes on the differences between the Florence of the nineteenth century and of the Renaissance; on the city's streets and their often quaint histories; and on the history of Florentine architecture, in connection with which Eliot mentions Leon Battista Alberti, who is recalled in *Romola* in chapter XXXIX, the chapter set in the Rucellai Palace, a building designed by Alberti.

Much of the action in *Romola* takes place in and around the Mercato Vecchio, and Eliot made a particular effort to acquaint herself with that part of Florence as it had once been. Some of her notes in the *Quarry* on the Mercato Vecchio are taken from the *Delizie degli eruditi Toscani,* in which, for example, she found information on the goods sold in the Old Market and their prices in 1300; but the authority on the Mercato was clearly the fourteenth-century Florentine poet Antonio Pucci, ancestor of the Giannozzo Pucci who appears in *Romola.* It is Antonio Pucci Eliot cites as her source the first time we enter, with Tito and Bratti, the area of the Mercato Vecchio (I, p. 14). On January 24, 1862, just as she was about to write the scene described in that first chapter, Eliot entered in her Diary that she and Lewes had walked to the British Museum to copy Pucci's poem on the Old Market (Yale MS 3). From that poem, much of which is quoted in the original in the *Quarry,* Eliot gathered a vivid account of the details of daily life in what was then one of the city's most important and flourishing centers.

It is not in the Mercato Vecchio, however, that Eliot suggested the central conflict of cultures in Florence. As the geometric imagery makes clear, there are two cities in Eliot's book that, taken separately, describe two distinct circles. To Nello the barber, around whom finally the pagan city revolves, Florence is a second Athens (III, p. 31). In a letter from Florence to William Blackwood, Eliot had called the city "this Italian Athens" *(Letters,* III, 300), and it is as the second Athens that Florence has been traditionally known. It has been called also the second Rome. Nerli speaks of it as the "new Rome," and Villani, as "the daughter and creation of Rome." The epic implications of those comparisons were not lost on Eliot. In the history of civilization, especially in the etymological sense of "civilization" as the history of cities, Florence, heir to both Athens and Rome, was not only the center of

Western civilization in its day, as Athens and Rome had been in theirs, but a reincarnation, at a later stage, of those ancient cultures, just as nineteenth-century England became a reincarnation, at a later stage yet, of the Renaissance. Eliot's point was not that history repeats itself (although to a degree and in an important way it does) but that the present moment assimilates the past into itself, that history is always the implied presence in any age, and that every place is the end, as well as the beginning, of an epic journey.

Appropriately, it is in Nello's shop that we find the pagan center of Florence, and it is for that reason that Nello proudly declares his shop to be the "focus of Florentine intellect" (III, p. 35). Nello's shop is the ancient *agora,* and in it we may meet nearly everyone associated with the intellectual life of the city, including the young Machiavelli, to whom we shall return in Chapter VI. Nello's shop is also Tito's favorite meeting place, and its affiliation with paganism, and with Hellenism in particular, is perhaps in no way so thoroughly enforced as in the fact that Nello becomes fiercely attached to Tito from the moment they meet.

The other focal point of Florence is the Cathedral of Santa Maria del Fiore, the cathedral with which Savonarola is associated. In contrast to Nello's view that Florence is a second Athens, Savonarola conceives of it as the *Civitas Dei,* and the cathedral functions as the city's Christian center. Nello's shop and Savonarola's cathedral, the first in the Piazza San Giovanni (III, p. 32), and the second in the Piazza del Duomo that almost adjoins it, face one another as though on opposite sides of the line of battle. That this was Eliot's intention is clear. Eliot modeled Nello on the barber-poet of the earlier fifteenth century, Domenico di Giovanni, commonly known as Il Burchiello. She could have learned something of Burchiello in Lastri's *Osservatore fiorentine,* but she had read also Domenica Maria Manni's *Life of Burchiello* (Cross, II, 254), from which she copied many entries into her *Quarry.* From Manni, for example, Eliot entered into the *Quarry* the note that Burchiello's barbershop was a retreat, in the style of the Platonic Academy, for the first men of letters—the source, obviously, of Nello's boast that his shop is the "focus of Florentine intellect." One of the questions that much concerned Eliot in the *Quarry* was the location of

Burchiello's shop. From a book entitled *Firenze antica e moderna illustrata* (1795), in which she read of other barber-poets in Florentine history, Eliot settled that Burchiello's shop had been located in the Via Calimala, which is near the cathedral but does not face it and in which, for that reason, she did not want to place Nello's barbershop.

Nello and Savonarola here, as representatives of the pagan and Christian traditions, are in reality engaged in a war. It is perhaps in this connection that Eliot, in preparing to write *Romola,* reviewed Herodotus on the Persian Wars, whom she entered in her *Commonplace Book* under "Books for Historical Studies" alongside others of more obvious relevance (Yale MS 6). Herodotus, with whom Eliot compares herself in *Middlemarch* when she suggests that Dorothea's story might be compared with Io's (chap. XI), was a great favorite with both Eliot and Lewes. Each of them seems to have owned a copy of Adolf Sholl's German translation of Herodotus (no. 1010, 1011), and both seem to have had a hand in marking the Greek text with Latin translation in their library (no. 1012). It was, of course, the role Athens assumed, in Sparta's default, at the beginning of the Persian Wars Herodotus records that granted Athens its leadership in Greece and introduced its great age; and possibly Eliot was thinking of the great Hellenic age of this second Athens that followed the war between the two cultures in Florence.

The Hellenic and Christian circles in Florence remain distinct. Unintentionally, Nello had used the right geometric word. From Manni, Eliot had written in the *Quarry* that Burchiello had claimed that the Calimala was the "center" of the city, but Nello calls his shop, not the center, but the "focus"; this is a significant substitution, for the center of each of the circles becomes a focus in an ellipse, the ellipse that describes the line one may draw around the land on which the Piazza San Giovanni of Nello's shop and the Piazza del Duomo of the cathedral are situated. Together, the two form the center of the old city of Florence, but each remains a separate circle distinguished by the difference between the Hellenic and the Christian points of view.

Another geometric contrast further elaborates this distinction. Each of the circles is a geometric translation of the concept of history that informs its culture. The Piazza San Giovanni is described in terms of plane geometry, since the Greek concept of history is cyclical and brings us back again and again to the same point. There is movement here but not progress. Since to the Christian however history implies progress, the evolution from creation to judgment, the geometry of the Piazza del Dumo takes on a third dimension. That is suggested in "Giotto's incomparable campanile," as Eliot had called it in her Diary on her first trip to Florence, "beautiful as a jewel" (Cross, II, 167). This campanile, Eliot wrote in *Romola,* leads "the eye upward, high into the clear air," and is therefore a "prophetic *symbol,* telling that human life must somehow and some time shape itself into accord with that pure aspiring beauty" (II, p. 33; my italics). Similarly, the cupola of the cathedral forms a circle at its base but rises into a dome, "Bruneleschi's mighty dome," as Eliot had described it in her Diary when she had first seen it (Cross, II, 167). It is on that dome that rests the great cross of the cathedral, visible in nearly every corner of Florence, and in that sense bringing visual order, as Christ will bring moral order, to the city as a whole. Thus, as private and public symbols continue to reflect one another, the cross of the cathedral becomes the public equivalent of the crucifix Dino had given Romola, the gift of the city's heritage.

There is one last ironic touch in the relationship between the two physical focal points in the city. The Piazza San Giovanni, in which we find Nello's shop, is the site of the cathedral's Baptistery, whose doors are the Gates of Paradise desgined by Ghiberti. Thus, as Bacchus is always examined in the shadow of the Christian vision, so Nello's shop stands in the shadow of the cathedral—in the shadow, in one sense, of the most important part of the cathedral. The Baptistery is, of course, dedicated to John the Baptist, after whom in fact the piazza itself is named, and it is John the Baptist who is the patron saint of the city of Florence.

Like Romola, Florence is confronted with a choice between the two gods, increasingly so as Tito and Savonarola become its two dominant political figures. Like Romola as well, the city seems unable to reconcile them. Indeed, although Romola has at least understood the distinction between Bacchus and Christ, Florence seems to have confused them; its political turmoil is merely a reflection of its deep moral anarchy. Nowhere is that moral anarchy more evident, or more symbolically suggested, than in the city's celebration of the nativity of its patron saint. As Eliot is careful to point out at the opening of the chapter in which that celebration is described, the nativity of John the Baptist happens to fall on the same day as Midsummer (VIII, p. 85), a day that commemorates ancient fertility rites. Although Eliot jotted down from Lastri in her *Quarry* that the celebration of the nativity of the Baptist was held in 1492 on June 25, perhaps she did not trust her source (rightly, it seems, for in 1492 the nativity of John the Baptist was apparently celebrated on June 26, as today it is celebrated on June 24), for she mentions no particular date in the text. Her concern there was merely to establish the coincidence of the nativity and Midsummer, for in that coincidence the calendar seemed itself to assume a symbolic purpose. Eliot might have found, and perhaps did find, information on the elaborate shows customary on the day of San Giovanni in many of the works she had read on Renaissance Florence, but her notes in the *Quarry* tell us that here she did rely on Lastri's *Osservatore fiorentine.* It is Lastri too who described the Carro della Zecca, the cart that carries through the city a living representative of John the Baptist but one who, curiously, carries Christ's cross but is dressed in tiger skins, the traditional costume of Bacchus (VIII, pp. 85-86).

Although Romola has not yet found a way to reconcile the clashing deities, for her the two cultures have at least found their symbolic relationship in the crucifix that is now locked inside the triptych. These two images also dominate the history of the city; Florence has in fact a peculiar custom that graphically translates into the city's architecture the two major symbols of the book. In the twenty-second chapter, we learn that on public occasions it was the habit in Florence to cover the Piazza del Duomo with a false sky of blue drapery when nature had provided a gray one. The contrast in color echoes the color imagery of the betrothal and wedding and distinguishes between the vibrant colors of Bacchus and the colorless world of Christ. The lily that was prominent in the symbolism of the betrothal returns here as well. But the blue drapery of the false sky is adorned not with white lilies but, a sign of the city's corruption, with yellow ones. There is, moreover, considerable irony in the coats of arms that are scattered over the blue drapery, whether we see them as aristocratic banners that contrast with the Christian principle of fellowship, or as weapons of war—tools of conquest, not of sympathy. Covered with this gilded and unreal sky, the Piazza del Duomo is in effect an enlargement of the triptych; although the blue drapery does not carry the Bacchic legend, in providing the illusion of fair weather it makes a Bacchic point. It is significant, however, that the cathedral is not enclosed by this false sky and that its cross remains outside this public triptych. Florence has not yet learned its proper place.

The event described in this chapter takes place on November 17, 1494. It is morning, the hour of the Advent sermon, and the holiday drapery makes an ironic comment on a city supposedly preparing to receive Christ, the Man of Sorrow. Like Tito, Florence shields itself from pain and decides to celebrate, instead of the Christian Advent, the arrival—also and literally an advent—of Charles VIII of France, not the spiritual, but, as some believe the French king to be, the political "savior." Indeed, to many Charles VIII seems, as Eliot draws another parallel between historical periods, the new Charlemagne, whose namesake he is, the "welcome conqueror of degenerate kings, regulator and benefactor of the Church" (XXI, pp. 214-15). No one supports this view of the French king more passionately than Savonarola, but ironically his followers do not seem to understand that to Savonarola Charles brings not salvation from suffering but the living hand of God's scourge on Florence, for the king is the very *Gladius Domini* of Savonarola's vision. While there is apparently no escape from the retribution of reality, the Florentines make every effort to hide from it. Perhaps this is the meaning of the old proverb Cennini quotes and that takes up on this larger, public scale one of the dominant images of the book: "Pisans false, Florentines blind" (VIII, p. 93). Incidentally, the Italian proverbs that appear frequently in *Romola* Eliot found for the most part in the nineteenth-century collection of Guiseppe Giustri, the *Raccolta di Proverbi Toscani,* a book she included in one of the bibliographies in the *Quarry* and in her own copy of which (no. 812) she underlined and commented on many passages.

The moral disorder is evident everywhere. The streets, the

narrator remarks with some irony, were not always a moral spectacle in those times (X, pp. 111-12). The image of San Giovanni is less influential, it appears, in the churches than on the gold florins where it has been unceremoniously stamped with no sense of paradox (VIII, p. 86). Like every other detail of Florentine life, the city's coinage is part of the book's symbolic structure. Chiefly in Varchi, as she acknowledged in her *Quarry* notes, Eliot discovered the suggestive fact that the florin, named after, and therefore symbolic of, the city itself, carried on it the image of John the Baptist. And where indeed "could the image of the patron saint be more fitly placed" in such a city, the narrator asks (VIII, p. 95), for Florence has become greedy and materialistic. God and Mammon are the same. It is the coin, not the image, the Florentines worship. As Giannozzo Pucci predicts, the silver saints of Antonio will "some day vanish from the eyes of the faithful to be worshipped more devoutly in the form of coin" (XXXIX, p. 352).

The youth of Florence have gone wild, not only in vain pursuits, but in unbridled mischief and worse. All of Italy, in fact, suffers from general depravity. The apparent "peace and prosperity" make a "handsome establishment" only for the "few who were lucky or wise enough to reap the advantage of human folly." It is a world "in which lust and obscenity, lying and treachery, oppression and murder, were *pleasant, useful,* and when properly managed not dangerous. And as a sort of fringe or adornment to the substantial delights of tyranny, avarice, and lasciviousness, there was the patronage of polite learning and the fine arts, so that flattery could always be had in the choicest Latin to be commanded at that time, and sublime artists were at hand to paint the holy and the unclean with impartial skill" (XXI, pp. 216-17; my italics). There is much for the few and little for the many, and even the few prosper only materially. What has brought about this decay is suggested in the two words I have italicized. For the Florentines as for Tito, the only criteria of judgment are the Bacchic and utilitarian criteria of pleasure and utility. Surely, the narrator argues, such a condition justifies Savonarola's zeal for reform (XX, pp. 202-13), his cry for a Christian brotherhood of all men, and his perennial admonition that "God will not have silver crucifixes and starving stomachs," that "the church is best adorned with the gems of holiness and the fine gold of brotherly love" (XXXIX, p. 352).

The "life of mankind at large makes a moral tradition for the race," the narrator observes (XXXIX, p. 361), and the life of society gives form to the individual conscience. Certainly we have here the converse of the old Platonic thesis that the state is the individual writ large. Both are the premise of Romola's epic embodiment of her people, and similarly of Tito's role as a representative of the moral confusion. In fact, in characteristic Greek fashion Tito takes the state as his model. In this world in which he finds himself, Tito reflects, the "sentiments of society" are a "mere tangle of anomalous traditions and opinions" (XI, p. 121). Why, then, should he be different? The undermining of traditional values has brought, to the Renaissance as it was later to bring to the nineteenth century, liberation but at the same time the engulfing chaos of a moral vacuum that few can survive. In the midst, therefore, of this "strange web of belief and unbelief" (Proem), what moral path can the individual discern? Where all things are possible, none is certain. In such an age, only total skepticism seems appropriate, and the only fitting view of sin is as the subject of a sophistic pleasantry, such as Monna Brigida makes when she concludes that "one must sin a little . . . else what are the blessed sacraments for" (XII, p. 129).

Thus, the pleasure-pain calculus and the philosophy of self-interest that grows out of it—not in a very enlightened form in this case—have brought Tito and Florence to a state of moral anarchy. This anarchy is one that reason is entirely powerless to overcome, since it is reason itself that is its ancient parent. While reason, the great gift of the pagans, can help Romola sift truth from falsehood in the Christian mystery, without that mystery it is no less prone to corruption than Bacchus himself.

Although Eliot's quarrel here seems to be with Apollo, it is in Tito that she embodies the moral chaos because it is through Bacchus that we discover the flaw not only of Bacchus but of Apollo as well. The argument is developed in part through Nello, "the priest of all the Muses," as he calls himself (XLV, p. 406), and therefore none other than the god Apollo incarnate. Nello is the thoroughly rational man, as his very trade suggests, for in shearing the beard Nello's hand controls the immemorial symbol of that most irrational and compelling of all mysteries, the Bacchic mystery of the generative power of nature. In her *Commonplace Book,* Eliot had copied from Horace, a poet she probably knew better than any other Latin writer, the line "[iussit] sapientem pascere barbam" (Yale MS 6), "he ordered wisdom to feed the beard" (Horace, Satire II, 3, 1. 35). Here, however, Eliot seems to have taken Bardo's qualified view of Horace's worth (V, pp. 59-60), since it is the exact opposite that Nello argues to Tito. In bringing Tito into his barbershop to be shaved, Nello promises to Bacchus himself the Apollonian gifts of "the sudden illumination of understanding and the serene vigour of inspiration that will come to you with a clear chin" (III, p. 35). It is not, then, without a hint at images of castration that Eliot has named Nello's shop "Apollo and the Razor," although the name was undoubtedly suggested to her by a poem, to which she referred in her *Quarry,* written by Burchiello and entitled "The Battle Between Poetry and the Razor." Nello boasts that the "Apollo and the Razor" is located "at the navel of the earth" (III, p. 35), a variant of the phrase "the navel of Tuscany," which Eliot had used in the *Quarry,* in noting once again the endless arguments among the old Florentines over the exact center of the city, to describe the site of Burchiello's shop. But "the navel of the earth" is the term bestowed by the Greeks on Delphi, the site of the most important of Apollo's temples. Indeed, as Nello holds his barber's mirror for Tito to see his reflection, he calls it the "true *nosce teipsum*" (III, p. 38), the Latin translation of the motto, "Know Thyself," inscribed on Apollo's temple at Delphi.

From the *Firenze antica e moderna illustrata,* Eliot noted in her *Quarry* that under Burchiello's portrait in the Reale Galleria was to be found a drawing of Burchiello's shop, which consisted of two rooms, one for his trade, and one dedicated to food, song, and poetry. Like Burchiello's, Nello's shop too has an inner sanctum; and this room in what is symbolically the Delphic temple of Apollo houses, strangely, a statue, not of Apollo, but of Hermes, or Mercury. Nello himself, in fact, is called the "mercurial barber" (III, p. 33), and we must conclude here that somehow Hermes explicates Apollo. On reflection, it seems a fair equation. Like

Hermes, the restless god of thieves and travelers, the reason of Apollo is unrooted and therefore morally anarchical. It may move unerringly from premise to conclusion, but it is, like the beardless Tito who leaves Nello's shop, impotent to distinguish morally between one premise and another. Reason too, it seems, conceals an inner vacuum. Apollo and Bacchus, in this respect at least, are intimately connected, just as Nello becomes passionately attached to Tito, whom he often calls, not Bacchus, but "my Apollino." It is this intimacy Eliot suggests when Tito takes up lodging in a room above Nello's shop (IX, p. 102), even as Bacchus, for two or three months every year (or every other year, as some think), took up residence, in the god's absence, at the temple of Apollo at Delphi. Apollo points to Bacchus, just as the Apollonian Nello becomes, in his "mercurial" role, the Hermes who conveys the souls of the dead to the underworld, whose ruler, Hades, is one of the many traditional alter egos of Bacchus himself.[3]

We are not surprised to learn therefore, that Nello is a complete skeptic. "I share no prejudices," Nello boasts. "Heaven forbid I should fetter my impartiality by entertaining an opinion" (III, p. 39). Opinions, indeed, are hard to arrive at and often inconvenient. As Niccolo Ridolfi says later, quoting Luigi Pulci, opinions "corrupt the saliva—that's why men took to pepper. Scepticism is the only philosophy that doesn't leave a taste in the mouth" (XXXIX, p. 352). Eliot began reading Luigi Pulci in August 1861 and did not finish until March 1862 (Yale MS 3). Her copy of Pulci's chief work, *Il Morgante Maggiore,* is heavily marked, by both Eliot and Lewes (no. 1753), perhaps another instance of Lewes's contribution to Eliot's research; and Pulci appears often, in references and quotes, in the *Quarry.* So much attention suggests that he was a figure of some importance in Eliot's mind, and the various references to him in *Romola* identify him as a central figure in Eliot's philosophic argument. Undoubtedly, as John Addington Symonds observed in his study of Italian literature of the Renaissance, Pulci's standing in nineteenth-century England had been seriously debased by the assessments of Hallam and Heeren, both of whom Eliot studied for *Romola,* not only on Roman law in the Middle Ages and the general outline of the fifteenth century, respectively, as Cross cites (II, 254), but also on literature, certainly in the copies to be found in the Eliot/Lewes library (nos. 927, 973). Eliot's volume of Hallam's *Introduction to the Literature of Europe, in the Fifteenth, Sixteenth and Seventeenth Centuries* is heavily marked, once more by both Eliot and Lewes, and it was Hallam who was primarily responsible for the low regard in which Pulci was held.

Eliot's estimate of Pulci, which perhaps did not do the Florentine poet justice, is spoken by Bardo, who calls the *Morgante Maggiore* "a compendium of extravagances and incongruities the farthest removed from the models of a pure age, and resembling rather the *grylli* or conceits of a period when mystic meaning was held a warrant for monstrosity of form; with this difference, that while the monstrosity is retained, the mystic meaning is absent; in contemptible contrast with the great poem of Virgil, who . . . embodied the deepest lessons of philosophy in a graceful and well-knit fable" (VI, p. 65). Bardo's comparison with Virgil is apt. Also an epic poem of sorts, Pulci's work stands in the shadow of Virgil's as a sign of the corruption of the times, a corruption, as Bardo significantly suggests, of both form and meaning. In Pulci, the "lessons of philosophy," as Bardo says, have lost their meaning. Hence, the skeptical remark Ridolfi quotes.

If Bardo holds Pulci the degenerate heir of the great Virgilian tradition, Eliot held him the true heir of another poet of Virgil's day. Suggesting once more the vast historical parallels that make men of different ages spiritual contemporaries, in the Proem Eliot joins Pulci's name to that of Lucretius. Eliot knew Lucretius well, as did Lewes, who owned and marked the copy in their library (no. 1334). As the chief Roman exponent of the philosophy of materialism, it is Lucretius who gives the philosophic warrant for Pulci to be, as Eliot described him in the Proem, a man "who was suspected of not believing anything from the roof upward." The end of ancient materialism must, of course, be the skepticism of the Renaissance, which leads inevitably in its turn to the empiricism whose subjectivity begets at last the utilitarian philosophy of the nineteenth and twentieth centuries. All are the children of Bacchus, who stood long before them as the mythic symbol of the sensory, material world in which the only intelligible criteria are pleasure and its sister, utility.

We stand here on the brink of nihilism. Although Eliot offered a very different solution, she anticipated Nietzsche in predicting that the death of God in the nineteenth century threatened to usher in the age of nihilism. For what indeed is there to believe in? Powerless to answer the basic ethical questions, rationalism makes way for empiricism. "All the disputes concerning the Chief Good," Tito remarks, echoing David Hume, "have left it a matter of taste" (XI, p. 123). But empiricism itself leads to a moral dead end, for all it has been able to prove is that "ginger is hot in the mouth" (XXXV, p. 325). The sensory world of Bacchus triumphant seems to be all that is left. If it is impossible to hypothesize beyond the senses, and if there is no valid moral claim we can make, surely we may, and perhaps must, accept the spontaneous promptings of the self as our basis for action. Bacchus may be welcomed not only as a natural impulse but as a moral criterion, a paradox mirrored in Tito's reflection, in which he is entirely unaware of self-contradiction, that he would be "equal to any sacrifice that was not unpleasant" (XXX, p. 288). On the current of a long historical stream, we arrive finally at the pleasure-pain calculus—by default.

6.

Bacchic and Christian Mysteries

A wonderfully subtle and alluring figure, Tito is remarkable in the gallery of Victorian villains because he is a villain only in the consequences of his choices, as is only too appropriate in a character in whom the utilitarian ethics of consequences is embodied. But he is not a gross pleasure seeker, as Eliot reminds us (XXXIV, p. 311), nor is he vain, arrogant, or malicious. When we first meet Tito, it hardly seems possible to imagine the corruption to which such a soft and pliable nature is inclined. Indeed, at the beginning Tito wants only to seize the day, in the spirit of Lorenzo de' Medici's *carpe diem* song we find Tito singing in Nello's shop (XIII, p. 137). Tito has a lovely voice, on which we will have reason to comment in Chapter VIII, and plays the lute, as Bacchus played the lyre.

It was certainly for this scene that Eliot read not only Guiseppe Tigri's anthology *Canti Popolari Toscani*, a marked copy of which we find in the Eliot/Lewes library (no. 2157), but the collection of *Carnival Songs or Poems Sung in Florence at the Time of Lorenzo de' Medici* (no. 372), undoubtedly the book she entered into her Diary in November 1861 as *Canti Carnascialeschi*—and I think the one to which Cross refers in error as *Conti Carnivaleschi* (II, 254)—and, more especially, the *Poesie del Lorenzo de' Medici; e di altri suoi amici e contemporanei,* a book she cited in one of her bibliographies in the *Quarry,* and one she owned (no. 1428). The *carpe diem* theme runs through the songs composed for the carnivals, which tended, we recall, to Bacchanalian enthusiasm, and none more so than those of Lorenzo de' Medici. For that reason they seem an appropriate choice for Tito, all the more appropriate because Tito is, after all, young and gifted, and seems to claim only what is his due.

Like many characters in Eliot's fiction, Tito arrives in a strange city in which he is alone, without ties, apparently free. Indeed the natural self, which Tito represents in his Bacchic form, yearns for this freedom from obligations, for it wants only to follow its own inclinations. But, as Savonarola later tells Romola, the fact is that we are not free. We are all born to bonds that we have had no part in making, and we cannot live long without making more. As Tito will, soon after his arrival, choose to undertake relationships that incur responsibilities, so he arrives in a profound sense already bound by the past.

This past is especially represented, appropriately, in Tito's father. Baldassarre's claim on Tito raises for Eliot the question of justice and introduces related issues that will be resolved only in Romola's story. What is pertinent to Tito's story is his own view of these issues. One's definition of justice depends on one's definition of man and the universe he inhabits, and Tito's corresponds precisely with his philosophic stance. He takes an entirely individualistic perspective, for justice to Tito is something to be worked out in his own personal relationship with the universe. His just due, therefore, is what he can, by talent and wit, win in the game of life.

But the Bacchic life can be lived by some, if at all, only at the expense of others. Hence, the Bacchic choice of conquest over sympathy. In exploring that choice, the narrator speaks in language that echoes Eliot's own words in her letter to John Morley. If it is the aim of morality to "lighten the pressure of hard non-moral outward conditions," as Eliot had written to Morley, it is necessary that each of us "divide the common pressure of destiny with his suffering fellow-men" (XXIII, p. 233). Tito, however, had "chosen to make life easy to himself—to carry his human lot, if possible, in such a way that it should pinch him nowhere" (XXIII, p. 232). The premise of Eliot's remark to Morley is that between nature and morality there are some conflicts that are irreconcilable. But it is nature that is Tito's moral criterion. In "that large and more radically *natural* view by which the world belongs to youth and *strength,"* Tito decides in considering whether or not he is bound to offer Baldassarre's gems as ransom for his father, those gems "were rather his who could extract the most *pleasure* out of them" (XI, p. 121; my italics).

The Bacchic and utilitarian premise of pleasure is joined here to another development in nineteenth-century thought, for surely there are echoes of Darwin in Tito's argument. Although unlike many of her contemporaries, Eliot was not in the least troubled by the religious questions Darwin had raised, she was quite troubled by the moral implications of the theory of the survival of the fittest, implications that Darwin himself did not wish to urge but that were nevertheless inescapable. In an extremely rare refusal to accept scientific evidence, and hiding most uncharacteristically behind vague sentiments, Eliot wrote to her friend Barbara Bodichon, shortly after the publication of *The Origin of Species,* "to me the Development theory and all other explanations of processes by which things came to be, produce a feeble impression compared with the mystery that lies under the process" *(Letters,* III, 227). The theory of the survival of the fittest hit at the very core of Eliot's conviction, the conviction that is the epic premise of *Romola*—that human evolution is, if not in every respect in some sense at least, moral evolution. Eliot was not without allies in that belief. Comte, Spencer, and others held with her that one of the characteristics that defines fitness in evolution is the sympathy that makes humankind as well as other creatures capable of acting communally, and thus of combining their individual strengths and compensating for their individual weaknesses. In identifying Tito, therefore, with the rival, Darwinian, theory of evolution, Eliot identified him, as she had already and would again in countless ways, as the regressive principle of civilization.

Tito comes very naturally to rest on his conclusion. Originally, he had said that if he were assured that Baldassarre were still alive and if he knew his whereabouts, he would not for a moment hesitate to rescue him. In one sense, we would expect no less from Tito, for it is his Bacchic function, which Eliot translated here into a literal case, to "ransom" the dead, to bring them back to life. "But, after all, *why* was he bound to go?" Tito asks himself on receiving Baldassarre's letter. "What, looked at closely, was the end of all life, but to extract the *utmost sum of pleasure?*" (XI, p. 121; my italics). Tito does not wish Baldassarre ill. He is never gratuitously callous. Quite the contrary. He wishes his father, as he wishes everyone, "prosperous and happy" (XXVI, pp. 247-48). But Tito is prepared to bestow these Bacchic gifts only if he can do so without trouble to himself. When he asks himself, "Do I not owe myself something?" (IX, p. 106), he sees no possible answer beyond the exclusive allegiance he is by nature inclined to give himself.

Here, private and public lives once more reflect one another. The political life of Florence at the time offers Tito many possible choices, but Tito does not distinguish among them. Having perceived "the equal *hollowness* of all parties," Tito "took the only *rational* course in making them subservient to *his own interest*" (XLVI, p. 415; my italics). As is evident from the italicized words, what Tito sees in the public arena is his own reflection. Some men among his political acquaintances pretend to other motives, as Tito knows, but surely, he thinks, they are unintelligible, foolish, cowardly, and, in fact, hypocrites. Secretly, Tito is convinced, all men share his convictions: "what motive could any man really have, except his own interest?" It would be absurd to think otherwise. "Men did not really care" about issues "except when their personal spleen was touched. It was weakness only that was despised; power of any sort carried its immunity" (LVII, p, 491). I leave the obvious Machiavellian echoes for later discussion, for it is not merely Machiavelli but much of the city's political life that confirms Tito in his view. At various stages of corruption, most of the political parties in Florence are engaged in a scramble for power on the supposition, articulated by Niccolo Ridolfi, that "there are but two sorts of government: one where men show their teeth at each other, and one where men show their tongues and lick the feet of the strongest" (XXXIX, p. 357). Like Tito, most of the political figures in Florence have chosen conquest over sympathy.

It is important to Eliot's case that Tito does not merely act egotistically but argues the philosophic grounds of his position. In the purely instinctual egotists of her fiction (Hetty Sorrel, Rosamond Vincy, Harold Transome, for example) Eliot probed the psychology of egotism. In Tito she did that and more. Along with a study of the egotistic instinct, we find here as well an inquiry into ethics. Yet the inquiry is not itself in a sense philosophic. The ethical dialogue in this book does not in fact constitute a philosophic argument. Here, the issues are concretely instantiated in the individual consciousness, and it was part of Eliot's purpose that they should be.

It is not only because Eliot was an artist and not a philosopher that she translated the philosophic question into psychological terms. It is at least equally because her point was precisely that to such philosophic questions as Tito asks we can make only a psychological answer. In theory, Tito's arguments are flawless. In the absence of divine or metaphysical imperatives, what can prove egotism wrong? That it is wrong is the testimony, not of logic, but of vision and imagination. Tito is not a scoundrel; he is not vicious. His problem is merely that he cannot see. Thus, Tito pursues the question of justice in his own mind and concludes, in all honesty, that it would be unfair "that he, in his full ripe youth . . . should turn his back on promised love and distinction" (IX, p. 104). He knows well that some think otherwise. But such knowledge comes to him merely as information and corresponds to nothing in his own consciousness. One might as well expect him to know the flavor of a fruit he has never tasted. The triptych identifies Tito as a hollow man, and the crucifix that might interpret that knowledge to him is not there. Intelligent enough to demand that the world make sense to him, Tito studies the views of others but is forced by his own nature to restate them in the only terms he understands. Any maxims, he concludes, "that required a man to fling away the good that was needed to make existence sweet, were only the lining of human selfishness turned inward; they were made by men who wanted others to sacrifice themselves for their sake" (XI, p. 122).

The distinctions Eliot has suggested here are essentially the distinctions between ethics and morality. Ethical questions may be uncertain, but in a fundamental sense moral questions are not.

Whether the virtue of an action is inherent in it or can be determined only by its consequences may be open to speculation. That to betray a trust is wrong is not a question of speculation but of moral conviction. Rational, secular, philosophic, ethics is the Hellenic road to rectitude. It is a road we may travel with much profit, but it is one fraught with dangers as well, as Tito illustrates. The surer road is morality, and morality is in a sense religion, religion not as a divine system, which can prove no less dangerous than ethics, as Dino shows, but as a mystery that, without appeal to the supernatural, transcends the obstacles of reason. However resolute we may be to resist an ethical error, it is not until we feel it not as an error but as a sin that we are armed against temptation.

When Tito argues with Romola over selling Bardo's library, for example, he remarks that any "*rational* person looking at the case from a due distance will see that I have taken the wisest course" (XXXII, p. 299; my italics). Tito does not share the "sentimental scruples" he attributes to Romola, for these, as he had "*demonstrated* to himself by a very rapid course of *argument,* had no relation to solid *utility*" (XXXI, p. 286; my italics). Speaking to Tito once about Dino's betrayal, Bardo had called Dino's faith a "dim mysticism which . . . eludes all argument" (XII, p. 134). Argument is precisely the point here, for as Dino's mysticism had allowed him to escape his obligations to Bardo, so too have Tito's arguments.

It is somewhere between religion as supernatural law and ethics as rational judgment that we find Eliot's morality. In one sense, her morality attempts to embody the advantages of both but to avoid their disadvantages. Like ethics, it is human and secular, and despite the fact that it is not open to the kind of philosophic speculation through which ethics may lead to total skepticism, it is flexible in the sense that it is informed not by divine fiat but by human considerations. Unlike ethics, however, morality is inspired not by reason, which is its handmaiden only, but by something that for the lack of a better word we must call feeling. It would be well if we could avoid that word, for in hearing it we are tempted to conclude that we have here once more the old Victorian quarrel between the head and the heart. But in fact we do not. Eliot herself had difficulty defining her meaning, although she knew precisely what she had in mind. She made one attempt in the narrator's observation that Tito's "mind was destitute of that dread which has been erroneously decried as if it were nothing higher than a man's animal care for his own skin: that awe of Divine Nemesis which was felt by religious pagans, and, though it took a more positive form under Christianity, is still felt by the mass of mankind simply as a vague fear at anything which is called wrongdoing. Such terror of the uneseen is so far above mere sensual cowardice that it will annihilate that cowardice: it is the initial recognition of a moral law restraining desire, and checks the hard bold scrutiny of imperfect thought into obligations which can never be proved to have any sanctity in the absence of feeling" (XI, p. 122). The heart, whose blind inclinations are enough to make moralists despair, has some connection with feeling; but in Eliot feeling is as acquired and cultivated as knowledge. It is, indeed, as Adam Bede says to Dinah Morris, "a kind of knowledge" (Chap. LII).

That knowledge is, in the mythic sense of the word, a mystery. It is in this context that we must understand the religious vocabulary in which Eliot expressed, in all her fiction, a thoroughly atheistic vision. We must not imagine that Eliot was merely calling things by their old, residual names that continued to haunt her secular philosophy with ghosts, personal and cultural, of an abandoned faith. The faith is indeed abandoned, but the religious vocabulary is deliberate in that it distinguishes morality, Eliot's morality, from mere ethics, and places it in this halfway house of myth.

Eliot anticipated the difficulties her readers might have with these subtle distinctions and took considerable care to define the central moral line through a contrast between the dangerous territory that lies on either side. This contrast forms one more of the many antitheses in the book, here an antithesis between reason and passion. Unlike the antithesis between vision and blindness, to which it is related, this one does not divide the pagan and the Christian worlds. The analysis here is more complex, and it acts as an elaboration and a qualification for the theme of vision.

As a Stoic, Bardo is the pivotal example of reason without passion. We have seen already what this implies in individual and private life in the imagery of death that everywhere characterizes Bardo's world. What it implies in public life is suggested in Bardo's friend, Bernardo del Nero, and in his friends the Mediceans, all of whom are, like Bardo, men of reason untouched by passion. In one respect they differ from the rational Nello, since they do commit themselves to a point of view: they take a political stand. But that stand is not inspired by passion, and it is therefore liable to the inherent corruption of reason. As the Mediceans form their conspiracy against Savonarola, in itself a morally definitive act, Tornabuoni articulates their position when he remarks that a "wise dissimulation" is "the only course for *moderate rational* men in times of *violent* party *feeling*" (XXXIX, p. 356; my italics). Tito, whom the Mediceans here commission to implement their plot against Savonarola, reflects their views. Indeed, like Endymion, Tito is the least passionate of men, and wiser—less passionate, that is—even than Tornabuoni thinks the Mediceans, for Tito dissimulates even with his allies.

It is ironic, but not a contradiction, that in Tito, Bacchus, the god of passion, should prove to be the most passionless of men. From a moral point of view, Apollo and Bacchus, in their intimate relationship, are often indistinguishable, two aspects of the same moral void, and they often so completely replace one another, even as they did at Delphi, that one seems transformed into the other. This is precisely the case with Baldassarre, in whom Eliot embodied one such transformation. In one sense, Baldassarre is Bardo's antithesis, an antithesis, however, in which we see Bardo himself from another perspective. Once like Bardo a man of reason and a scholar, Baldassarre is now consumed by a passion that has replaced both his reason and his knowledge. Bacchus has supplanted Apollo, as the imagery makes clear. Baldassarre's surname, Calvo, is Italian for "bald," an image that takes us back to Nello the barber and identifies Baldassarre as a hairless and therefore Apollonian figure. Similarly, it is significant that Baldassarre is captured by pirates and lost on his pilgrimage to Delos (VI, p. 64), the island that was the birthplace of, and remained sacred to, Apollo. It was precisely in that pilgrimage that the Apollonian Baldassarre became the Bacchic. The event itself is Bacchic, not only because of its violence, but because it imitates, as the ancient Bacchic worship imitated in ritual, the capture of Bacchus by Acoetes while he sailed with his ship to Delos, a story told in the same third book of Ovid's *Metamorphoses* in which is described the scene Tito asks Piero to paint on the triptych. In the logic of this amoral world, Bacchus proves to be the destructive side of Apollo, Apollo's own restrained passion unleashed.

Balance and proportion, however, remain the keys. "Nothing in excess," as was also written on the temple of Apollo at Delphi. Passion uncontrolled by reason, even the passion for Christ, is equally dangerous. If Baldassarre is lost on his pilgrimage to Delos, Dino is lost on his pilgrimage to Christ. And, ironically, in his extreme religious passion, Dino becomes passionless (see, for example, XV, p. 162), just as Baldassarre had become passionate and irrational.

Between the pagan and the Christian extremes lies the mystery Romola will discover. That mystery inherits from pagan ethics its humanism and from religion its passion, its "moral energy," as Romola later defines it (LII, p. 458). Only in their union is morality, a morality such as Eliot would accept, possible, just as only in the union of the two cultures that engendered them is the progress of Western civilization possible. Such a union, which brings together reason and religion, is the genesis of myth, a vision whose truth is no longer literal to us but symbolic. To apprehend that symbol, however, requires a special faculty; if ethics is the province of reason and religion is the province of faith, the symbolic truth of myth is the province of mystery. Myth is not allegory in which the mind can discern, sometimes with mathematical precision, a set of equations, but a perception that must be internalized. It is not an exposition but an experience in which the word must be made flesh.

One of Eliot's earlier experiments in the poetic use of myth, a small but important passage in *The Mill on the Floss,* may help to illuminate in its simplicity Eliot's far more complex and comprehensive exploration of that mystery in *Romola.* I allude to the myth of St. Ogg in which the Virgin Mary appears, in disguise, and asks the ferryman Ogg to take her across the river one bleak and stormy night. To the other ferrymen, the request had seemed irrational and obstinate, especially since the Virgin refused to give her reason for it. But it did not seem so to Ogg, who does not even ask her reason but agrees, without question, to take her across, saying, "It is enough that thy heart needs it" (Book I, Chap. XII). Foolish as Ogg seems to the other ferrymen to risk so dangerous a crossing, to Eliot his reply is precisely the right one. In it Ogg acknowledges the unintelligible otherness of another self, whose motive is consistent only with itself and whose need therefore cannot, as Lear said, be reasoned.

There is no mysticism in this mystery, in which, on the contrary, Eliot further explored imagination by rooting a mythological reading of Christianity itself in an empiricist foundation. In a sense, in his reply to the Virgin, the ferryman Ogg makes the final concession to an empiricist psychology in recognizing that it is impossible for one self-contained bundle of perceptions, in Hume's phrase, to enter into the experiences of another. Yet, paradoxically, in this resignation to individual isolation lies the language of fellowship. Ironically, reason, in accepting only what is objectively demonstrable, divides and separates individuals, locking each in his own consciousness. But the knowledge that is feeling confesses every mind to be a mystery, a mystery in which each of us recognizes the reflection of his own mystery, and in whose needs we acquiesce not because they are our needs but because we know that our needs are equally unintelligible to others.

In this argument, Eliot found the psychological and moral basis for the historical inevitability of Christianity. Here was the very moment of transition from the pagan gods to Christ, the transition from the pagan knowledge that there is sorrow to the Christian knowledge of sorrow. Between the two there is little connection. The first is rational, statistical. It recognizes human agony as a proposition, an objective fact in the external world. In Eliot's view, the second was a mystery, the mystery of Christ's incarnation. Comte argued that Positivism taught the true function of feeling even better than Catholicism, and perhaps in this similarity Eliot found the pivotal point that connects the two in her book. But in expounding the mystery of the crucifixion, Eliot was indebted far more to Feuerbach than to Comte.

In Christ, Feuerbach argued in *The Essence of Christianity,* the objective and subjective points of view become one. God had, of course, always known human suffering, for his knowledge was, by definition, infinite. But he had known it only from a divine point of view, as it were, objectively, as mere information, as the experience of another. Yet the knowledge of pain and sorrow is precisely such as can be had only in the experience of them. Thus, it was to participate in that human experience that God became Christ. In becoming man, God gained the only knowledge of human experience that makes the human agony intelligible, sensory, empirical knowledge. The incarnation was, of course, a myth for both Feuerbach and Eliot, and therefore an emblem of our capacity to transcend the barrier of our senses somehow through our senses, and so to identify in imagination with others, to feel not, as God had before he became Christ, for them but, as Christ himself felt in the crucifixion, with them. It was only in this identification, Eliot argued, that sympathy could be born, and it could be born then because the very egotism that makes us indulgent to our own pain can make us compassionate to the pain of another when we have come to feel it as our own. When Savonarola urges Romola to return to Florence and to her husband, he says: "you, my daughter, *because you know the meaning of the cry*" of anguish, "should be there to still it" (XL, p. 375; my italics). It is for this reason also that the Madonna dell' Impruneta, to whom the Florentines always turn in their hour of need, is called the Mother "rich in sorrows and *therefore* in mercy" (XLII, p. 383; my italics).

But if experience of pain is a necessary, it is not always a sufficient condition for sympathy. We are not all capable of imagination, and experience without imagination is a moral dead end. That is the essence of Tito's story. It is a moral dead end, not only because the sympathy Tito cannot feel would have spared those with whom he is associated considerable pain and suffering, but because it would have been, had he known it, the only path for his own salvation. Bacchus, ironically, proves to be as poor a savior of himself as of others. Although Carole Robinson argues that in Baldassarre, in whom Tito's retribution is chiefly embodied, Eliot created a character who replaced the banished Victorian God, a divine retribution presented in secular terms, as it were,[1] the imagery through which we trace Tito's destruction makes Baldassarre, it seems to me, not a divine but a natural retribution. As I have already suggested, in his pilgrimage to Delos, Baldassarre becomes a Bacchic figure, and the ultimate irony of the image of

Bacchus triumphant is that Tito is himself the last victim of the Bacchic commitment to conquest rather than sympathy.

I have already quoted the passage in which the narrator speaks of the dread that is the "awe of Divine Nemesis" (XI, p. 122). Throughout the book, this dread, to which the narrator alludes often and by which Tito is little touched, is contrasted with fear, something quite different. Tito's nature, the narrator remarks at one point, was "too joyous, too unapprehensive, for the *hidden* and *distant* to grasp him in the shape of *dread*" (X, p. 107; my italics). But fear "was a strong element in Tito's nature—the *fear* of what he believed or *saw* was likely to rob him of pleasure" (XI, p. 123; my italics). In some sense, fear and dread reflect one another, but as the italicized words suggest, they are distinguished in that fear belongs to the visible, the amoral, sensory world, whereas dread belongs to the invisible moral world. Dread is the first stirrings of "a moral law restraining desire," while fear is just what the narrator had said dread was not, "a man's animal care for his own skin" (XI, p. 122).

Piero di Cosimo had early recognized that it was not dread but fear that characterized Bacchus when he had chosen Tito as his model for the portrait he was painting of Fear, fear in its very essence. We hear of this portrait for the first time when Tito comes to Piero's studio to commission the triptych from him, and the portrait of Fear becomes thus the secret truth concealed in the legend on the triptych. As in the triptych, Piero envisions Tito in the portrait of Fear in an attitude of triumphant joy, right hand uplifted and holding a wine-cup, but "with an expression of such intense fear in the dilated eyes and pallid lips" that Tito himself, looking at this other and uncommissioned likeness, feels as though a cold stream were running "through his veins" (XVIII, p. 197). Although Piero had begun the portrait of Fear soon after he had met Tito, it is not, appropriately, until he witnesses Tito's meeting with Baldassarre that he understands what it is that Tito fears. Piero is the first to recognize that it is Baldassarre who is the "ghost" (XXII, p. 229) who threatens "my bland and smiling Messer Greco" (XXV, p. 241).

The form in which Baldassarre appears to Tito is, however, entirely Tito's choice. Potentially at least, Baldassarre could represent either dread or fear. He is a "ghost," as Piero calls him, in the sense that he is a phantom from Tito's past, but also in the sense in which Dino is a ghost, as a messenger who comes from the invisible moral world of the book. And he comes from that world, not because the retribution he brings is itself moral, but rather because he proves that to deny a moral claim, a claim that to Eliot was nothing more than mankind's attempt to resist as far as possible the devastating impact of nature, is tantamount to accepting nature and all the consequences that entails. Yet this is the alternative Tito chooses, and Baldassarre appears to Tito in the form of fear only because Tito cannot willingly yield to the moral claim of dread. Against moral dread "no chain-armour could be found" (XXXII, p. 298), the narrator observes. When Tito buys the chain-coat he henceforth wears as a protection against Baldassarre, he assumes "The Garment of Fear" (XXVI, p. 245).

Here again chronology is instructive. Abandoned by Tito, Baldassarre, after many adventures, is brought to Florence among the French prisoners who follow the entrance of Charles VIII. It is November 17, 1494, the hour of the Advent sermon. As Charles is, in Savonarola's mind at least, the agent of God's retribution on Florence, so Baldassarre is to be the agent of natural retribution on Tito. In both Charles and Baldassarre, in their literal advent, the meaning of Savonarola's Advent sermon is fulfilled. The preparation for the coming Christ foreshadows Tito's alternatives, for in Christ there is either salvation or the judgment of sin. The imagery suggested by the calendar is elaborated in the topography as Tito and Baldassarre meet for the first time in Florence. Running to escape from the French soldiers, Baldassarre makes his way from the Baptistery to the great marble steps of the Duomo. In her own tour of the Baptistery, Eliot had been especially impressed by its mosaic dome ceiling, from which she had singled out to note in her Diary the "pale large-eyed Christ surrounded by images of Paradise and Perdition" (Cross, II, 168). Those images are Tito's alternatives now. The moment of their meeting is a public one, and Tito has the opportunity to make the kind of public confession that so often purges the Dostoevskian hero of his sins. But Tito does not make it. By rejecting Baldassarre's claim on him on the very steps of the Duomo that Baldassarre has finally reached, Tito repudiates the salvation Christ offers, and although Tito does not realize it, so challenges Baldassarre implicitly to a Bacchic contest. It is appropriate, therefore, that having been denied by Tito, Baldassarre buys the dagger through which he intends to be revenged exactly one week later, on November 24 (XXX, p. 284), in that year Christ the King Day. The Bacchic retribution, seen from the book's moral perspective, proves to be the Christian judgment Tito had unwittingly chosen.

The same point is made in connection with Baldassarre, for he too, in choosing revenge, has taken a Bacchic course. To buy this dagger of revenge, Baldassarre must sell the only valuable he has left, a sapphire he wears in an amulet around his neck. Like all the gems in the book, the sapphire has a symbolic significance. Often called the "holy sapphire," it is held to have the power to confirm the soul in its good works and to prevent wicked thoughts. It is also the stone of the cardinal's ring in which it is a symbol of the cardinal's marriage to the church. Thus, when Baldassarre sells the sapphire to buy the dagger, he too, like Tito, exchanges the protection of Christ for a Bacchic weapon.

This event recalls two others. Tito had made the same exchange when he had sold the ring that symbolized his bond with Baldassarre and bought, with that money, the triptych on which he had first announced himself Bacchus triumphant. Here, to both Tito and Baldassarre, the contrast is Tessa. Baldassarre's sapphire had been concealed, as is appropriate for a holy gem, in a *breve* his mother had once given him as protection for his soul (XXX, p. 282). Tessa too wears a *breve,* which she believes will bring her the protection of the Virgin. Tessa, however, does not part with hers, and her faith, as we shall see, is rewarded in Romola's patronage.

As Bacchus and Apollo had at some point become indistinguishable and had seemed to assume one another's roles, so, strangely enough, do Bacchus and Christ in an ironic extension of the pleasure-pain calculus. In calculating not only between his own pleasure and pain but between his own pleasure and another's pain, Bacchus, the god of joy, becomes the god of sorrow. In precisely the opposite way, Christ, the Man of Sorrow, becomes also the god of joy. It had been in this paradox that Tito had assumed satanic proportions. Similarly, as Baldassarre increasingly plays his Bacchic part, he too assumes satanic dimensions. Bacchus and Satan are joined here in the image of the serpent, the central image the two myths share. On their first meeting, for example, Tito feels as if "some magical poison had darted from Baldassarre's eyes," a poison he experiences, like the chill he had felt when he had first seen Piero's painting of him as a portrait of Fear, "rushing through his veins" (XXII, p. 229). Not long afterward the image becomes more concrete, as Tito feels that "a serpent had begun to coil round his limbs. Baldassarre living . . . was a living revenge, which would no more rest than a winding serpent would rest until it had crushed its prey" (XXIII, p. 231). Slowly, the two figures become synchronized in a Bacchic ritual as Baldassarre's movements mirror Tito's. Although Piero remarks that when Baldassarre clutched Tito, Tito had looked "as frightened as if Satanasso had laid hold of him" (XXIX, p. 268), it is in Tito that Baldassarre sees the "diabolical prompter" (XXX, p. 275), the creature favored by some "diabolical fortune" (L, p. 441). Indeed, Baldassarre is Tito himself, the embodiment of his own past (see, for example, XXXIV, p. 317; LXVII, p. 564). And from that no escape is possible.

Eliot took great care to identify Baldassarre with the images of the Bacchic ritual, images that had for the most part already been suggested in the legend on the triptych. In the triptych, Tito had asked Piero to paint, among other things, leopards and tigers, both traditional Bacchic adjuncts (XVIII, p. 194). As Tito is subsequently called the leopard (XLVIII, p. 430), so Baldassarre becomes the other "wild beast" (XXX, p. 275), the "mysterious old tiger," as Piero always calls him (see, for example, XXV, p. 241; XXIX, p. 267), "mysterious" in both the popular sense and the religious sense appropriate to the mystery cult of Bacchus. The image of the tiger recurs many times in Baldassarre's pursuit of Tito (see especially XXIII, p. 229; XXIII, p. 232; XXXIV, p. 318). In this context, the moment in which Tito irrevocably denies Baldassarre's claim on him and so incurs his revenge takes on special significance.

Tito disclaims Baldassare when Tornabuoni asks Tito who the strange man clutching Tito's arm might be. Trapped in the necessity of making an instant decision, Tito replies, *"Some madman, surely*" (XXII, p. 229). It is those words that transform Baldassarre's confusion and doubt into madness. What takes hold of Baldassarre in that moment is a Bacchic *mania,* as Tito himself realizes later (XXXIX, p. 363). This is not madness in the ordinary sense of the word that Tito had at first meant to suggest. The monks who later take Baldassarre in and help him to escape recapture by the French soldiers do not think him mad in the common sense, but they do recognize him as belonging to the tribe of Bacchus when they remark that Baldassarre seemed distracted as though he were "planting a *vine* twenty miles off" (XXIX, p. 267; my italics). That distraction is one aspect of Baldassarre's amnesia, and the amnesia itself is Bacchic, for the loss of memory is one of the most common characteristics of the Bacchic *ekstasis.*

Ordinary madness would have been far less devastating. The *mania* that takes hold of Baldassarre is a passion so blind and intense that, as Tito instantly recognizes, it "subjugates all the rest of the being, and makes a man sacrifice himself" to it "as if it were a deity to be worshipped with self-destruction" (XXII, p. 231). A deity it indeed is, Bacchus himself, and self-destruction is precisely the point of this Bacchic worship. Ironically enough, self-sacrifice is a far more total annihilation, as Tito himself seems to know, in the Bacchic than in the Christian mystery.

If Baldassarre is Tito's reflection, as he is, his self-destruction must then be Tito's also, and it is Tito who is the chief actor in that last Bacchic rite. For Baldassarre is the Maenad (XXXVIII, p. 348) to Tito's Bacchus, and the Maenad is the spirit of Bacchus himself. This equation is stressed in Tito's identification with Orpheus, a figure with whom Nello associates him (XIII, p. 138). But Tito plays not only the role of Orpheus, who was torn limb from limb by the Maenads, but the Maenads themselves, as we see when he renders so well the Maenad chorus from Poliziano's Orfeo (XXXIX, p. 361). In Baldassarre (and in Dolfo Spini, as we shall see), the merciless beasts Tito had so long let loose on others turn finally on himself.

Early in the book, Nello had referred to the *"audacia perdita"*—the "Incorrigible impudence"—which had been attributed to the Greeks by Juvenal (III, p. 40). Along with many others, Juvenal was one of the ancients Eliot reread for *Romola,* returning to him many times between November 1861 and April 1862 (Yale MS 3), not, I think, in the two English translations included in the Eliot/Lewes library (nos. 1140, 1141) but probably in a Latin text. Juvenal's phrase, terse as always, suggests a form of hybris, a blindness, that is, to the human limitations beyond which man may not step in safety. Apparently, Greeks had not much altered since Juvenal's day by the time of the Renaissance. For ironically, while Tito is vulnerable to fear, he is entirely ignorant of the nature of hybris, whose consequences should make all men tremble. Yet his ignorance is not surprising, for hybris and dread are parallel perceptions, and to be impervious to one is often to be impervious to the other.

Dread, the narrator had said, is an expression of moral awe. Similarly, a sense of hybris is an expression of natural awe, a confession of human impotence against the power of nature. To transgress either is to incur an inevitable Nemesis. Nemesis, in fact, functions in *Romola,* as in all of Eliot's fiction, on both a natural and a moral level. " 'It is good,' sing the old Eumenides in Aeschylus, 'that fear should sit as a guardian of the soul, forcing it into wisdom—good that men should carry a threatening shadow in their hearts under the full sunshine; else, how should they learn to revere the right' " (XI, p. 122). Of this moral Nemesis, which the Eumenides represent, Tito knows nothing. But before the Eumenides became the agents of that moral Nemesis that weighs the heart of the wrongdoer with guilt, they were the Furies, the agents of natural retribution, the fiends who drove to madness and death those who, like Tito, had betrayed their blood bond with the past. Like Aeschylus, Eliot too believed that we cannot elude these eternal guardians of Justice and Time and that if we cannot hear their song as the Eumenides, as the "Well-Intentioned Ones," they will repeat it more forcefully as the Furies.

The moment Tito shows himself incapable of feeling the benevolent guilt of the Eumenides, he incurs the wrath of the Furies, whose role Baldassarre (and later Spini) assumes. For if there is no just God, as for Eliot there was not, who brings all things in the end to their moral fruition, there is something else, something far more implacable, the natural laws of consequence, from which no man can escape. Our "deeds are like children that are born to us," the narrator observes; "they live and act apart from our own will. Nay, children may be strangled, but deeds never; they have an indestructible life" (XVI, p. 170). Tito wonders at one point whether he cannot "strip himself of the past, as of rehearsal clothing, and throw away the old bundle, to robe himself for the real scene" (LVII, p. 492). But the rehearsal, in this case, is the real scene. The play is performed only once.

That natural order governed by the laws of consequence, while perfectly indifferent to moral questions—the very order of the "hard non-moral outward conditions" Eliot had described to Morley—is nonetheless not entirely unconnected to morality. It is that connection Baldassarre illustrates when he is transformed from a moral claim to a retributive agent. Baldassarre perceives the link when he concludes about Tito that "the heart that never quivered with tenderness for another had its sensitive fibres that could be reached by the sharp point of anguish. The soul that bowed to no right, bowed to the great lord of mortals, Pain" (XXXVIII, p. 347). Even for Tito, who is willing to sacrifice others to his own pleasure, pure joy is unattainable. Neither the laws of nature nor of human nature permit it. Betrayal breeds revenge. It is impossible to resign from the fellowship with suffering without being exiled from the fellowship of sympathy.

To say this is to say that Tito is, in Eliot's terms, a gambler. Eliot's fiction numbers many gamblers, literal gamblers such as Dunstan Cass, Fred Vincy, and, of course, the most frenetic of all, Gwendolen Harleth who opens *Daniel Deronda* in a casino; and even more commonly metaphoric gamblers, characters like Dinah Morris in *Adam Bede,* for example, who plays dice with the universe when she preaches that things will somehow turn out as they should and that we must not, therefore, trouble ourselves with making plans. Tito is not a literal gambler, and he does indeed make plans. But he always speaks of life as a game[2] and always prays to the god of fortune to deal him the winning hand. [3] He is a gambler because he believes, ironically for a man of utilitarian persuasion, not in consequences but in luck. Yet it is precisely those committed to the pleasure-pain calculus who are the most likely to fall into this trap; for here Eliot suggests that the greatest threat to utilitarian ethics is the psychology of the utilitarian himself. Indeed, the pleasure-pain calculus is very deceptive. Distant pain, however certain, is often less vivid to the present imgination than imminent pleasure. The love of pleasure that commits Tito to the calculus makes him far more susceptible to the anticipation of immediate pleasure than to the fear of subsequent pain. Many of Tito's greatest errors, including his entanglement with Tessa, are made in a dreamlike indifference to consequences not yet envisioned. Thus, although to implement the pleasure-pain calculus with success it is necessary to foresee and act on all possible consequences—"perfect scheming," the narrator remarks, "requires omniscience" (LXIII, p. 535)—it is clear that the calculus is of little use not only to characters of limited intelligence, such as Tessa, but even to a character so intellectually remarkable as Tito, in whom, however, judgment is often far from desire.

Psychologically, the calculus also troubled Eliot for another reason. For we do not come to our choices, Eliot maintained, without a past. Often, it is not our judgment but rather the habit of our characters that speaks for us in our actions. A mere moment's reflection shows Tito, for example, how poorly he had handled his first meeting with Baldassarre. He might have acknowledged him; he might have explained his failure to search for him with a few clever lies. Very likely, Baldassarre in his love would have believed him. But it is the very habit of lying, the inclination always to escape consequences, that prompted Tito's outright denial. We "prepare ourselves," the narrator observes, "for sudden deeds by the reiterated choice of good and evil that gradually determines character" (XXIII, p. 231). Thus, in these ways, the ethics of utility is psychologically subverted and leads to disutility. Ironically, Tito, who considers himself a child of nature, who believes that his moral code is written in nature's cosmic laws, fails to discern the inherent paradox in them.

But for Tito the world is a game in another sense as well, one that also derives from the pleasure-pain calculus. Here, the explicating analogue is Bratti. Although not a historical figure in the same sense as Savonarola or Machiavelli, Bratti is historical in that he is a composite of a legendary character in Renaissance Florence. Eliot seems to have taken great delight in tracing the origins of his name, Bratti Ferravecchio, in which the legend is suggested. In the

Quarry, she noted that when the woolcarders of Florence were out of work, they did not learn a new trade but became secondhand dealers in rags, old iron, and glass, and went about the city crying their wares. From one such cry, "Chi ha ferri vecchi?" ("Who has old iron?") they came to be known as Ferravecchi. Bratti's first name has a similar origin. Its history, which Eliot entered in her *Quarry,* is reproduced in Bratti's cry in the text, which, as each word slurs and shortens the preceding one, gives every stage of its etymology: "Chi *abbaratta—baratta-b'ratta*—chi abbaratta cenci e vetri—b'ratta ferri vecchi?" ("Who will exchange rags and glass, who will exchange old iron?" [I, p. 12; my italics]).

Such minute concern to re-create the actual sounds of Florence is, we recall, what sent Eliot to read Varchi's *L'Ercolano* in which the Florentine vernacular is both illustrated and discussed. Varchi was not, however, the only defender of the vernacular, nor Eliot's only source. We recall that Poliziano and Lorenzo de' Medici had greatly contributed to making the vernacular acceptable; and even the historian Villani, who had written in the Tuscan vernacular, had been instrumental in establishing the Tuscan tongue as the standard of Italy. Already familiar with those works and with many others, Eliot read a number of other volumes, chiefly for their contemporary idiom. Recognizing rightly that comedies were among the best examples she could find, she studied not only Michelangelo's *La Tancia,* as we have seen, but Bernardo Dovizi's *La Calandria* (Cross, II, 260), a Florentine version of the *Menaechmi* of Plautus, full of lively and colloquial dialogue, and Machiavelli's *La Mandragola,* reread, she noted, "the second time for the sake of Florentine expressions" (Cross, II, 260). Eliot may also have studied Giovanni Maria Cecchi's comedies, although their library copy seems to have been Lewes's (no. 402). In the summer of 1861, Eliot was reading Antonio Francesco Doni's *I Marmi* (Yale MS 3), a book she owned (no. 606) and one she entered into one of the bibliographies in the *Quarry.* In addition to its wonderfully rambling conversations, *I Marmi* was especially appropriate, for its dialogue takes place, as the title suggests, on the marble steps of the Cathedral of Santa Maria del Fiore, the steps on which Baldassarre had confronted Tito.

Accuracy in the Italian expressions that appear everywhere in

Romola was only one of the reasons Eliot concerned herself with the Italian vernacular, for in her linguistic research too historical verisimilitude had an epic purpose. Indeed, in its transformation from the ancient Latin to the Renaissance vernacular, the Italian language was a mirror of European history, and as such assumed a symbolic significance. The heated Renaissance controversy, therefore, over whether the ancient or the modern tongue was to be preferred implied for Eliot, what in a sense it was, a conflict between the static and the dynamic views of history, and scholars who wished not only to rediscover the ancients but to return in the Renaissance to their life and language were, like Bardo, men who repudiated evolution, progress. Eliot favored the vernacular as the language of the Renaissance and turned in her linguistic studies without exceptions to those who were its most vigorous defenders. Varchi was only one of those she read in this connection. In February 1862, Eliot and Lewes went to the British Museum to look up various items and consulted, among other sources, Vincenzio Maria Borghini's *Discorsi,* a sixteenth-century work that provided Eliot with information on the "simplicity of the Florentine table equipage" *(Letters,* IV, 15), but a book which has among its chief objects a comparative assessment of the Greek, Latin, and Italian languages. Her best choice for the colloquial speech of Florence was the *Novelle* of the fourteenth-century writer Franco Sacchetti, whom Eliot seems to have been reading from July through December 1861 (Yale MS 3) and who is cited several times in the *Quarry.* It was Sacchetti's "intensely idiomatic" dialogue that Eliot gave as her authority in arguing an idiomatic point with T. A. Trollope *(Letters,* III, 432). It is surely not without some irony, then, that Eliot has Monna Brigida remark in *Romola* that she has not read Sacchetti's book because someone has told her it was "wicked" (XII, p. 131); it was precisely because he wished to address himself to just such ordinary people as Monna Brigida that Sacchetti, fully aware of his radical purpose, wrote the *Novelle* in the simple and lively vernacular that made them so valuable to Eliot. Apparently not content with examples only, she also studied the history of the Tuscan language in Pier Francesco Giambullari's *Origine della lingua Fiorentina,* a book she entered into one of the bibliographies in her *Quarry.* The author of the first

Tuscan grammar, Giambullari, a sixteenth-century scholar and a contemporary of Varchi and Borghini, was not only one of the first to trace the history of the Tuscan vernacular but was one of its most eloquent supporters.

To return to Bratti. Although a cheerful and colorful character in the book, Bratti is nevertheless another symptom of the moral disintegration of Florence. Nello remarks that Bratti "has a theory, and lives up to it," namely, he "means to extract the utmost possible *sum of pleasure,* that is to say, hard *bargaining,* out of this life, winding it up with a bargain for the *easiest* possible passage through purgatory, by giving Holy Church his *winnings* when the *game* is over" (III, p. 30; my italics). Like Tito, therefore, Bratti looks for the Bacchic path of "ease," and in that is implied the utilitarian criterion that calculates the "sum of pleasure," a criterion that makes life for Bratti, as for Tito, a "game." Eliot noted in the *Quarry* that one Ferravecchio, commonly known as Bratti Ferravecchio, was reputed to have died a very rich man. In a comic, and therefore more innocent, modulation of the theme, Bratti's position suggests that the attitude of Bacchus triumphant, the attitude that life is a game in which we must try to be winners, is one that sides with the hard, nonmoral outward conditions against everything mankind has done to resist it. And it is to urge that resistance that Daniel Deronda tells Gwendolen Harleth, when he lectures her on her gambling, that there "are enough inevitable turns of fortune which force us to see that our gain is another's loss—that is one of the ugly aspects of life. One would like to reduce it as much as one could, not get amusement out of exaggerating it" (chap. XXIX).

In his private revenge, Baldassarre is joined by a public revenge embodied in Dolfo Spini. For Tito has sinned publicly in precisely the same way as he has sinned privately. The varied political parties to which Florence falls prey at the death of Lorenzo de' Medici are, by their very number and multiplicity of purpose, divisive. Yet, although these parties dismember Florence, they are not themselves morally equal. Between the extremes, each represents a bloc of interest, and even here some are worthier than others. The Milanese, the pope, and the French are all outsiders and have chiefly an acquisitive interest in the city. The loyal Mediceans, among whom Romola's godfather Bernardo del Nero is one of the best, believe, some more honestly than others, that Florence's salvation lies in them. None of these conceives of Florence as a *polis,* as a city in which every aspect of life is comprehended in a unified whole. That is the vision of Savonarola, whose purpose it is to make the city a Christian utopia of moral purity and brotherly love.

It is in this context that we can understand one more of the many reasons Eliot chose 1492 as the year in which to open her book. That date was, for Eliot, a turning point, not only in Florentine, but in Western and world history. This is also the year in which *The Spanish Gypsy* is set, and in its introductory lines Eliot made clear in what way she considered it a symbolic moment in mankind's evolution. In one sense, 1492 is the year in which the pagan and the Christian traditions finally flower:

> The fifteenth century since the Man Divine
> Taught and was hated in Capernaum
> Is near its end—is falling as a husk
> Away from all the fruit its years have riped.

At the same time, however,

> The West now enters on the heritage
> Won from the tombs of mighty ancestors,
> The Seeds, the gold, the gems, the silent harps
> That lay deep buried with the memories
> Of old renown.

As in *Romola,* the Renaissance of the fifteenth century sees the fruit of the two traditions, and their collision as well, for in *The Spanish Gypsy* too

> the vine-wreathed god
> Fronts the pierced Image with the crown of thorns.

In man's growing knowledge of himself and in his deeper awareness of his humanity, he has reached the stage at which his "soul . . . is widening toward the past," in which he is "More largely conscious of the life that was." The "horizon widens round him," therefore, but it extends not only into the past but into the future, to the "untracked waves" toward the West that Columbus "watches, or he sails in dreams."

Like the year that made him famous, Columbus, to whom Eliot also alluded in the Proem of *Romola,* becomes the symbolically pivotal figure, "the pulse of all mankind," as Eliot called him in *The Spanish Gypsy.*[4] Columbus had always been a particularly important figure for English history, since the discovery of America placed England, which had until then been at the very edge of European civilization, at the center of the Western world. But for Eliot he had a more spiritual significance, and Eliot not only read books on Columbus, such as Johann Georg Kohl's *A Popular History of the Discovery of America from Columbus to Franklin,* published in 1862 and very likely purchased for her research for *Romola* (no. 1169 in the Eliot/Lewes library), but she also used Columbus in a figurative way when she spoke of pioneers who broke new ground in other areas. In *Middlemarch,* for example, in speaking of Lydgate's hope to discover the primal tissue and thus make a pioneering contribution to medicine, Eliot wrote: "we are apt to think it the finest era of the world when America was beginning to be discovered, when a bold sailor, even if he were wrecked, might alight on a new kingdom; and about 1829 the dark territories of Pathology were a fine America for a spirited young adventurer" (chap. XV). Like Antigone, then, and like Christ, Columbus is one of those who take us into our future; and all the more so because the discovery of America, which Eliot once called the "cradle of the future" *(Letters,* II, 85), enclosed the earth within a known circumference and therefore brought all men into one world. In her chronology of Florentine history, Eliot noted in the *Quarry* that the two chief events of 1492 were the discovery of America and the death of Lorenzo de' Medici. Lorenzo's death closes an age, and Columbus begins a new one. The year 1492 is the first year in history in which Savonarola's dream—and it was surely Eliot's dream as well—of a world united in brotherly love, symbolically represented in Florence, is actually possible. It is the beginning of the last arc of the circle of light and glory.

It is that dream that Tito threatens, not intentionally, but simply because in the political upheaval, Tito too is a party, like the others, but unlike the others a party of one. While most have come to recognize Tito's motives and thus to consider him a dangerous ally, they are nevertheless aware that he is useful, and utility is the primary criterion of Florentine public as well as private life. As members of the Special Council debate whether or not to use the services of this "ingenious and serviceable Greek," they conclude that "unprincipled men were useful, enabling those who had more scruples to keep their hands tolerably clean in a world where there was much dirty work to be done" (LVII, pp. 489-90). Yet the bonds of mutual utility are not only very loose ones that must dissolve with the shifting centers of power; they are also very dangerous ones. Maximal utility is clearly to be gained in making use of every party and wagering on the possible success of none. Whatever their failures, every other group has at least taken some political stand. But Tito has learned the disutility of commitments, and his political game is to win no matter who loses.

In short, Tito is a man who practices already what Machiavelli will later preach. Machiavelli, who is in fact a friend of Tito's, if either can be said to have a friend, is only twenty-three when the book opens, but young as he is, he has, the narrator observes, already "penetrated all the small secrets of egoism" (XLV, p. 406), and is even now proclaiming the doctrine that the "only safe blows to be inflicted on men and parties are the blows that are too heavy to be avenged" (LX, p. 511). Eliot alludes of course to Machiavelli's thesis in *The Prince,* a well-marked copy of which was included in the Eliot/Lewes library (no. 1352), along with a volume of Machiavelli's minor writings (no. 1354) and one that contained his complete works (no. 1353). Although the chief exponent of these views, Machiavelli was not Eliot's only source for them. At the time she was reading Machiavelli, in October 1861, she was also reading the works of Donato Giannotti (Yale MS 3), whose political convictions were very similar to Machiavelli's. Eliot's copy of Giannotti (no. 801 in the Eliot/Lewes library) is heavily marked in her hand, and both Giannotti and Machiavelli are assimilated generally into the condition of Florentine politics as well as more specifically into Tito's arguments.

Of Machiavelli and Giannotti, and therefore of Tito, Dolfo

Spini is a grotesque mirror. A despicable man in every respect, Spini leads a group known as the Compagnacci, or Evil Companions. In the *Quarry,* Eliot had copied a description of the Compagnacci from Nardi, who called them a company of vicious and impudent youths created to crush Savonarola and his form of government. In her book, Eliot described them as "the dissolute young men belonging to the old aristocratic party, enemies of the Mediceans, enemies of the popular government, but still more bitter enemies of Savonarola" (XLV, p. 405). Like Tito, they are part of the regressive principle of history. Spini is a suitable leader of this riotous band. Although unlike Tito he is vulgar and vain, Spini recalls the satyr of Piero's sketch, and indeed both Spini and his young men are, like Baldassarre, Bacchic reflections. Himself identified as a tiger (LXVI, p. 556), brother therefore to Baldassarre, Spini, like his men, spends his time banqueting and carousing, and above all in indulging his taste for the Bacchic grape (XLVI, p. 415). They too share Tito's love of pleasure (XLV, p. 405) and prefer it in its most primitive form. In their mythological character, therefore, the Compagnacci are a Maenad chorus, the chorus that will pursue Tito in the last stages of the Bacchic rite, a rite whose end is fast approaching.

The end of the Bacchic ritual is the *sparagmos,* literally a dismembering, a rite in which the Maenads tear apart the god, symbolically represented in the sacrifical animal, and consume him, thus—and literally—internalizing the divine being and becoming one with him. Here again, Eliot calls our attention to the parallels between the Bacchic and Christian mysteries, parallels that suggest their differences all the more strikingly. The *sparagmos* is reenacted in the Eucharist in which the worshiper consumes the body and blood of Christ and so shares in his divinity. The historical authority for the Eucharist is the Last Supper, and it is clearly to the Last Supper that Eliot alludes in the title of the thirty-ninth chapter, "A Supper in the Rucellai Gardens."

That supper does not, however, take place at Easter; Eliot's imagery here is more complex than simple analogies can imply. It is at Easter that Tito dies, for the last day of his life is Palm Sunday, 1498. Appropriately, Tito does not survive to take part in that year in any of the rituals that mark the last four days of Easter Week—the Last Supper of Holy Thursday, the crucifixion of Good

Friday, the Harrowing of Hell on Holy Saturday, and the resurrection of Easter Sunday. Each event presupposes the former, not only in the sequence of Christ's last days, but in their symbolic reenactment in the ritual. Thus, without the Eucharist, resurrection is impossible.

It is not the Eucharist, however, but its pagan antecedent, the *sparagmos,* that Tito celebrates at his Last Supper in the Rucellai Gardens, and he celebrates it therefore before the Christian era of the book begins, on the evening, before the day on which Savonarola converts Romola, and so mankind, to Christianity. It is when Romola is converted to Christianity that Tito loses her, and in not following her into the Christian era Tito loses, with Romola, his last link to moral order. This is suggested in the date of Tito's Last Supper, December 23. It is the date of the winter solstice, the darkest night of the year. For the Bacchic Last Supper, which promises no resurrection, takes place, ironically, not in the fertile spring but in the very dead of winter. Thus, although Tito dies at the very beginning of the Holy Week of 1498, he has by then already celebrated his Bacchic rites of spring in a Bacchic perversion of the Eucharist of which the *sparagmos* that ends his life is, as we shall see, a more literal reenactment.

It is significant, as Sullivan points out, that the Rucellai Palace is the site of the Platonic Academy of Florence,[5] for Tito's Bacchic Last Supper is indeed the end of the Apollonian road. The Greek philosophers were very much on Eliot's mind while she was writing *Romola.* For example, on July 24, 1861, Eliot noted in her Diary: "Walked with George. . . . We talked of Plato and Aristotle" (Yale MS 3). It was not because Eliot thought ill of Plato that he fares so unhappily in this scene. Eliot was indebted to Plato in various ways, not the least of which is her analogy in *Romola* between the individual and the state. And the meeting in the Rucellai Gardens is haunted in fact by ghosts that recall a more honorable Platonic tradition, when "a company of scholars and philosophers" had "met to eat and drink with moderation and to discuss and admire, perhaps with less moderation, the doctrines of the great master" (XXXIX, p. 350). We are reminded of Pico della Mirandola, who had begun by being "astonished at his own powers" but had come finally "to find the universe more astonishing" even "than his own cleverness" (XXXIX, p. 350). We are reminded of Leon Battista

Alberti, a man of "universal mind, at once practical and theoretic, artist, man of science, inventor, poet" (XXXIX, p. 351). And we are reminded of many others "whose names are not registered where every day we turn the leaf to read them, but whose labours make a part, though an unrecognized part, of our inheritance, like the ploughing and sowing of past generations" (XXXIX, p. 351). The work of these Platonists, Eliot acknowledges, is part of the legacy of Western civilization.

In contrast, we are also asked to recall men like Marsilio Ficino, still alive at the time of this meeting although not present, who had been one of the most influential exponents of Platonism in Florence, and had indeed been chosen by Cosimo de' Medici to head the Platonic Academy. Eliot had read Ficino's *De christiana religione,* which she had entered in one of the bibliographies in the *Quarry,* but her estimate of it may be guessed from her description of Ficino in *Romola* as a man "fed on Platonism in all its stages till his mind was perhaps a little pulpy from that too exclusive diet" (XXXIX, p. 351). In contrast too, the reader may recall here earlier references to other Platonists or pseudo-Platonists, such as the reference to Agnolo Firenzuola (XIX, p. 199) whose *Novelle,* which Eliot owned (no. 719 in the Eliot/Lewes library), were preceded by an introduction that is a tangled mass of disintegrated Platonism. Earlier too, we had been introduced to the "popular poet" Francesco Cei, whose *Rime* falls far short of his model, Petrarch, and indeed replace the coherent Petrarchan vision with a trivial but pretentiously abstract Platonism. That he appears in *Romola* only to denounce Savonarola is symbolically definitive (VIII, p. 91).

It is obvious in Eliot's survey that there is, if not an undeviating line, at least a general tendency to deterioration in the Platonism of the Florentines. Yet such corruption could not have been possible had its potential not existed in the beginning, in Plato himself and again at the very height of Florentine Neoplatonism. Perhaps the greatest patron of Neoplatonism was the Magnifico himself, the center of the most illustrious company of genius ever assembled since the Golden Age of Athens, but a company not always above moral suspicion, despite several significant exceptions. It had been at Lorenzo's home, as Eliot mentions in the thirty-ninth chapter, that the Platonic Academy had first gathered, and only at Lorenzo's death had it been moved to the Rucellai Gardens where, as Eliot noted in the *Quarry* from Nerli, who had himself attended those meetings, some of the old and many young Platonists, including Machiavelli, met annually on November 13, the "reputed anniversary of Plato's death," as the narrator apostrophizes (XXXIX, p. 350). The quality of Eliot's historical research is suggested, incidentally, in her concern over this minor detail of the date of Plato's death. In her *Quarry,* she entered various opinions on the dates of Plato's birth and death, including Heeren's, whose conclusion she rejected, and Lastri's, which she finally accepted.

A bust of Plato, prominently placed, looks down on this Bacchic gathering, and while it was generally accustomed to survey a better company, it had no objection, the narrator speculates, to the group that met in the Rucellai Gardens on December 23, 1494. While Plato himself would surely not have sanctioned its activities, Platonic rationalism, especially in its Neoplatonic decline, offers no safeguards against moral chaos, as Nello had proved. We recall that Manni had described Burchiello's barbershop as an intellectual retreat something in the style of the Platonic Academy (see p. 132), for as Sullivan rightly suggests, it is in Nello that we realize the final decay brought about by Florentine Neoplatonism.[6]

Once more, the end of the Apollonian worship is suggested in Bacchus himself. Eliot took great pains to emphasize the Bacchic character of the setting in this scene. A little earlier, the narrator had connected the etymology of Rucellai's name with the color imagery of the book. Apparently in Lastri, from whose *Osservatore fiorentine* she entered those notes into her *Quarry,* she discovered that the family had gained both its wealth and its surname by bringing the secret of a dye derived from a little lichen called "oricella" or "roccella" from the Levant to Florence, a journey that echoes part of the survey made by the angel of the dawn in the Proem, and so traces part of the geographic progress of Western civilization. This lichen, which is significantly native to the Greek isles, yields the color of Bacchus, a reddish purple dye (XXXVIII, p. 343).

It is not the Christian wine of the Eucharist, therefore, but the Bacchic wine of forgetfulness that flows freely at the Rucellai supper. And as the wine is passed around the table, it is not the Christian but the Bacchic ritual that is celebrated. Eliot makes her moral point here by playing on the etymological meanings of the religious rites. In rejecting the Christian rite, the *communion* of the Eucharist, Tito and the Mediceans reject the Christian principle of fellowship (Latin *communio).* Indeed, in celebrating the Bacchic rite, they practice the very opposite of fellowship, the dismemberment, the tearing apart that is the etymological meaning of the culminating moment of the Bacchic ritual, the *sparagmos.* It is fitting then that the business of this company is to conspire against its political enemies by ingenious elaborations on the Bacchic art of treachery and that Bacchus himself should outdo all the rest by planning to deceive not only Savonarola but the allies who sit with him at this table. These political events are symbolically reflected in the entertainment. The plot perfected, Rucellai calls for more wine, and Tito engages to entertain the company by singing the Maenad chorus from Poliziano's *Orfeo.*

At this moment, Tito's portrait on the triptych is in essence fulfilled: he is just about to be transformed into the image of Bacchus triumphant. Indeed, it is at this moment that Tito begins to sing the "soft low-toned" notes of the traditional Bacchic cry of triumph: "evoè, evoè." Much to his surprise, however, it is at this moment also that Piero's other portrait, the portrait of Fear, comes to life, for just as Tito utters the words of triumph, the tiger Tito had asked Piero to paint on the triptych suddenly appears in the person of Baldassarre.

Immediately before his arrival, Baldassarre had been stirred to memory and, awakened as though to life again, had felt like a "maenad in the glorious amaze of her morning waking on the mountain top" (XXXVIII, p. 348). His eyes had then fallen on the pages of Pausanias, which, to his surprise, he had once again found himself able to read. Those pages which Baldassarre's eyes had scanned so eagerly fully justified Dino's charge, made long before to Bardo, that "worldly ambitions and fleshly lusts made all the substance of the poetry and history" of the pagans whom Bardo had wished him to study (XV, p. 163). It is indeed a brutal world Baldassarre finds in Pausanias, a Bacchic world of conflict and conquest, in which Tito himself seems to appear in the story of the traitor Aristocrates. In that story too Bacchic betrayal breeds the Bacchic passion of revenge, and as Baldassarre reads it he reflects, thinking of Tito, that if "baseness triumphed, if it could heap to itself all the goods of the world and even hold the keys to hell, it would never triumph over the hatred itself awaked" (XXXVIII, p. 348). It is that hatred, awake like the Maenad on the mountain, that brings Baldassarre now to the Rucellai Gardens.

Although a Maenad in that the spirit of Bacchus has entered in him, and a tiger in that the Bacchic spirit has inflamed him to a savage passion, Baldassarre appears at the Last Supper in the Rucellai Gardens as a Bacchic perversion of Christ. Entering, he denounces Tito in a paraphrase of Christ's words to the disciples at the Last Supper: "I wish you and your honorable friends," he says to Bernardo Rucellai, "to know in what sort of company you are sitting. *There is a traitor among you*" (XXXIX, p. 362; my italics). Then, explaining himself at length, he concludes in a paraphrase of Christ's words to Peter: "he left me in slavery; he sold the gems that were mine, *and when I came again, he denied me*" (XXXIX, p. 362; my italics). Perhaps Eliot remembered as she wrote this scene a fresco, believed to be by Raphael, which she had seen at the Egyptian Museum at Florence, of the Last Supper in which the figure of St. Peter had struck her with particular force (Cross, II, 178). But it is clear that although a Bacchic figure now in every respect, Baldassarre, as an embodiment not only of a moral claim but of the historical past, must speak for the moral vision and the progress of civilization, at this moment at least, in the voice of Christ.

And though in a strange and perverted way, Baldassarre's revenge, while Bacchic, asks us to consider a moral point, not the point that wickedness is punished, but the point that moral law grows out of necessity, out of the hard and imperfect world we inhabit, and that to disregard the law is not to escape the necessity. Thus, precisely because Baldassarre embodies that necessity, he points, by contrast, to Christ. This is evident in the central significance of Baldassarre's name, which suggests not only the myrrh that is life's bitterness but the resurrection to which it can lead. Here the imagery is appropriate for the Christmas season, for in following Tito to the Rucellai Gardens Baldassarre reenacts the Epiphany.

In tracking Tito to the Rucellai Gardens in a symbolic parallel to the journey of the Magi, Baldassarre is led not by a star but by something very close to it. The evening is a dark one as Baldassarre shadows Tito through the streets of Florence. And in the dark night, the figure of Bacchus is invisible except intermittently, as it "crossed the occasional light of a lamp suspended before an image of the Virgin" (XXXVIII, p. 344). From Nardi, and even more from Lastri, Eliot had noted in her *Quarry* that the Florentine streets had been commonly lit by candles that burned under the sacred images that were displayed in public. It is these lights, which successively reveal Tito on his journey, that Baldassarre follows, like the star of Bethlehem, to the Ruccellai Gardens, to an epiphany in which not Christ but Bacchus is to be discovered.

Thus, as in the Christian calendar Easter is implied in Christmas, in that the crucifixion and the resurrection are implied in Christ's birth, so in the pagan calendar in this Bacchic Last Supper is implied the *sparagmos* that is to be more literally fulfilled in Tito's end. That end evolves now with ruthless logic. Anticipating Eliot's quotation from Aeschylus, Nello had, on first meeting Tito, declared that the old Furies had gone to sleep (III, p. 39). They awake now, however, with a vengeance. In a chapter significantly called "A Masque of Furies"—a title that recalls Piero's sketch as well—Tito is led finally to the last frenzied rite of the Bacchic worship. Baldassarre and Spini, the two tigers that recall the savage end of the Bacchic mystery, join in pursuit as Tito, trapped beyond extrication, attempts to flee the city. The pursuit begins late into the night of Palm Sunday, ironically on the day on which Christ entered his ministry in Jerusalem, the first day of the Holy Week that brought the other savior to death as well, but a death that was to be, in Eliot's view, a resurrection for mankind.

Tito too believes that he can retrieve his life. When Spini and his men, now driven by a manic rage that has appropriately turned them into a band of Maenads, press Tito to the Ponte Vecchio, he looks for safety in the waters of the river Arno below. His immersion suggests a baptism and parallels, as we shall see, the baptism Romola will experience on the waters that take her to her salvation. Salvation had of course been the promise of the vegetation god, a god whose joyous ritual had indeed seemed to repudiate, even to transcend, death. But that had been the greatest of all the illusions in the Bacchic worship. And Tito's baptism, like the supper that has finally brought him to this savage end, proves to be only a parody of the Christian sacrament. For Tito had refused the sacrament of baptism when he had long before rejected the patronage of John the Baptist.

We recall that Eliot had taken special care to stress that the day that celebrates the nativity of John the Baptist also celebrates the festivities of Midsummer. In the same way, she took special care to stress that it is on that same day that Dino brings Tito the letter in which Baldassarre asks to be ransomed. For on that day, John the Baptist had symbolically, as history and ritual required, given Tito the opportunity to act in the Christian spirit of fellowship, and so absolved to prepare himself for the coming Christ. But in not ransoming Baldassarre, Tito had rejected the baptism, had chosen to celebrate the day in its pagan rather than its Christian aspect, and had thus committed himself to a relationship, not of sympathy, but of conquest. Tito's answer to Baldassarre then must be John the Baptist's answer to Tito now.

It is, in fact, under the auspices of a patron very different from John the Baptist that Tito now finds himself. In ancient times, the narrator had told us early in the book, the patron of Florence had been the god Mars, the god who "as he saw the gutters reddened with neighbours' blood, might well have smiled at the centuries of lip-service paid to his rival, the Baptist" (V, p. 46). Although in the Christian era Mars had been replaced by the Baptist as the city's patron, the Florentines, mindful even of remote possibilities, had wished to avoid offending the pagan deity, and so as not to oust him completely had assigned him the post of guarding the river Arno (VIII, pp. 85-86). It is therefore under the far more suitable eye of the god of war, who understands all about the Bacchic world of conflict and conquest, that Tito now tries to escape. Long before, the narrator had remarked that Tito's "little rills of selfishness" had at last united to "make a channel" (IX, p. 106). That channel has now become the current of the Arno, the current that carries Tito to the shore where Baldassarre waits for him. And here, the past Tito had refused to accept in life claims him in death. The next morning, the two dead bodies of Tito and Baldassarre cannot be separated. They will be buried in a common grave (LXVII, p. 545).

It is past midnight, far from the color and light he had lived in, when Tito dies, early on the morning of April 9. It had been on April 9, six years earlier, that Tito had first arrived in Florence. At the end of a full cycle, the savage Bacchic ritual is complete. Although for a time Tito's presence had been deeply felt, he leaves no legacy. One of the most striking ironies of the book, and one of its most compelling moral statements, is that Romola's marriage to the fertility god was sterile. That it would be so had been predicted in their betrothal, in the masqued procession Tito and Romola had encountered in the street in which an image of Winged Time surrounded by his winged children, the Hours, had been strangely followed by what seemed like a company of the sheeted dead chanting the wailing strain of the Miserere (XX, p. 211). It was time, and therefore history, that Tito had betrayed. In its end, which recalls its beginning, Tito's life in Florence has been a barren interruption in the progress of civilization.

7.

Conversion

If in Tito Eliot suggests the negative forces of civilization, in Romola she embodies not only the positive forces but the progress itself, in its successive stages, and even at last an answer, Eliot's answer, to the dilemma of modern man.

The scene of Romola's formal transition from Bacchus to Christ, the conversion scene in which Romola begins her Christian pilgrimage, is one of the most important scenes in the book. On the narrative line it seems simple enough: Romola tries to leave Tito, meets Savonarola, and, converted, is persuaded to return. The imagery and the structure, however, imply something considerably more complex.

This point marks the historical beginning of Christianity. It is surely this that is implied in the fact that Romola is converted by Savonarola on the road out of Florence just as Paul of Tarsus, the founder of Christianity, was converted by Christ on the road to Damascus. It is appropriate, therefore, that Romola enters her Christian era on the eve of Christ's birth, December 24. But as Tito had begun his Bacchic cycle in April, at the beginning of the Bacchic year, so Romola begins her Christian cycle at the beginning of the Christian year, not at Christmas, but at Advent, when she first hears Savonarola preach the Advent sermon of November 17, 1494 (XXVII, p. 251). Despite her resistance, the Advent sermon leads Romola to her spiritual nativity. While Romola had long felt those first stirrings of the moral law that were not unknown to the pagans, as the narrator had remarked, it is her conversion that acknowledges, sanctions, and gives them a coherent voice. Her conversion, therefore, witnesses the birth of Romola's soul, and it was that soul, Eliot argued, that was born in history in the Christian era.

As in her study of the pagan world Eliot had assessed the ancient civilizations and shown why, in her view, Christianity was necessary as a further step in the growing moral consciousness of the race, so in this Christian era Eliot will evaluate the Christian vision and show why it too must yield to the next. Although in one sense Christ will remain forever the "genius of the future," a symbol not of an age but of an atemporal vision of perfection that lies forever ahead of any specific "present," the Christian era—the era, that is, of faith and religious institutions—must like all ages come to an end. Thus, what Romola learns from the Christian experiment will suggest what Eliot considered the contribution of Christianity, and what at last alienates her from Savonarola will show in what ways Christianity failed. Between Romola's conversion and her apostasy, Eliot will explore what role the Christian discipline plays in the formation of the communal and the individual conscience.

It seems at first surprising that while Eliot does not ignore the Protestant era, she gives it so little space in the narrative—or rather she hints at it only indirectly. It is not, I think, only because fifteenth-century Florence happened to be Roman Catholic that Eliot concerned herself primarily with that stage of Christianity, but far more because it was Roman Catholicism that engaged her imagination. In this Eliot was not alone. If only to the degree that the unending quarrel of the Victorian with Roman Catholicism was voiced nowhere perhaps more vehemently than in the last Protestant words of John Henry Newman, historical moments, as it were, before he embraced the Catholic church, that century-long tirade against papism seems less inspired by religious or other considerations than by the terror of fascination. Although Eliot never participated in that tirade, she shared the fascination because, like many of her contemporaries, she understood that Roman Catholicism offered what no Protestant faith could—authority and coherence—and what few Protestant faiths do—mystery. In an age in which intellectual and moral uncertainty threatened society with anarchy, and in which Renaissance humanism had at last triumphed in a secularism that permitted neither wonder nor awe, Roman Catholicism, like the Middle Ages that embodied it and that became for men like Carlyle and Ruskin the Eden forfeited by modern man, seemed indeed the last sanctuary of intellectual, moral, and spiritual order. Writing to Sara Hennell once about Nuremberg, where she had stayed, to her regret for only twenty-four hours, Eliot described the city as "a real mediaeval town, which has grown up with the life of a community as much as the shell of a nautilus has grown with the life of the animal. . . . A pity the place became protestant, so that there is only one Catholic church where one can go in and out as one would. We turned into the famous St. Sevald's for a minute, where a Protestant clergyman was reading in a cold formal way under the grand arches. Then we went to the Catholic church, the Frauenkirche, where the organ and voices were giving forth a glorious mass, and we stood with a feeling of brotherhood among the standing congregation, till the last note of the organ had died out" *(Letters,* II, pp. 451-52). It is not surprising that Eliot associated the sense of community, of coherence, in Nuremberg with a nostalgic vision of a medieval town, nor that, in consequence, it seemed incongruous to her that the town was no longer Roman Catholic, like the church in which the glorious mass and the music filled the congregation with a sense of brotherhood in contrast to the cold and formal sermon of the Protestant clergyman. Although in Romola's development Eliot recognized as a moment of progress the declaration of independence of the individual conscience, in a sense she saw perhaps that Protestantism, like the other children of the Renaissance, marked the beginning of the end of a "coherent social faith and order."

Early in her plans for her "Italian novel," Lewes had, we recall, suggested Savonarola as a fine figure for a historical romance, and although Savonarola did not finally remain Eliot's central figure, something of Lewes's suggestion characterizes the structure of the book. The terminal dates of the action are the dates of Savonarola's public career in Florence, and in the chronology of Florentine history Eliot entered into the *Quarry* for those years, Savonarola is the dominant theme.

Eliot's research on everything that concerned Savonarola was extensive. She read Savonarola's own writings, of course. I have already cited her study of Savonarola's commentaries on the Psalmo Miserere that was important in her writing of the betrothal scene. Late in July 1861, as she noted in her *Quarry,* Eliot was reading Savonarola's sermons. At the same time, she indicated in her Diary that she was studying Savonarola's treatise on government (Yale MS 3), undoubtedly in her own copy of Savonarola's *Poesie,* to which was appended his *Trattato circa il Reggimento e Governo della citta di Firenze* (no. 1929 in the Eliot/Lewes library). September and October 1861 were devoted chiefly to Savonarola's *Prediche* (Yale MS 3), her volume of which is very heavily marked (no. 1930). On the afternoon of December 13, 1861, Eliot and Lewes walked to Molini's and brought back Savonarola's *Dialogus de Veritate Prophetica* and his *Compendium Revelationum* (Cross, II, 253). Both remained in her possession until her death (Appendix I, no. 255). Eliot turned to both works eagerly. She began reading the *Dialogus* on the next day, December 14, finished it on the fifteenth, and on the sixteenth read the *Compendium* (Yale MS 3), to which she returned for a second reading exactly a year later, as she noted at the end of her volume, just as she was writing about Savonarola in her book, and perhaps as she was preparing to quote from the *Compendium* (XLIV, p. 402).

Certainly the study on which Eliot relied most in her readings on Savonarola was Pasquale Villari's *La Storia di Girolamo Savonarola e de' suoi tempi.* A nineteenth- and early-twentieth-century historian and statesman, Villari wrote on Machiavelli, Dante, and many others, and Eliot could not have found a more knowledgeable or more readable book on the subject. She seemed to think so, for she read Villari intently through the summer and fall of 1861, made chronological notes from his history (Yale MS3), perhaps the chronological notes we find in her *Quarry* on Savonarola, and marked her copy of the book in great detail (no. 2226). By that time she had already consulted François T. Perrens's *Jérôme Savonarola,* a book she had bought in May 1860 in Florence *(Letters,* III, 296), and that she seems to have found of some use (no. 1666 in the Eliot/Lewes library). Characteristically, Eliot tried to get historically closer to the events of Savonarola's life by reading a much earlier account as well, the sixteenth-century *Vita con alcuni scritti di Fra Girolamo Savonarola urso in Firenze l'anno 1498,* a work attributed to Fra Pacifico Burlamacchi, which she read, again in her own copy (no. 344), not once but twice (Yale MS 3). In the same summer of 1861, Eliot looked through Audin de Réans's introduction to Savonarola's poems (Yale MS 3), poems, we recall, she was reading at that time; and finally, in November of that year she read F. Karl Meier's study, *Girolamo Savonarola, aus grossen Theils handschriftlichen Quellen dargestellt* (Yale MS 3) (no. 1430 in the Eliot/Lewes library).

Like Nerli and Nardi, many Florentine historians discussed Savonarola and his influence. As we have seen, Eliot had read widely, and continued to do so, in the history of religion. But in preparing to write about Savonarola and the monastic revival generally, she looked at a number of works on monastic history. In July 1861, she studied both Helyot's *Histoire des Ordres Religieux* and Charles F. Montalembert's *Les Moines de l'occident* (Yale MS 3). The Eliot/Lewes library contained also Jean Mabillon's *Traité des études monastiques* (no. 1342), to which she did not refer in her Diaries but which one suspects she had read, as well as various other volumes that would have been pertinent to her studies, volumes such as the *Manual of the Third Order of St. Francis of Assisi* (no. 755). As we have seen, Eliot found much useful information in Mrs. Jameson's *Sacred and Legendary Art,* in which, as in the account of St. Nicholas of Myra that may have inspired her to make Tito a native of Bari, religious history took a more anecdotal but at the same time a more personal form.

Although Romola's formal conversion takes place in her encounter with Savonarola, it is Bardo's death that marks the exact moment at which Romola crosses from the pagan to the Christian circle of the book. Yet Romola's transition, while it repudiates one aspect of her pagan heritage, proves to be an extension of another. In the metaphoric idiom of the book, Romola's conversion is a redefinition of her role as Ariadne, and a fulfillment of the image of Antigone.

In her quarrel with Tito over Bardo's library, Romola had realized that in the Bacchic world her identities as daughter and wife resisted fusion. She had hoped that Bardo's death would free her from her conflicting allegiances, but instead it had translated Bardo's pagan request into Christian terms. Alive, Bardo had commanded only filial loyalty. Dead, his wish had become for Romola a "*sacramental* obligation" (XXVII, p. 254; my italics). It had become, that is, a claim from that invisible world Bardo himself had rejected. The translation of the secular term into a religious one points once again not to the supernatural but to the psychological, for what this passage tells us, essentially, is that duty, internalized, becomes religion. In more secular terms, ethics becomes morality. The obligation we can debate and deny when it comes to us merely as an external duty becomes, internalized, irrefutable, inconsistent not with duty but with ourselves. It is that psychological transformation Eliot suggests in the imagery that assumes now a religious dimension. Antigone becomes the nun.

In preparing to leave Tito as a result of their disagreement, Romola removes her Bacchic wedding ring—annuls her marriage, as it were—and returns to the role she had played earlier, before Tito had tempted her. It is as Antigone that she puts on the nun's habit in which she leaves Tito, and it is in the identity that synthesizes the two images that she begins to understand, for the first time, what Dino had so inadequately tried to tell her long before. Now for the first time Romola understands her brother. She understands why men like Dino would wish to leave the earthly delights of life and dwell on images of sorrow (XXXVI, p. 331). Herself now initiated into the mystery, Romola recalls the images of her last meeting with Dino, and these press on her "almost with the imperious force of sensations" XXXVI, p. 335). Eliot chooses her words very carefully here. Out of context, they could as easily describe Tito's empirical perceptions, and that is why Eliot chooses them. What distinguishes Romola from Tito from this pivotal moment on—what distinguishes Christ from Bacchus—is not the nonempirical world Dino inhabited but the power to feel, as the phrase implies, the invisible world as though through the senses.

It is clear that in one respect Romola comes to Savonarola a ready convert. Savonarola's words now evoke her own inarticulate knowledge of sorrow. Indeed, she could not understand them otherwise, for that is the very nature of mystery. His arguments seem to Romola "an interpretation of that revulsion from self-satisfied ease . . . which had already been awakened in her" (XL, p. 375). But in another sense, the nun's habit is just what Romola calls it, a disguise. For in an ironic reversal of the triptych-crucifix image, the Christian figure that meets Savonarola at the Porta San Gallo conceals a true pagan. We see it, and Savonarola sees it, in the "proud attitude" that jars so with the habit of gray serge (XXXVII, p. 341) Romola has assumed. Indeed, Romola is not only a pagan still but in many ways very much a Bacchic one. The Christian period Romola now enters will be a period of discipline and resignation, but her flight from Tito and Florence, although it is meant to signal her rejection of Bacchus, is prompted by an instinctual desire to escape, and it is therefore, itself a Bacchic act.

The conversion scene is dominated by the image of the wedding ring, for as it had been in Tito's relationship to Bardo, the ring is the symbol of the closest of possible bonds. Appropriately, Romola's ring begins as a Bacchic symbol and ends by becoming a Christian one. In the process of its transformation, Eliot expands on the concepts of freedom and law, and shows their connection to the question of justice, a question that had first been raised in Tito's story and that will be resolved in Romola's.

Although when Romola decides to leave Tito she removes her wedding ring as a symbolic repudiation of the Bacchic life, in that gesture she echoes the first of Tito's deliberate betrayals. The two scenes are structurally analogical. Romola believes she has ample justification for her act, for Tito had broken his word to Bardo. Ironically, however, in refusing to hold to her marriage vow, Romola too breaks her word. Indeed, at this moment Romola finds herself in a situation very similar to Tito's in some respects. Unguided by affection and bound yet by no sense of obligation beyond it, Romola is lost in a moral vacuum. She feels, in consequence, as free to obey "the instinct to sever herself from the man she loved no longer" (XXXVI, p. 333)—and "instinct" here is a clear Bacchic term—as Tito had felt to obey his instinct to abandon

Baldassarre to his fate. Although Savonarola does not yet know of Tito's betrayal, his argument to Romola when he stops her unwittingly alludes to it. "Of what wrong," he asks her, "will you complain when you yourself are breaking the simplest law that lies at the foundation of trust which binds man to man—faithfulness to the spoken word?" (XL, p. 371). It is this affinity Romola herself comes to perceive "between her own conduct and Tito's" that determines her to return to her husband (XL, p. 371). She has not yet discovered Tito's betrayal of Baldassarre, but his broken word to her father now seems to her a paradigm of her own broken marriage vow.

In calling it one of the "outward symbols by which our active life is knit together" (XXXVI, p. 332), the narrator defines the significance of the ring. One more of the book's circles, the ring graphically parallels the circle described around the old city of Florence by its walls and gates. It is within those walls and gates that "life is knit together," that mankind exists in its communal character, and it is at one of those gates, at the Porta San Gallo, that Savonarola stops Romola. Significantly, when Romola had decided to separate from Tito, she had also decided to leave the city. Without understanding the equation she had automatically made in her own mind, she had been able to envision her freedom only beyond the boundaries of the city (XXXVII, p. 341). Only beyond those boundaries is freedom possible, for in the communal life within them one cannot escape obligations. As the imagery suggests, social existence is a continuum of ever widening and interrelated circles. In rejecting her marriage vow, in its socially symbolic sense, Romola has rejected the very terms of social life. This is made evident in a second event that Romola's flight echoes.

When Romola tells Savonarola that she is now eager to "forsake forever the worship of the gods of beauty and joy" (XXXVII, p. 341), and that it is to hardship, not to happiness, she wishes to flee (XL, p. 372), she tells him exactly what in essence Dino had told her. As Romola intends to do now, Dino too had fled his home, his city, and all human responsibility. That is what Romola had accused him of. Ironically, beyond the city's limits, beyond the social circumference, Bacchus and Christ are indistinguishable. That is why Savonarola does not differentiate between his arguments to Romola to return to Tito and his arguments to her to return to Florence. One undertakes to live within the social circle or one does not. What Savonarola attempts to show Romola is that moral responsibility is not selective or optional.

It is clear that the Bacchic premise of conquest cannot function within the communal circle. By his very nature, Bacchus stands outside the social ring. It is not surprising, therefore, that the moment Romola passes through the Porta San Gallo, the moment she "turned her back on Florence," she feels "free and alone" (XXXVII, p. 342). Both are Bacchic terms, and both are the antithesis of the principles on which Christianity is founded.

In *Architects of the Self,* Calvin Bedient argues what must be the instinctive response of every reader of George Eliot's fiction when he states that the debts the individual is asked to honor to his community in Eliot's world are nothing less than a "life imprisonment." [1] It is to such a life imprisonment, it seems, that Savonarola condemns Romola when he stops her in her flight and persuades her to return to her city and to her husband. Romola herself argues along similar lines when she first attempts to resist Savonarola's view of the situation. Eliot knew well enough that we are all born worshipers of the Bacchic life, prizing freedom and independence from obligations as much as Tito does. We marry Bacchus before we marry Christ. But Romola does not return because Savonarola compels her to do so; she returns because she recognizes the truth of what he tells her. It is not a happy Bacchante that Savonarola attempts to wrest to the worship of the cross, but a very disillusioned one. Indeed, when Savonarola happens to come upon Romola, she is sitting under a cypress tree just outside the city's gate (XL, p. 368), and that tree, not only in Christian art but in pagan times as well, is traditionally a symbol of death.

To a nature like Romola's, it is death that awaits her in that lonely and isolated existence to which she flees. There is, as Carlyle had said,[2] a great difference between the material Ego and the spiritual Self. It had been, after all, the Bacchic pursuit of happiness that had proved to be Romola's prison. Savonarola's argument, translated into more secular terms, is essentially Eliot's argument: that joy is not all mankind needs, that we yearn, like the night-student of the Proem, for satisfactions that transcend the fulfillment of desire, and that the pursuit of happiness (as Tito and John Stuart Mill discovered) may very well be the best way not to find it. There can surely be no doubt that Eliot would prefer to satisfy both Ego and Self. But if conditions are such that we must choose between them—and often they are—it is wiser to choose Self, for in choosing Ego we satisfy neither.

Before Savonarola sorts out the confusions in her mind, Romola sighs with relief to find herself free and alone. But as Savonarola quickly perceives, Romola is quite mistaken about what she needs. The one thing that Romola does not want is to be alone. It is because in her marriage she had come to feel alone that she leaves Tito. On reflection, it seems to Romola that their marriage had effectively ended the day Tito had put on the chain-coat to protect himself against Baldassarre, for the chain-coat had changed his "sensitive human skin" into a "hard shell" (XXVII, p. 259). The egoism that had made it necessary for Tito to secure himself against revenge had equally built an impenetrable barrier to human contact. When Tito had enclosed himself in his prison of fear, he had left Romola entirely alone. It was Romola's awareness of her isolation that had turned her thoughts back more and more frequently to Dino. Dino's religion had appealed to her then for one reason only. Still repelled by his loss of natural affection, rejecting still his superstition and dogma and fanaticism, Romola had reached for the essential truth of the Christian vision when she concluded that there might be something more than madness in that supreme fellowship with suffering (XXXVI, p. 337). This sense of fellowship is the crucial element in Romola's reassessment of Dino's faith. The experiment with Bacchus had failed, as the imagery of Tito's downfall suggests, precisely because the joy he had promised had proved to be the very principle that made joy impossible. Perhaps, Romola begins to believe, and in a similar way, in the mutual support of fellowship, sorrow too can prove to be its own negation.

But this fellowship that is the most important promise, as it is the most important legacy, of Christianity is incompatible with the freedom Romola is seeking in her flight. Eliot explores two kinds of freedom in *Romola,* one a Hellenic, an individual freedom, the other a Christian, a communal freedom. To a great degree, the joy

Bacchus had promised had consisted in the complete freedom of the individual. Such freedom is so much a part of the Bacchic life that it is, indeed, one of the names of Bacchus, Eleuther in Greek and Liber in Latin. Yet in the end, that promise, like so many others, had been one Bacchus could not universally, and finally not at all, keep. For the price of Bacchic freedom is isolation. By the same token, the price of fellowship is, conversely, submission to communal law.

It is important to realize that Eliot's point is not a moral prescription but a psychological description. The moral argument, that is, rests not on an "ought" but on an "is." Given the facts of existence as they are—and that is what we are given, whether we like it or not—we cannot enjoy both happiness and fellowship, not both fully at any rate. Of the two, fellowship is the better bargain in the end, for it allows us to maintain an essential integrity of the self. That is what the narrator claims when he remarks that the "force of outward symbols by which our active life is knit together" makes, as the ring symbolizes, "an inexorable identity for us, not to be shaken by our wavering consciousness" (XXXVI, p. 332). That is also what Savonarola tries to tell Romola: "You wish your true name and your true place in life to be hidden, that you may choose for yourself a new name and a new place." You "are turning your back on the lot that has been appointed for you—you are going to choose another. But can man or woman choose duties? No more than they can choose their birthplace or their father and mother" XL, pp. 369, 370). Savonarola's words exactly describe Romola's experiences. When she had married Tito she had been given the choice of following Bacchic freedom. She had wanted that freedom, yet she could not accept it. The lot that had been appointed to her, implied in the image of Antigone, had resisted even her own instinct for the satisfactions of desire. It had not been an external enemy Romola had fought. External enemies can be conquered. The war had been with herself, against her own nature.

Savonarola warns Romola that she cannot escape the truth he tells her: "Either you must obey it, and it will lead you; or you must disobey it, and it will hang on you with the weight of a chain you will drag forever" (XL, p. 369). The chain of Savonarola's metaphor is thematically linked to Tito's chain-coat, but with this important difference, that the retribution that comes to Tito in the garment of fear will come to Romola in the far heavier burden of guilt. The Furies are indeed inescapable, but the Eumenides, though benevolent, are fiercer still.

Each of the two concepts of freedom entails a different concept of law. The subject of law was very much on Eliot's mind as she was planning *Romola.* As we have seen, in July 1861, Eliot studied Hallam on Roman law in the Middle Ages (Yale MS 3). She had already read Johannes Scherr's *Geschichte Deutscher Cultur und Sitte* in 1854, and, from her own well-marked copy (no. 1941 in the Eliot/ Lewes library) and from the entries in her Diary, we assume she found it extremely useful in many areas of her research, including her examination of Roman law in the Middle Ages (Yale MS 3). Finally, in October 1861, Eliot turned for another view of medieval Roman law to François Pierre Guillaume Guizot's history of civilization in France (Yale MS 3).

These studies were, however, only part of the informing knowledge of the book. Eliot had, in fact, among the characters in *Romola,* representatives of precisely the two concepts of law that concerned her. In Machiavelli, she had essentially the Bacchic concept of law and freedom, a concept that was the very basis of Machiavelli's political philosophy and that was in essence identical to Tito's choice of conquest over sympathy. In Savonarola, in whom it inspired a political philosophy directly antithetical to Machiavelli's, she had a full expression of the Christian law of sympathy. The historical Savonarola was deeply committed to the notion of law, as Eliot had learned in studying his treatise on government, and his views are very accurately conveyed in her book. And, as surely both men would have shuddered to realize, but as Eliot, finding once more a parallel that reflected one historical age in another, must have discovered with pleasure, on the subject of law and government Savonarola and Comte were very much in agreement. As for Comte philosophy had its natural completion in a political organization, so for Savonarola, in a religious version of the same thesis, religion had its natural completion in the structure of the state. It was to carry the Christian vision to what he considered its inevitable and necessary completion that Savonarola entered the political affairs of Florence, and to the Christian religion in both its private and its public form "the ideas of strict law and order," the narrator remarks, "were fundamental" (LII, p. 458). Nothing, however, is more inimical than law and order to the Bacchic law of unrestrained individual freedom; Bacchic freedom has political implications but no political extension. As Carlyle would say (and did as one of his most serious charges against the libertarian position), Bacchic law envisions society as an aggregate but not as a community.

At their best, of course, both the libertarian and the Christian visions require acquiescence in law. But it is not the same law. The law of the aggregate is defensive. It protects the individual against the encroachment of others for the sake of giving him as much freedom as is consistent with social existence. The law of the community is supportive. It attempts to bind the individual through mutual concern for the welfare of all. Unlike libertarian law, communal law declares each of us our brother's keeper. Taken to the extreme, both are subject to perversion. As Tito's egotism is the ultimate reduction of individualism, so Savonarola's vision of a communal good can in the end become entirely indifferent to the welfare of the individual. However, this is not yet evident either to Romola or to the reader; Eliot is not yet interested in exploring that extreme position. In the conversion scene, we find rather a yet untested and therefore pure statement of Savonarola's ideal of the law of sympathy. It is a demanding law, but by its very nature and unlike the law of the aggregate, it cannot be enforced. It can be effective only if one willingly submits to it. Comte argued that the success of a political organization depended on a spiritual rebirth of mankind's moral nature. This is essentially the substance of Savonarola's view. As the representative of the Christian life, Savonarola preaches spiritual resurrection as a precondition for political regeneration.

If the foundation of social life is communal law, the foundation of communal law is fidelity: here we are brought back to the image of Antigone, but Antigone's fidelity is the seed not the fruition of the communal vision Savonarola urges. That fruition begins as Christian images assimilate the pagan. As it had been Piero di Cosimo who had first identified Romola as Antigone, so it is he who first, and often after, identifies her as the Virgin when he brings the pagan and the Christian images together in another of Romola's epic epithets, "Madonna Antigone" (see, for example, XXVIII, p. 266; XLIX, p. 436). The evolution that realizes that epithet begins in Romola's decision to return to Tito and to Florence.

It had been the failure of the pagan concept of fidelity that had made Romola's flight possible. In her marriage to Tito, the image of Antigone had extended into the image of Alcestis, as we have seen, but the loyalty of neither had been sufficient to keep Romola faithful to Tito. Her loyalty had been the expression only of personal attachment and had lasted only while love lasted. But the bonds of love make a very small community. Beyond those bonds lies a vast world to which, as members of society and fellow pilgrims in the progress of civilization, we must become no less responsible than we are inclined to be to those we love. It is because the interdependencies that make the web of all human relationships lie wholly beyond our individual perceptions, in the invisible realm, that we cannot lightly decide what laws we may break and when. Although Romola does later break some fundamental laws, and with her creator's sanction, what Eliot wishes to stress here is that before we grant ourselves the right to rebel we must learn the reason for obedience. Unlike Tito, we cannot rely on calculating consequences; even if our ends are more moral than Tito's, most consequences must still lie far beyond calculation. At some point, vision must yield to trust, to the assumption that all will bear their shares of the mutual burden that falls to the lot of man. It is that trust that is formalized in law, which imposes on each of us, as it were in the name of all, a pattern of obligations that cannot easily be questioned because the subtle and intricate network of claims it represents can never be known. Each, as Savonarola puts it, must fill his "place" in the whole. Both Tito and Dino had vacated their places and had therefore made life harder for those who remained behind. Her own flight, Romola comes to see, would vacate another place.

Thus, the Christian freedom of which Savonarola speaks is the freedom that voluntarily accepts the rule of communal law. "The higher life," Savonarola argues, "begins for us, my daughter, when we renounce our own will and bow before a Divine law. . . . It is the portal of wisdom, and freedom, and blessedness" (XL, p. 374). Divorced from its religious idiom, translated into the humanistic terms in which Romola understands him, Savonarola's words reveal a mystery, the mystery that freedom is expressed in law and that law is entailed in freedom.

It is on this mystery that the Christian concept of justice is based. When Tito had received Baldassarre's letter and asked himself why he was bound to ransom him, it had seemed to him unfair that he should yield his own pleasure for the sake of an undesired, unfelt obligation. Similarly, when Romola had determined to leave Tito, she had asked herself why she was bound to remain with a husband she no longer loved and who, moreover, no longer deserved to be loved (XXXVI, p. 332). Both had claimed justice on their side. Justice it was, but it was the justice of Bacchus. It is a quite different sense of justice that grows out of Christian law. In exploring this question, Eliot takes us beyond the community, to the very limits of nature.

Of the many visions of justice presented in *Romola,* Tito's is the most primitive. It signifies nothing more, as we have seen, than the survival of the fittest. From this point, Bardo's seems far removed. Bardo has a characteristically Hellenic sense of the *polis,* and in theory at least he conceives of society as a community in which human relationships must be regulated by just laws. But to Bardo justice is essentially a matter of restraints. Like law, justice is designed to allow everyone an equal degree of freedom, and it is realized when the checks that must in consequence be imposed are distributed equally among the members of society. It is the libertarian view again. Eliot recognized that in one sense such justice is entirely egalitarian, but in another sense it is not, for it assumes implicitly an equality among society's members that is far from true. What, Dino had asked Romola once in arguing with her about their father's Stoicism, "were the maxims of philosophy to me?" They "told me to be strong, when I felt myself weak" (XV, p. 162). That weakness is not recognized in Bardo's world, and it is therefore given no protection. Although unlike Tito and Machiavelli, Bardo would never take advantage of weakness, in refusing to acknowledge it he condemns the weak, no less than Tito and Machiavelli, to be defeated by the strong. Bardo's views are not so different, after all, from the primitive theory of the survival of the fittest.

Savonarola realizes well, however, that not all men are born equal. Speaking in his own religious idiom, Savonarola tells Romola that paganism has cultivated her mind but not her heart. "What has your dead wisdom done for you, my daughter?" he asks. "It has left you without a heart for the neighbours among whom you dwell, without care for the great work by which Florence is to be regenerated and the world made holy; it has left you without a share in the Divine life which quenches the sense of suffering Self in the ardours of an evergrowing love" (XL, p. 375). Bardo envisions a community of rational men, and thus, in Bardo's world, in all but his rational self the individual is left to his own lonely struggle for survival. Savonarola accuses Romola of having lived, like her father, "in blindness." You have lived, he adds "with those who sit on a hill aloof, and look down on the life of their fellow-men" (XL, p. 371). Without knowing Bardo, Savonarola has described him most accurately, for Bardo has lived his life in the proud exile to which his own vision of life condemns us all.

It is not enough that each of us should undertake the same share of the burden of our human lot. Bardo's error had been that he had not realized that equal distribution to unequals is not justice. What Savonarola urges is that we must all bear as much as we can. If we do not, who will? The ultimate distinction, then, between the pagan and the Christian concepts of justice is the distinction between enforcing and resisting the injustice of nature. This is what Romola has understood when she says, to the rough-hewn men who threaten to take by force the food supplies she carries to feed the women and children of Florence during the famine: "You are strong men," and "if you do not choose to suffer because you are strong, you have the power to take everything from the weak" (XLII, pp. 387-88).

This point brings us back to Tito with a clearer understanding of Savonarola's insistence that Romola return to him. The imagination that is essential to moral perception is no more equally distributed by nature than are any other of her gifts. Eliot's books are filled with characters who are morally hopeless. Hetty Sorrel in *Adam Bede* is perhaps the most striking example, and in her story, as in those of other characters who share her deficiency, we are made to realize that we are dealing, not with wickedness, but with a blindness that is an innate limitation. Like floods and earthquakes, Hetty is an unfortunate cosmic accident. Certainly she did not ask to be made stupid and selfish. That decision was nature's. Like Hetty, Tito too is what he is, which is all he can be. It is not the weed's fault that it isn't a flower, and it is not Tito's fault that he is weak in imagination and self-centered. In the face of betrayal, the pagan sense of justice turns to retribution, as we see in Baldassarre. It is significant that the story on which Baldassarre focuses when he reads Pausanias is the story of the traitor Aristocrates whose stoning by the people he had betrayed was commemorated, Pausanias comments, in verses that tell "how Time had brought home *justice* to the *unjust*" (XXXVIII, p. 346; my italics). On this point, Bardo would have agreed. As Eliot noted in her *Commonplace Book,* summarizing the Stoic Cicero's view in his treatise on duty, *De Officiis,* "Cicero holds it an essential part of justice to punish (or avenge) a wrong" (Yale MS 6). It is from this view that Savonarola has converted Romola, holding before her a more sympathetic sense of justice. The Christian principle would be less different from the Bacchic if it excluded even Tito from the fellowship he himself betrays.

Romola's widening sense of human fellowship measures the degree to which she fulfills her epic role, for here too the substance shapes the form. In her symbolic role as a representative of mankind's historical progress, Romola assumes her epic dimension at the beginning of the book. As a representative of mankind's moral imagination, however, she does not achieve her full epic identity until the end, when she is in full possession of that imagination. And at each step in the book, Romola embodies just so much of human experience as she is herself capable of grasping. Thus, the chronology of events in Romola's personal life shapes an intricate relationship between character and structure.

This evolving identity had been one of the many prophecies of Piero's sketch. In the pagan period of her life, Romola has been awakened to her individual self. From Bardo, she had acquired genetic and also intellectual identity. Later, appropriately in the period of her adolescence, Tito had awakened her to her natural and physical self. Savonarola, the third figure of Piero's three visions, is the inevitable next step in that sequence. With Savonarola, Romola is awakened to her own soul. Although the Christian journey is a journey outward, in imagination, it is also a journey inward. As Romola is first stirred by Savonarola's preaching in the Duomo, the narrator observes that these "larger possibilities of her nature" now being called forth had lain in herself, "folded and crushed like embryonic wings" (XXVII, p. 255). In taking Dante's journey into her own soul, Romola discovers, like him, the divine potential within.

That inward journey, which is also outward, is chartered in Romola's development in a progression of religions, two progressions in fact, which explicate one another at different but related levels. One describes Romola's transition from the Bacchic to the Christian life. Over this pattern another emerges, similar but not identical, one that takes Romola through three religions: the religion of affection, the religion of sympathy, and the religion of humanity. Each grows out of the former but differs from it. Here, the influence of Comte is obvious not only in the substance but in the form of the book as well.

Like Eliot, and like most of his contemporaries, Comte had a profound and characteristically nineteenth-century faith, born in part of the optimism engendered by the march of science and its child the industrial revolution, in history as evolution, in time as progress. Like Eliot and many others too, Comte saw mirrored in the progress of the individual the progress of civilization. The motto of Positivism, therefore, "Love, Order, Progress," describes the successive stages of the history of both individuals and society. Although undoubtedly not as firmly convinced as Comte that progress was inevitable, and certainly by no means inclined to believe like him that the age of perfection was imminent, Eliot did agree with Comte's analysis of the stages of evolution. It is Love, Order, and Progress that characterize both Romola's and Florence's development. In Comte's scheme, love is centered chiefly where Eliot centered it, in the family, in ties to one's parents, one's husband or wife, and finally one's children. Out of such love grows a certain moral structure that becomes Order, Order that, once created, is, unlike Love, capable of surviving beyond affection and of extending to those to whom we are not directly bound in affection. The movement of Order becomes Progress, the Progress that takes us through a growing moral vision, along the circumference, in the metaphor of the Proem, of the night-student's circle of light and glory.

In this context too, as ever, Tito and Savonarola are the extreme antitheses. In them Eliot suggested the two forces whose constant conflict determines the condition of the world. Savonarola's association with Christ and Tito's with Satan reflect in Christian imagery the Comtean conflict between the positive principle of Order and the negative principle of Disorder, a principle whose root is egotism. Thus, Romola's transition from Tito to Savonarola is a transition from the forces of destruction to the forces of creation, from—to put Savonarola's words in a wider context—chaos to law. In the analogous development of civilization, the same is true of Florence. Although the years covered by the book is a period for both Romola and Florence of great uncertainty, the "mixed condition," the narrator remarks in a clear echo of Comte, is not "the sign of hopeless confusion, but of struggling order" (LVII, p. 490).

Comte's language echoes everywhere in Eliot's prose in her descriptions of Romola's progression of religions. The first of Comte's stages, Love, had characterized Romola's relationship to Bardo and Tito in that her fidelity to them had been prompted by nothing more than personal attachment. Both with Bardo and Tito, Romola "had endured and forborne because she had loved," and this had constituted the "religion of her life" (XXXVI, p. 333). But Bardo's death and her disillusionment with Tito had ended this stage of her life and had left her morally and psychologically suspended. For the "first time in her life," Romola was "alone, with no human presence interposing and making a law for her" (XL, p. 368). There is moral law in this first period, but it is only the spontaneous expression of love. That law functions well, almost as well as anything else, as long and as far as love extends. That, of course, is its limitation. Although love teaches Romola to discipline herself in relation to someone she loves, it does nothing more. At nineteen, Romola discovers that she must face life without the inspiration of love, without, in her experience therefore, law of any kind, and this presents itself "to her as an entirely new problem" (XXXVI, p. 333).

Romola passes from the religion of affection to the religion of sympathy and from Bacchus to Christ at the same moment, for the religion of sympathy and Christianity, in its symbolic sense, are identical. But while Christianity is not in its literal sense identical to sympathy, as we shall see, the historical period of Christianity embodied for Eliot the second step of the Positivist motto, Order.

Although the religion of affection and the worship of Bacchus had been, by their very natures, in opposition, the religion of sympathy is a natural extension of affection, and the image of the nun, in which Romola is initiated into Christianity, grows naturally out of the image of Antigone. At the moment of Romola's conversion, it is clear that while Romola had seemed to assume the role of the Bacchic Ariadne in her marriage to Tito, a submerged but developing self had foreshadowed the truer transition from Antigone to the nun. In fact, the gray serge in which Romola flees Florence fulfills a much earlier vision.

It had been Dino who had first hinted at the image of the nun. In his dying message, he had warned Romola against marriage as though, had he been able to finish his sentence, he were urging her to follow him to the monastic life (XV, p. 167). From this moment on, the image is taken up again and again by different characters and events like a recurring motif that will eventually swell to become a major theme. For example, shortly after her meeting with Dino, Tito had teased Romola away from her sober thoughts by declaring them fit only for "sickly nuns" (XVII, p. 188).

In that scene in Dino's cell had begun also the influence Savonarola comes to have on Romola. While she had then, as she does later in the conversion scene, resisted his claim to authority over her, he had awed her, as no one had before, and almost against her own will had brought her to submit so far as to kneel before the crucifix. Although that event had been nearly seduced from her memory by her joy in Tito, the sorrow to which Bacchus introduces her recalls in time that Christian seed. At first merely to understand the political affairs in which her husband is involved, Romola enters the Duomo to hear Savonarola's Advent sermon. Unconsciously, she too begins, appropriately, to prepare for the coming of Christ. Under her desire for pleasure, she begins to discover a ready "sympathy with something apart from all the definable interests of her life" (XXVII, pp. 255-56).

At last, when she leaves Tito, in choosing the nun's habit as her disguise, in placing around her neck the crucifix Dino had given her, in submitting to the guidance of Savonarola who had also guided Dino, Romola seems to be accepting the role Dino had once chosen for her. Indeed, she seems to take his very place, as she had with her father when Dino had abandoned him. The physical similarities between Romola and Dino are often remarked on, and when she first sees herself in the nun's habit Romola notices the striking resemblance she bears to Dino as she last saw him in San Marco (XXXVI, p. 331). Structurally, Romola is continuing Dino's work in taking up the search he had begun for a life in which meaning does not derive solely from the satisfaction of appetite. The structural point here makes a historical one. Although Romola entered her Christian epoch with Christ's birth, her Christianity takes a far later form than Dino's. Frenzied and fanatical, Dino's religion is characteristic of the very early years of the Christian era, while Romola's, more ritualistic, more institutional, is the faith of a much later age. Indeed, like Tito, to whom he is often an analogue, Dino is historically regressive, for he worships Christ, not as "the genius of the future," but as the spirit of the past, and he would, if he had his way, take mankind back a thousand years.

It is precisely because many centuries have passed between Dino's faith and Romola's, centuries in which Christianity has been progressively humanized, that Dino's faith is unacceptable, whereas Romola's, in her time, is not. Despite the many similarities, therefore, Romola does not follow Dino into his wilderness. Unlike Dino, she can never accept the monastic life. The thought of entering a convent repels her now as it always has (LVI, p. 484). It is not to withdraw from the world but to join in its fellowship that she accepts Christianity, and not to contemplate her own wickedness but to contribute to the world's good that she submits to its discipline. Between Dino's formal and Romola's substantial conversion to the Christian concept of life lies the difference between the death and the life of the spirit.

Thus, it is a nun only in a metaphoric sense that Romola becomes, and that metaphoric sense is suggested in a startling metamorphosis in the image of the wedding ring. But this transition is intimately connected to another; as the central figure of the religion that succeeds Romola's religion of affection, Savonarola replaces both Bardo and Tito.

Romola has three fathers in the book, each of whom brings her metaphorically closer to moral perception, and in leaving each of which, as we shall see, Romola makes her way forward in her historical pilgrimage. Literally, it is only Bardo and Savonarola who have a genuinely important effect on Romola's growth, but symbolically the progression moves from Bardo, her biological and intellectual father, to Bernardo, her *god*father, to Savonarola, her spiritual father. The sequence traces her development from the secular to the divine, from the physical to the spiritual, from reason to mystery. Thus, in Savonarola, Romola finds her last and most significant father.

And in Savonarola, too, Romola finds her second husband. The marriage with Bacchus ended, a new one with Christ begins. Once more, it is Piero di Cosimo who conceives the image in which this marriage is suggested when he remarks that Romola seems to him a suitable model for St. Catherine of Egypt (XLIX, p. 436). From Mrs. Jameson, Eliot had entered the story of St. Catherine of Egypt into her *Commonplace Book* and had there noted what is the most common and often retold tale of St. Catherine's life, how she came to be married to Christ (Yale MS 6). The marriage of St. Catherine to Christ was, in fact, an extremely popular subject in medieval and Renaissance art. At the Pitti Palace, Eliot had seen Titian's *Marriage of St. Catherine* and had called it a work of "supreme beauty" (Cross, II, 175). At Naples, she had seen Correggio's *Marriage of St. Catherine* and distinguished it as one of the few good pieces of art in the city (Cross, II, 162). Perhaps she recalled those and other paintings on the same subject when she devised the image in *Romola.*

It is as one marriage replaces another that the wedding ring is transformed. When she had left Tito, Romola had removed her Bacchic wedding ring, thus ending her marriage. When, persuaded by Savonarola, she replaces the ring on her finger, it is another

Romola who returns to Tito, and a new marriage she has undertaken. In the note Romola leaves Tito as she prepares to leave Florence, Romola writes, "Tito, my love for you is dead, and therefore, *so far as I was yours, I too am dead. . . . The Romola you married can never return*" (XXXVII, p. 339; my italics). Indeed, the Bacchic Romola died in her conversion, and in that moment a Christian one was born. The transformation is emphasized as Romola puts away the wedding clothes in which she had married Tito and puts on the habit of the nun. When he had locked the crucifix inside it, Tito had called the triptych a "tomb of joy." And the Bacchic wedding clothes now seem to Romola, in a way that Tito never intended, the "shroud of her dead happiness" (XXXVII, p. 339). As the sun of Tito's joyous life is darkened for her, Romola replaces the white of her wedding dress with the gray of the nun's habit. But the habit is also a wedding dress, for the nun is the bride of Christ. The marriage of sympathy now replaces the marriage of conquest. Looking at her reflection in the mirror in her new costume, Romola remarks that "Ariadne is wonderfully transformed" (XXXVII, p. 339).

Although Savonarola acts as both spiritual father and husband to Romola, he performs different functions in each capacity. The distinction is a traditional one. Through Savonarola, Romola becomes the bride of Christ and the daughter of the church. Both are necessary stages of transition and are themselves interdependent. In her union with the church, Romola's spiritual union with Christ becomes rooted in the human community, and as a result she escapes being lost in Dino's distantly invisible realms. Not surprisingly, Dino had proved as poor a son of the church as he had been to Bardo. In contrast, Romola's human bond with her father prepares her for this second filial role.

The double relationship to Christianity is even more important to Romola in another way. It is perhaps not facetious to wonder whether the nun's habit in which Romola's transformation takes place is a pun, since the most important lesson of this period of her life is her development of the "habit" of sympathy. Here, the church serves a very special function. When Romola at last passes to her final stage of moral independence, she will repudiate the formal and dogmatic elements of Christianity. But the Christian era of history—that period in which not only the moral but the supernatural aspects of Christianity inspired faith—had a vital contribution to make, in Eliot's estimate, to mankind's progress. For the religion of sympathy, symbolized in Christ, must be accompanied by the second step of the Positivist motto, Order, and that order was first expressed historically in the structure of the church. It was in the church, therefore, that the universal implications of the myth of Christ became a historical reality.

From the beginning, Eliot places great stress on the efficacy of habit. In one more epic analogue between the individual and mankind, the narrator remarks that "our lives make a moral tradition for our individual selves, as the life of mankind makes a moral tradition for the race." The specific object of the narrator's observation, Tito too makes a tradition for himself, an amoral tradition from which he can have at last no "sense of falling" (XXXIX, p. 360). Choice, Eliot argued everywhere, is not merely the decision we reach after assessing a situation or weighing consequences; it is often far more the habit of the past determining our present apart from our own will. Just as Tito's egotism becomes finally a "habitual choice" (XXIII, p. 233), so, in contrast, in her apprenticeship to Savonarola and the church, Romola learns to "habitually reject the impulsive choice" (LII, p. 457). Habit, as Eliot conceived it, is not something that, once established, becomes second nature; in a sense, it becomes, or can become, nature itself. Like civilization, we are individually creatures in the constant process of changing, and like history, what we are at any given moment is the sum of cumulative antecedents. Thus, action can often inspire feeling just as feeling can inspire action. The continued performance of an act to which we are not inclined may give rise to the inclination, as a therapeutic machine might move a limb until the muscles move themselves.

Comte was fond of observing that sympathy grows with exercise. It had proved so in Romola's relationship to Bardo. The habit of conduct inspired by love had carried her over many moments of rebellion and weariness. Through Bardo's sometimes peevish demands and surly complaints, Romola had found herself able to minister to him because she had acquired a "habitual patience" (V, p. 52). That habit of patience and endurance had been formalized in Romola's Stoical education, and as she now envisions her "solitary loveless life," she determines to face it with "a stoical heroism" (XXXVI, p. 335), which, if it cannot make her happy, will at least not allow her to become ignoble. When, therefore, after Bardo's death and her growing isolation from Tito, her habit of love could "no longer spend itself in the woman's tenderness for father and husband," Romola inevitably seeks another outlet for it in the "enthusiasm of sympathy with the general life" (XLIV, p. 400). But for this transition neither the religion of affection nor Bardo's Stoicism proves to be a sufficient bridge; generalized love is considerably more difficult to sustain than the love that has a single immediate object. Thus, while Romola has the will, she does not have a rule of conduct to inspire her when love itself fails. It is precisely this gap that the rituals of the church offer her. The church helps to "keep alive that flame of unselfish emotion by which a life of sadness might still be a life of active love" (XLIV, p. 401). In time, the sense of fellowship becomes as "habitual" to Romola "as the consciousness of costume to a vain and idle woman" (XLIII, p. 394).

This moral discipline acts as an antidote to intellectual uncertainty. When Romola had first questioned the clashing deities, she had been unable to reconcile them. She had made a choice but had not solved the problem. When she leaves Tito, the same clashing deities return to challenge her. Again, although she makes a choice, she does not resolve the dilemma. But it is Eliot's point that the answer cannot be theoretic, or at least that the theoretic answer, if there is one, is not accessible to us. In the absence of a solution, Tito had chosen total skepticism and committed himself to the pursuit of pleasure. But the Roman Catholic church has this advantage, that it openly declares its vision a mystery, a mystery that need not be rationally intelligible, that may be accepted without being understood, and that may even be followed with uncertain faith. The rituals of the church transcend both desire and confusion and create, in the constant practice of the acts of sympathy, a moral habit. It is for this reason that the narrator says, in another connection, that there "is no kind of conscious obedience that is not an advance on lawlessness" (XLIX, p. 435).

Paradoxically, the Christian freedom Romola accepts when

Savonarola converts her is expressed in the Christian gesture of submission. The physical act not only symbolizes but transforms the psychological state of mind. At Dino's death, Savonarola had commanded Romola to kneel, and while she had at first resisted, in the end the authority of Savonarola's voice had subdued her into compliance. Dino had spoken to her of passivity, a state in which "our souls are as an instrument in the Divine hand" (XV, p. 165), and in the act of kneeling, "in the *renunciation* of her rigid erectness, her mental attitude seemed changed, and she found herself in a new state of passiveness" (XV, p. 166; my italics). Nearly an identical scene is enacted again in the conversion. Although she faces Savonarola at first as a proud, erect figure, with eyes directed straight before her, the force of Savonarola's presence brings her to her knees once more. It is, once again, an act of "renunciation," for at this moment the conversion scene has become a confession, and Romola appropriately identifies the experience as a "sacrament" (XLI, p. 377).

The narrator speaks at one point of a "region of trust and resignation which has been in all ages called divine" (XLIII, p. 395). The pagan life had rested on the certainty that the universe was within man's power to know and understand, and even to a large extent to control. But if uncertainty is chaos, certainty is surely blindness. The religious faculty, which Romola here acquires, is characterized among other things by an openness to possibilities, even to the possibility that knowledge and power are ultimately beyond human grasp. The pagan world, moreover, had forged civilization in a perennial challenge of the universe. And indeed it had produced much. But its pride—and pride is the dominant trait of the Bardi character—had been blind to that portion of the human condition that must forever remain unalterable. It is therefore part of Romola's religious conversion to accept resignation as a necessity inherent in human existence. The sense of place Savonarola had talked of is not only social but cosmic. Religious awe places man in the perspective of all creation.

8.

Creon and Antigone

In calling Romola "Madonna Antigone," Piero di Cosimo had not only fused the two dominant images of Romola's best heritage but had also suggested the nature of her Christian role. For a brief time after her conversion, Romola subdues the critical intelligence she had inherited from the pagans in submission to Savonarola's guidance. Fearing that the services the church is rendering her may prove on inspection falsely founded, Romola avoids theological issues and accepts the spiritual gift without question. But her fear is an expression of her judgment, and in time it awakens, as historically it awakened in the Renaissance, to act once more as a touchstone against which mankind may measure its more passionate inspirations. Reborn as a Renaissance humanist, Romola is saved from succumbing to the dim mysticism to which her brother had fallen prey.

We enter here, in short, the Protestant era. In this transition, Eliot seemed to follow the conventional view that it was the pagan rationalism and individualism, reborn in the Renaissance, that was ultimately responsible for the Reformation. In the late fifteenth century, Romola lives at the culmination of that rebirth. Martin

Luther is in fact only eight years or so younger than Romola herself. Without the prophetic advantages of hindsight, the historical Savonarola recognized the enemy. His opposition to Lorenzo de' Medici was not so much political as cultural. Political parties come and go, and it was not their brief tenure Savonarola feared. It was classicism, so encompassingly patronized by Lorenzo, the Renaissance itself, in which Savonarola saw the end of the Roman Catholic church, and with it the end of his own world.

Although Protestantism fired Eliot's poetic imagination far less than Roman Catholicism and took up far less of the book (although one should add that it has taken up less of history too), this epoch was, like the last, a significant advance for Eliot along the night-student's arc. Eliot did not trouble herself to cite those endless vices that many leaders of the Reformation cited against the officers of the church. What concerned her was something far more central to the question than those vices, more central because, unlike them, it was irremediable. For Roman Catholicism, in Eliot's judgment, concealed, like the Bacchic legend if in a different form, an inherent and corrupting paradox.

How far Eliot believed Savonarola and his church to be from embodying the best of the Christian vision becomes clear in the fact that Romola assumes her highest Christian identity in the moment in which she rejects Savonarola's judgment entirely. At this moment, although she continues for a time to be the bride of Christ, Romola is no longer the daughter of the church. The role of the daughter, a role Romola had enacted almost without interruption, first with Bardo and then with Savonarola, is a dependent one. In dissociating herself from it, Romola takes a large step toward the independence she must, like modern man, assume in the final stage of her evolution. In this emancipation, we see a progression characteristic in Eliot's fiction, although in *Romola* we see it from a historical as well as a personal perspective.

Twice in the book, Romola passes through the center of indifference. Each time is a period of despair in which she finds herself suspended between a life with which she has become thoroughly disillusioned and a new life she has not yet been able to realize. Each time, she comes close to wishing for death and, symbolically, dies to the old to be born again to a new. And each time, the precise moment of transition is marked by a paralysis of the will. What makes it possible for Romola to be recalled to life a second time, when she awakens on the shore of the plague-stricken village, is the moral energy, the habit of sympathy, she develops as Savonarola's disciple. Thus, although the two moments of indifference are parallel, they are far from similar. Romola survives the second time only because Savonarola saves her the first.

When Romola first leaves Florence and Tito, the narrator observes that she has now a choice between "the path of reliance and action which is the path of life" and the path of "loneliness and disbelief, which is no path, but the arrest of inaction and death" (XXXVI, p. 338). At this point, Romola needs to be inspired to live, for she is physically, morally, and spiritually dying. Romola's crisis suggests that human life is a persistent struggle in which we require not only the support of our fellow men but, more particularly, the support and guidance of those who have already found their way on the road on which we are still stumbling. We require too the inspiration of those who have found the strength to endure the trials under which we have begun to fall. Romola herself will become such a support later, in the village and with Tessa and her children. She is indeed meant to function in the same way for the reader; for we invest, Eliot always argued, much of our idealism and hope in heroes on whom we rely for strength in our weakness. For Romola, Savonarola is such a hero.

In this sense, Romola's relationship to Savonarola is a relationship we find in all of Eliot's fiction. It appears in many forms, sometimes dominating an entire book, as in the case of Daniel Deronda and Gwendolen Harleth, or serving as a subplot in the less classic case of Mary Garth and Fred Vincy in *Middlemarch.* Sometimes it is beneficial and successful, as in the examples above, and sometimes neither, as in the case of Dorothea Brooke, who looks for such a figure in Casaubon. Often it is a complex mingling of all these possibilities, as in the Reverend Mr. Irwine's influence, in *Adam Bede,* on Arthur Donnithorne. This hero-teacher-father is usually present in his own person, but sometimes he is not, as in the case of Thomas à Kempis in *The Mill on the Floss.* Next to its archetypal form in *Romola,* Kempis is perhaps the best example of the pattern. In defining his relationship to Christ, he defines the essence of the relationship between the hero and his disciple. As Kempis attempts to live in imitation of Christ, so Maggie Tulliver attempts to live in imitation of Kempis. Thus, through a hierarchy as it were, we reach toward perfection. The relationship in *Romola* is very similar to that in *The Mill on the Floss.* Romola imitates Savonarola, who in turn imitates Christ. Each hero, at his own level, is a parable, as Christ is the ultimate parable, whose example, as the narrator of *Romola* remarks, makes us "almost believe in our power to attain the highest ends" (LV, p. 472). Thus, Savonarola fulfills in its most essential meaning the role of the priest, the role of the mediator between the divine and the human, which in a more secular sense is a mediation between a present and a future, better, self and historically between the present and the time that draws us nearer to the "genius of the future."

But the role of the hero-teacher-father—all of which Savonarola enacts for Romola—is at its best a self-negating one. His success is measured by the degree to which he can render himself progressively useless. If he is completely successful, he will become entirely unnecessary. This is in essence what Daniel Deronda tells Gwendolen Harleth when he leaves for Palestine and assures her that she can now survive without him. It is what Romola tells Savonarola later when she leaves Florence a second time. The period between the first moment of independence, historically the moment of the Reformation, and the last moment of complete freedom, historically the threshold of the modern era, is for Romola, as for mankind, an exercise in self-reliance, for it is as an exercise in self-reliance that Eliot distinguished the Protestant epoch.

When Romola's path begins to diverge from Savonarola's, Eliot makes it clear through the imagery that she considers Romola's a purer perception of the Christian vision. Ironically, it is only when Romola enters her Protestant period that she assumes the role of the Virgin that culminates the Christian imagery, a role that grows quite naturally out of the image of the nun. Romola's progression through the images of Antigone, the nun, and the Virgin is one from daughter to sister/wife to mother, a natural evolution of her womanhood. It had always been Romola's "maternal instinct," the narrator observes, that had made the largest part of her "passionate tenderness" (LVI, p. 474), and it is in the role of the mother that Romola, as the Virgin, takes Tessa and her children under her protection at the end. Bernardo del Nero, who little understands the Christian period of Romola's life, remarks glibly that her conversion must be her way of compensating for a childless marriage (XLV, p. 403). In a sense, although not in Bernardo's, this is quite true.

Here we reach the last stage of the progression Comte had described, on the pattern of the family, as the evolution of the individual into moral consciousness. As the child's love for a parent had engendered the individual's capacity to love something other than himself, and as married love had extended that capacity to a contemporary, and so to society at large, so parental love is directed toward the next generation and becomes, by implication, a universal love for all those yet to come, a love for the future of mankind. Eliot followed the Comtean sequence, but in a metaphoric way. As we shall shortly see, when Romola adopts, as it were, Tessa's children, she does so in the role of the Virgin, and especially in relation to one of the children, Lillo, who assumes, although in function only, the part of the Infant Jesus. It was in the Virgin's love for her son that her universal compassion for mankind was born, and in a symbolic reenactment of that same story Romola becomes the compassionate mother to all the needy in Florence. Two years after her conversion, and as though in answer to Dino's and Savonarola's charge that the Bardi family had lived aloof from the life of the city, we see that Romola's figure has become a common and welcome sight to the helpless and the hungry (XLIII, p. 390). One of those helpless creatures is Tessa, and the sympathy Romola is now cultivating takes, as is characteristic in Eliot, both a universal and a very specific form.

Like Romola, Florence too is by now subjecting itself more and more to the purer light of Christianity under the political leadership of Savonarola, to a large degree because it has been more and more discovering the inner corruption that taints its apparent prosperity. The pestilence and famine that rapidly succeed one another in 1496 are symbolic symptoms of the moral disease. As hunger and disease decimate the city, the Florentines as always turn for help in their time of need to the Virgin, to the Pitying

Mother embodied in the statue of the Madonna dell' Impruneta which was brought into the city in all times of crisis (XLIII, pp. 392-93). We know from Eliot's penciled references at the back of her copy of Nardi's *Istorie della Citta di Firenze,* where she jotted down the page of his description of the procession of the Madonna dell' Impruneta, as well as from one of her chronologies in her *Quarry,* in which she entered the date, October 30, of this procession, that one of Eliot's sources for this scene was Nardi's history. Surely a more extensive source must have been a book in her own library, Francesco Rondinelli's *Relazione del Contagio stuto in Firenze l'anno 1630 e 1633, con un breve ragguaglio della miracolos a imagine della Madonna dell' Impruneta* (no. 1869), a book that, although a narrative of the pestilence that struck Florence a century and a half later, gives a vivid account of its effects and includes, as the second half of the title states, a brief report of the miracles performed by the image of the Madonna dell' Impruneta.

For Eliot, the greatest, and indeed the only, miracle of the Madonna dell' Impruneta is Romola. While the work of the "Unseen Madonna," as she is called, is equally invisible, Romola, the "Visible Madonna," who is the Virgin's incarnate manifestation, is seen everywhere, feeding the hungry, tending the sick, comforting the forsaken, bringing relief and receiving thanks as though she were, indeed, the Holy Mother (XLIII, p. 399). Here, of course, one of the chief metaphoric implications of the image of the lily, the Virgin's flower, the symbol of the Annunciation as we have seen, is finally fulfilled. As it had been Nello who had first conferred on Romola the epic epithet "the Florentine lily," so it is he who, repeating it now, elaborates its religious significance when he remarks that Romola is "constantly going about like a sunbeam amongst the rags that line our corners—if indeed she is not more like a moonbeam now, for I thought yesterday when I met her, that she looked as pale and worn as the fainting Madonna of Fra Giovanni's" (XLV, pp. 406-7). Even Nello, it appears, realizes that Romola has moved from the Bacchic sunlight into the shadows of Christ.

But such universal sympathy as Romola now practices must be rooted, in Eliot's view, in the specific and the concrete. To cultivate either, the universal or the concrete, exclusively, can lead only to moral corruption, as we shall see shortly in Romola's quarrel with Savonarola over Bernardo del Nero. Romola's opportunity to integrate the two comes, ironically, in her encounter with Tito's other "wife," an encounter, however, that finds its full symbolic significance at the end of the book.

Once more, the calendar brings us to the Easter ritual. It is Shrove Tuesday of 1497, the day that is the last day of the pre-Lenten carnival. That carnival seems to Bratti no merrier than Holy Week (L, p. 433), and certainly it is, as the narrator observes, an epoch in carnival-keeping (XLIX, p. 432). Savonarola, who is preaching the last Lenten sermons he will ever be allowed to preach in the Duomo, has, despite the spiritual and political crises that have already begun for him and that will defeat him in the end, managed so far to conquer the pagan and mercenary elements of Florence as to substitute, for the traditional mayhem on the last happy day before Ash Wednesday, a ceremony known as the Pyramid of Vanities. In that ceremony, Florence is to be purified by throwing into a gigantic bonfire all its Anathema, all its earthly adornments (XLIX, p. 434). For this scene too, as Eliot indicated at the back of her volume, Nardi was one of her sources. Another, as she noted in the *Quarry,* was Lastri. But nearly every history that covers the period alludes to the Anathema, and for her description of the event Eliot must have gathered details from many of them.

The scene is an extremely important one. In calling the carnival a "sacred parody" of the old pagan ritual (XLIX, p. 434), the narrator had already begun to suggest not only that Christianity, contrary to Savonarola's belief, had not in this case been able to suppress or assimilate the pagan spirit, but indeed that it had, in a historical reversal, begun to imitate its ancient rival, and not to imitate it well. This is made evident in the chief event of the Anathema, in the Procession of Children. Organized by Savonarola, these children have been charged with the task of collecting the vanities from the crowd, and they return time and again to the bonfire with the jewelry, the wigs, the opulent garments, and all the other adornments they have been able to gather. Inspired to frenzy by their holy purpose, they are a fierce and merciless lot. When the narrator calls them a "regiment" of "beardless inquisitors" (XLIX, pp. 433-34), we realize that Eliot is recording another historical event. From Helyot, Eliot had entered into her *Commonplace Book* that the officers of the Inquisition had been, like these children, chiefly Dominicans (Yale MS 6). And it is the Inquisition that we have here in the Procession of Children. In their sadistic holiness, as in the Inquisition, we see the flaw inherent in religious enthusiasm, and we discover, as we will again shortly in Savonarola, the deadly offspring of the union between spiritual authority and temporal power.

It is by these children that Tessa is pursued when Romola finds her. Long before, Tessa had bought a *breve* to wear as an amulet around her neck, and she had then felt certain that in consequence the Holy Madonna would come to her rescue should she ever need it (X, p. 115). Romola's arrival now seems to her a fulfillment of that certainty, and Tessa falls here, without doubt or reflection, into calling Romola the Holy Madonna (L, pp. 445, 447). It is as a child turns to its mother that Tessa turns to Romola for help, and in their relationship the image of the "Mother and Babe," which is the carnival's banner (L, p. 447), is fulfilled.

Yet in helping Tessa escape the children's holy pursuit, Romola has for the first time defied Savonarola. The incident marks a milestone, not only in Romola's growing independence, but also in her growing moral perception. The action Romola takes in relation to Tessa can be subsumed under no category that can be generalized into the form of law. Although the Christian period is one that instructs Romola in law, Eliot shows here once more that form must always be perceived through substance. In the end, it is not rules of moral conduct that we must acquire but the soul that will guide us to make moral decisions in the unique circumstances of every individual case. Moral vision is too subtle for prescription. The "sensibilities which are our deepest life," the narrator observes, can never be codified even in language and must remain forever "inarticulate" (XXXVII, p. 341).

Every situation requires its own moral solution. Thus, the moral perceptions to which society and the individual can arrive are, by their very natures, different. Society can achieve law, and in society every member can be guaranteed the protection of law. But such law cannot meet the unique needs of each individual. The law of the state assumes, like the justice of the pagan and the libertarian, a hypothetical equality that reality does not confirm. Even religion, when it is formalized in law, as it is in the institution of the church, cannot offer the true balm of the spirit. It is only when we act, not on principle, but informed by vision that we act morally. Ironically, this is geometrically implied in Savonarola's own Pyramid of Vanities, for although the pyramid has a broad base, as law has in society, at its highest level it rises to a single point, a point that geometrically has no physical dimension but exists only in perception. In turning her back on the Pyramid of Vanities, Romola has far surpassed Savonarola, to whom now the disciple becomes a contrast.

Here Savonarola and Romola exchange places, for now Romola inherits from Savonarola the function of representing the Christian center of the book's circles. This too is suggested in the imagery. The great Duomo with which Savonarola has been associated is only one part of the Cathedral of Santa Maria del Fiore, "Sacred Mary of the Flower." Thus, when Romola assumes the role of the Virgin, the "Florentine lily" becomes the embodiment of the Madonna to whom the cathedral is dedicated, and therefore the center of Christian Florence. At the same moment, and for the same reason, Romola assumes here her full epic dimension. In becoming the moral center of Florence, which is the symbolic human community, the "Florentine lily" is now wholly identified with the city that has been traditionally known as the "Lily of the Arno."

It is, then, Romola and not Savonarola who now moves in the mainstream of history, in whom "the genius of the future" is embodied. As Savonarola had been before her, it is Romola who is becoming the book's "moral pioneer," a role that recalls the image of Antigone. And Antigone does indeed return here, in her broadest implications, for as before, Romola's best vision is a synthesis of both her pagan and her Christian heritage. It is in fact Romola's pagan heritage that rescues her from the corruptions of power and enthusiasm that Savonarola cannot escape. This is illustrated in the fact that while Romola was able to find the moral solution in Tessa's individual case, Savonarola cannot find it in the case of Bernardo del Nero, the case in which Romola enacts once more the part of Antigone, not of *Oedipus at Colonus* this time but of *Antigone.*

In the events concerning Bernardo del Nero, Eliot suggests a far broader assessment of Savonarola's entire political career and identifies the flaws of Christianity as a political system, not in Florence only, although that is the specific point at issue, but in the whole history of Europe's Christian kingdoms, implied in *Romola* in that Most Christian King, in whose arrival Savonarola appropriately rejoices, Charles VIII of France. For Eliot, the political aspect of Christianity was the antithesis of the mythical, and both were latent possibilities in the institutional church. As in its spiritual essence the church embodies the mystery of imagination, so in the structure in which it codifies its formal doctrine it provides the basis of a political organization. As Romola discovered in the Pyramid of Vanities, to the degree that the institutional church cultivates form, it violates substance. Thus, although the period of Savonarola's influence on Florence is for the city as for Romola a period of purification, in Savonarola's political government Eliot saw an inherent danger, which is the exact opposite of the danger toward which Tito leads. As Tito's political career revealed the potential Bacchic tendency toward chaos, so Savonarola's political career reveals the potential Christian tendency toward tyranny.

This was a question that profoundly concerned Eliot in her research for *Romola.* It was indeed a question that very much concerned Italian and European historians. The struggle for liberty was, we recall, the theme of Leonardo Bruni's history of Florence. It was an important theme too in Guizot's *Histoire de la civilisation en Europe,* which had been one of Eliot's sources for Roman law in the Middle Ages, but in reading which Eliot seems to have been even more engaged in tracing the tradition of liberty, for it was that subject that she annotated at the end of her volume (no. 907). Perhaps she had also read Guizot's study of the evolution of democratic institutions, the *Histoire des origines du gouvernement représentatif en Europe,* a copy of which Eliot and Lewes owned (no. 908).

In this area, however, it is to Muratori and above all to Sismondi that Eliot seems chiefly indebted. As Eliot's extensive entries in the *Quarry* show, it was the conflict between liberty and tyranny in Italian history that most interested her in her reading of Muratori, and she traced it, from Muratori and others, to its ancient beginnings. It was not only Eliot's thoroughness that called for so long a retrospective, for the question of political heritage was a burning one to the late-fifteenth-century Florentine. Whether Florence had been founded in the days of the Roman republic or its empire was heatedly debated. The "daughter and creation of Rome," as Villani had called Florence, the city was either the child of the free people of the ancient republic or the already decadent offspring of the enslaved people of the empire. Villani chose to identify Florence with the republic, while Machiavelli outraged many of his contemporaries by declaring Florence to have been founded in the days of the empire.[1]

Perhaps in this connection, Eliot read at least some of the many volumes on Roman history in the Eliot/Lewes library. In addition to Gibbon, which she had read, she had at her disposal such general studies as Prosper Merimée's *Etudes sur l'histoire romaine* (no. 1438); studies of the Roman republic such as Horace Moule's *The Roman Republic* (no. 1520) and Jules Michelet's *Histoire Romaine Republique,* heavily marked by both Eliot and Lewes (no. 1454); and studies of Rome's decadence such as Charles Louis Montesquieu's *Grandeur et decadence des romains* (no. 1502) and Francis W. Newman's *Regal Rome,* a gift of the author to George Henry Lewes (no. 1556). Eliot's love of chronological tables, of which she herself made many, might have interested her too in another volume, the *Chronological Tables of Ancient History* (no. 430). Among the Eliot manuscripts at the Beinecke Library at Yale University there is a very small volume, nine centimeters tall, marked "Quarry," in which Eliot copied the barest outline of a chronology of ancient history (Yale MS 18).

It was surely Sismondi's thesis, however, that chiefly influenced Eliot's study of Savonarola in his political aspect, for his is certainly the most thorough and persistent exploration of the opposition of the Roman Catholic church to Italian liberty. In reading Machiavelli, who shares Sismondi's view, Eliot had already read, in an account contemporary with her setting, many of the same arguments; but unlike Machiavelli, Sismondi is a profound believer in liberty and argues his case with a deep personal passion.

There is considerable irony in Eliot's analysis of Savonarola's government. Himself in conflict with the pope, and arguing against the pope for a popular government, Savonarola seems to be not the spokesman for the church but its challenger. So certainly he seems both to himself and the pope. Indeed, in that conflict Eliot took Savonarola's side, for the pope seemed hardly a figure fit to assume the spiritual leadership of Christianity. In contrast to his politically inspired motives, Savonarola's are clearly purer. In fact, Savonarola's political ends are in theory at least not unworthy. To work for a political organization that rules a city united in brotherly love is no mean ambition. Such a government is indeed, as Savonarola claims, the highest form of democracy in being truly an egalitarian government of the people (XLV, p. 407).

But if in encouraging a communal sense of fellowship the Christian government counters the egotism and isolation of pagan law in its vision of the whole, it is potentially inclined to disregard the rights of the individual. That question is put to the test in the case of Bernardo del Nero, and in the two stages of the conflict between Bernardo and Savonarola, Romola is each time further alienated from the church, as Savonarola, following the political Christian path, fails to discern the moral one.

The first stage is inaugurated by Camilla Rucellai, who claims to have seen a vision in which Bernardo's death is the only means of rescuing Florence from imminent peril (LII, p. 457). Although Romola's immediate response is to declare Camilla either "mad" or "detestably wicked," clearly the only sensible alternatives in this case, Savonarola has not only failed to denounce her but, in fact, has countenanced her vision (LII, p. 548). Thus, her deadly fanaticism becomes a gloss on Savonarola. It is not because Savonarola believes Camilla's vision—for indeed he is very doubtful—nor because he particularly sanctions its message, that he cannot speak against it (LII, p. 458). Savonarola's dilemma reveals rather an inner inconsistency, a potential to lawlessness, in the formal structure of his religion. As Savonarola rightly estimates, in impeaching the credibility of any vision whatever its moral value, he would inevitably lay the foundations for the skepticism that might impeach his own visions. Like the other Christian characters in the book, Savonarola too is given to receiving messages from the invisible world. Eliot had, of course, read Savonarola's expositions of his visions in his own writings and in commentaries on them in biographies of Savonarola, especially in Perrens's. In December

1861, she had even read a passage pertaining to visions in Emil Heinrich Du Bois-Reymond's essay commemorating Johannes Müller (Yale MS 3), the *Gedächtnissrede auf Johannes Müller* (no. 621 in the Eliot/Lewes library).

That Savonarola's visions happen in many ways to be grand ones is incidental to the problem that troubled Eliot. The problem is not the nature of the vision, but rather that there is, in formal Christianity, no external criterion by which one vision can be distinguished from another. That is what Savonarola realizes. One accepts no visions, or one must accept all. Although Camilla's is the last extreme, the final extension, of Dino's, it is a vision that, despite its distinctly anti-Christian sentiments, suggests the inevitable if extravagant variation on the unchecked tendency to the perception of the invisible.

The incident of Camilla's vision raises two other, related questions, one that pertains to Savonarola's attempt to translate his passion for purity of conscience into the cause of public reform, and the other, implied in the first, that pertains to the irreconcilable conflict between individual and general welfare. Here, the interdependence between psychological and moral issues introduces more complications. It becomes evident that one of the difficulties with visions of any kind is that there are no visions apart from visionaries.

In a very early letter to her teacher Maria Lewis, Eliot once wrote on the subject of egotism: "But where is not this same ego? The martyr at the stake seeks its gratification as much as the court sycophant, the difference lying in the comparative dignity and beauty of the two egos. People absurdly talk of self-denial—why there is none in Virtue to a being of moral excellence—the greatest torture to such a soul would be to run counter to the dictates of conscience, to wallow in the slough of meanness, deception, revenge or sensuality" *(Letters,* I, 127). In many ways, Savonarola derives from this early portrait, but the older Eliot knew as the younger had not the complex and mixed elements of human nature. That purer egotism she described in the imaginary martyr Savonarola shares, but it is mixed with another, less attractive egotism and warped by the blindness no one eludes, the conviction that the best light we have is also the best light there is. Thus, although as Tito's antithesis Savonarola argues for a view entirely opposed to Tito's egotistic principles, Bacchus to some degree seems inescapable even for Savonarola; the monk is not, after all, so clear a contrast to Tito in this respect as he himself believes.

Although Savonarola has great visions for Florence, his is a "power-loving soul" (XXI, p. 218), and while he is ennobled by "piety," by "active sympathy," and by a "clear-sighted demand for the subjection of selfish interests to the general good" (XXIII, p. 224), he has a terrible "need" for "personal predominance" (XXIII, p. 224). As his virtues have a regenerative effect on Florence, and on Romola, so his inner conflict too has its public ramifications. Savonarola envisions himself the sole instrument of divine favor, a priest on a cosmic scale, as it were; and he thus considers his government too important, his cause too great, to be sacrificed to such small considerations as the lives of a few individuals.

It is not only Savonarola's character and the conflicts in his own heart that bring him to this moral impasse. Quite apart from motives, the act of translating religion into politics, morality into law—because it is an attempt to codify the inarticulate—incurs the risk of tainting both. George Levine rightly remarks that in Savonarola's story we have the beginning of Eliot's explicitly dramatized distrust of politics, hinted at first in "Janet's Repentance" and fully explored in *Felix Holt.*[2] Public life is invariably corrupting. Precisely because to achieve its ends it must gain and hold power, Savonarola's party, like every other party, begins to subject itself to the exigency of practical compromise. It is impossible to have an effect otherwise, but such compromise corrupts the purity for whose sake Savonarola entered into public conflict.

Power, indeed, tends to corruption, in more ways than Lord Acton cared to mention. From the first, Savonarola's attempt to find a secular arm for God's retribution had proved misguided. The French king whom Savonarola had welcomed as "the instrument elected by God" (XXI, p. 219) is characterized as a man peculiarly ill-suited to assume that high office. As the narrator observes, Charles VIII had "come across the Alps with the most glorious projects; he was to march through Italy amidst the jubilees of a grateful and admiring people; he was to satisfy all conflicting complaints at Rome; he was to take possession, by virtue of hereditary rights and a little fighting, of the kingdom of Naples; and from that convenient starting-point he was to set out on the conquest of the Turks, who were partly to be cut to pieces and partly converted to the faith of Christ. It was a scheme that seemed to befit the Most Christian King" (XXI, p. 215). Unlike the narrator, Savonarola does not see the irony.

Savonarola himself, translated from the monk who had retired from the world because he had been disillusioned by perceiving the "contradiction between men's lives and their professed beliefs" (XXI, p. 217) to the leader of temporal power, undergoes the very corruption he had wished to escape as his actions begin to contradict his beliefs. In the political arena, the conflicting selves of his nature are "brought into terrible evidence" (LII, p. 455), and it becomes increasingly difficult for him to distinguish "Self" from the "purpose which is not selfish" (LXV, p. 458). Later in his trial, the succession of confessions, retractions, retractions of retractions, reveals the same conflict as Savonarola searches desperately for a way to reconcile his own glory with the principles he cannot choose to betray.

Savonarola can no longer distinguish clearly between God and himself. In her volume of his *Prediche,* Eliot had copied onto the end papers Savonarola's words, "Dio mio, io non voglio altro che te" ("My God, I do not wish anything but you"). Yet in Savonarola's mind, God's will and his own are very confused. Although he does not wish to wish it, he does in fact wish for much in addition to God. He wishes for temporal power. Arguing with Romola over Bernardo, Savonarola declares that the cause of his party is the cause of God's kingdom (LIX, p. 508). Yet although "in that declaration" Romola "heard only the ring of egoism," Eliot does not allow us to make so simple and one-sided a judgment. For in their collision over Bernardo, Eliot suggests the collision of Creon and Antigone, and while Eliot's reading of *Antigone* was not entirely Hegelian in that the two opponents are not in the end equally right, it was Hegelian enough for her to insist that we recognize some merit in Creon's, Savonarola's, argument as well. "Perhaps such words," the narrator comments, "have rarely been uttered without that meaner ring in them; yet they are the implicit formula of all energetic belief. And if such energetic belief, pursuing a grand and remote end, is often in danger of becoming demon-worship, in which the votary lets his son and daughter pass through the fire with a readiness that hardly looks like sacrifice: tender fellow-feeling for the nearest has its danger too, and is apt to be timid and sceptical towards the larger aims without which life cannot rise into religion" (LXI, p. 517). Earlier, the narrator had remarked that Romola had begun to shrink from Savonarola's "right" when she realized that it was bound "to so much narrowness." (LII, p. 459). But there is both narrowness and largeness on Romola's side as well; in her loyalty to Bernardo she gives too little thought to the general good. Thus, like Polynices in Sophocles' play, Bernardo becomes the victim of a "collision between two kinds of faithfulness" (LX, p. 513).

It is not, therefore, because Eliot did not see the point of Savonarola's case that she finally awarded the moral victory to Romola. It was rather because Eliot saw the collision as irreconcilable. In her "Notes on 'The Spanish Gypsy,'" Eliot defined tragedy as embodying either an "irreparable collision between the individual and the general" or, in an obvious echo of Hegel, the clash of "two irreconcilable 'oughts.'" Often, she wrote, a tragedy embodied both, as Greek tragedy did (Cross, III, pp. 33-34). It had been in just these terms that Eliot had discussed the tragedy of *Antigone* in her essay, in which she had written that the essence of Sophocles' tragedy was: "two principles, both having their validity, . . . at war with each other." It is precisely because the collision is irreconcilable that Eliot concluded her essay on *Antigone* by saying that perhaps "the best moral we can draw is that to which the Chorus points—that our protest for the right should be seasoned with moderation and reverence, and that lofty words—*μεγάλοι, λογοι* [sic]—are not becoming to mortals." [3]

In the passage that contains the words Eliot quotes, the Chorus refers to Creon's pride, to his lack of reverence and moderation, and it is this, finally, which weakens Savonarola's case. In calling Bernardo the victim of a "collision between two kinds of faithfulness," Eliot draws the incident into the larger theme of fidelity, and in that context the moral issues become a little clearer. While in his passionate desire for the good of the state Savonarola seems the very antithesis of Tito, in this case Savonarola betrays Florence in its spiritual character just as Tito had betrayed it in its temporal character. This is evident in the fact that it is, indeed, both Savonarola and Tito together who are ultimately responsible for betraying Bernardo.

As Tito is the chief agent in the disclosure of the Medicean plot against Savonarola's party, so Savonarola is the chief voice that sanctions the execution of the Mediceans—or the chief silence, rather, since it is easier for Savonarola to "repose on a resolution of neutrality" and continue correcting the sheets for his *Triumph of the Cross* (LIX, p. 502). It is that "neutrality," so wholly inappropriate in a spokesman for Christ, and so ironically reminiscent of Tito's moral skepticism, that makes it difficult for us now to distinguish in Savonarola's actions between the Bacchic and the Christian visions. Indeed, the title of Savonarola's book fully captures the inner contradiction; while it alludes to Christ, it echoes the image of Bacchus triumphant.

How Savonarola came to mirror Tito can be explained only by recalling Dino, who resembles both and is therefore the bridge between them. In the comprehensive sympathy that characterizes his political vision, Savonarola has stepped over that dangerous boundary that divides the concrete from the abstract. Abstracted, Dino's Christ had become incompatible with human claims. Abstracted, Savonarola's Christian state becomes equally incompatible with the claims of the individual. Florence must be saved, Savonarola's argument runs, since a "good government is needful to the perfecting of the Christian life" (LIX, p. 502). But for Florence to be saved, Savonarola concedes, some Florentines may have to be sacrificed. The narrator had spoken of the ease with which the martyr yields his children to the flames. With the same ease, Savonarola remarks to Romola that the "death of five men—were they less guilty than these—is a light matter weighed . . . against the furthering of God's kingdom upon earth" (LIX, p. 507).

If Tito follows the principles of egoistic utilitarianism, admittedly in their worst form, it is difficult to distinguish Savonarola's conclusion here from the universalistic utilitarianism that the narrator had parodied in the mood of the Florentine crowd during the feast of San Giovanni, a crowd eager for some riotous merriment, and "ready to sacrifice a stray individual to the greater happiness of the greater number" (X, p. 108). There "is a mercy," Savonarola cautions Romola, "which is weakness, and even treason against the common good" (LIX, p. 504). To make Christ's cause prevail, it seems, it may be necessary to transgress one or two of his principles.

This contradiction is inherent in Savonarola's political purpose. When Savonarola speaks of the "furthering of God's kingdom upon earth," it is impossible not to hear Christ's words: "My Kingdom is not of this world." Any attempt to institutionalize the Christian experience is in its very conception an error. Christianity, as Eliot saw it, is a private and internal perception, the mystery of the soul, not of the state. It belongs and must remain in the invisible world. It is here therefore that Savonarola fulfills at last the Magdalen prophecy of Piero's sketch. The paradox in Savonarola's position is aptly translated into the image of the pure prostitute, pure in heart but not in deed. When Romola had recognized that the contribution of Christianity was to be found in its moral energy, she implicitly realized that it was a motive for, not a system of, action. In arguing with Savonarola now, she understands better than he what the nature of that motive is. Romola had begun in the religion of affection, and she sees now that love, transformed by experience and imagination, is still the essential truth of the religion of sympathy. In answer to Savonarola's identification of God's kingdom with his own political party, Romola replies, "God's kingdom is something wider–else, let me stand outside it with the beings I love" (LIX, p. 508). As Eliot wrote to Charles Bray a few days after the Christmas of 1862, while she was writing *Romola:* "I am happy to believe that no philosophy will expel from the world" the *"Caritas"* which is "the highest love or fellowship" *(Letters,* IV, 72).

This contradiction between the form and substance of Christianity is illustrated not only in the contrast between Savonarola's success in teaching Romola the inward sympathy of the heart and his failure to practice that sympathy in his political decisions but even more pointedly in Eliot's resolution of the question of law and justice that had been raised in Tito's story. Very concerned, as we have seen, with the law and order of the state, Savonarola had been active, in his struggle to bring the outward form of law into harmony with the inward light of justice, in setting up a procedure for an appeal from conviction that now proves to apply to cases exactly like those of the five Mediceans. It seems that it is only in theory, however, that law and justice can become one. Although the appeal is the fruition of his own ideals, Savonarola in this instance argues against granting it, on the basis, he claims, of a justice higher than that which law embodies. His concept of justice is now parodied in one of the two handbills that come into circulation at this time. The one called "Justice" follows Savonarola in demanding the speedy execution of the five. It is the one called "Law" that urges that the appeal be granted (LIX, p. 499).

The incident demonstrates both the necessity and the insufficiency of law. In divorcing itself from law, Savonarola's concept of justice has become lawless, ironically the very subject on which Savonarola had once lectured Romola in another context. But Romola's concept of justice in Bernardo's case is equally lawless, since she is willing to excuse his offense to save his life. Yet the two lawless conclusions are very different, and out of their dialectic comes Eliot's resolution. For the purpose of law, Eliot concludes, is to act as an external restraint when the internal restraint fails. Where the mind has escaped the sympathy of the heart, as in Savonarola's case, law is essential. But where there is sympathy of the heart no external law is required, for sympathy, in passing beyond the harsh formality of law, is indeed better than law. That is precisely what the Eumenides sing in a passage that Eliot had quoted earlier, that outward law will become needless when duty and love have united in one stream and made a common force (XI, p. 122). That stream is not law but justice. As the narrator remarks when Tito and Baldassarre both die on the shore of the Arno, "Who shall put his finger on the work of justice, and say 'It is there'? Justice is like the kingdom of God—it is not without us as a fact, but within us as a great yearning" (LXVII, p. 565).

Like so many other threads in the book, the question of law and justice returns us once more to those inarticulate sensibilities that underlie all moral questions. This inarticulate world stands in contrast to language, itself a subject in the book, and indeed the paradigm for all the distinctions between form and substance.

As the property of the community rather than of the individual, languages expresses, like law, the form that clothes but also disguises the substance of meaning. Early in the book, Nello had foreshadowed the question when he had remarked that "we Florentines have liberal ideas about speech, and consider that the instrument which can flatter and promise so cleverly as the tongue, must have been partly made for those purposes; and that truth is a riddle for eyes and wit to discover, which it were mere spoiling of sport for tongue to betray" (III, p. 39). On different levels, Nello's remark is both true and ironic. In saying that it is for the eyes and wit to discover truth, he identifies for Eliot the two instruments of perception the book explores: Christian vision and pagan reason. But that truth is something the tongue "betrays." Recalling perhaps Tennyson's "For words, like Nature, half reveal/ And half conceal the Soul within" in *In Memoriam,* Eliot uses the word that picks up once more one of the book's major themes to suggest the ambivalence of language that codifies and for that reason misrepresents meaning.

Elaborating this metaphor, Eliot once again links Tito and Savonarola. At first, it seems that the two are distinguished rather than identified in the quality of their voices. Tito's voice, with its soft liquid sound, is, as the voice of Bacchus would be, extremely pleasant to hear. Everyone is charmed by it. Ironically, it is Bratti who first hints at its moral implications when he remarks that the words come out of Tito "all melting . . . so that a Christian and a Florentine can't tell a hook from a hanger" (I, p. 12). Later, Tessa expands on Bratti's hint when the "strange voice" seems to her "a thing to make her cross herself" (II, p. 27). No such diabolical overtones are suspected when we first hear Savonarola's voice, a voice that seems to speak of divine inspiration. Its power moves Romola the first time she hears it in San Marco. Later, she tells Tito that Savonarola's "very voice seems to have penetrated me with a sense that there is some truth in what moves them; some truth of which I know nothing" (XVII, p. 187). It is Savonarola's voice again, the "Arresting Voice" of the conversion scene, that stops Romola in her flight from Florence.

But on November 17, 1494, this distinction between Tito's and Savonarola's voices begins to blur strangely. As Bacchus stands outside the Duomo, where his fluent tongue welcomes the French invader, inside Savonarola prepares for the arrival of Charles VIII by preaching the impassioned Advent sermon. Graphically, the scene echoes the antithesis between the triptych and the crucifix, but the irony is that at this moment the inherent paradox in language begins to contradict the apparent moral contrast, for it is language that betrays them both and through which they both betray Florence. Increasingly, it is his great skill as an orator that both impels Tito to seek a public career and brings him success in it. After his initial triumph, it occurs to Tito that it is very easy, and very pleasant too, "this exercise of speaking to the general satisfaction: a man who knew how to persuade need never be in danger from any party; he could convince each that he was feigning with all the others" (XXIX, pp. 272-73). In this realization that he can "tickle the ears of men with any phrases that pleased them" Tito's political ambition is born (XXXV, p. 324). But it is the same gift of eloquence that gives Savonarola his hold on Florence, and it is his public eloquence that begins to betray his inner vision. "In the career of a great public orator who yields himself to the inspiration of the moment," the narrator observes, "the conflict of selfish and unselfish emotion . . . is brought into terrible evidence: the language of the inner voices is written out in letters of fire" (LII, pp. 455-56). When later Savonarola tries to distinguish in himself the subtle encroachment of false on true motives, language proves too coarse to catch the faint, uncertain light of conscience. In his public sermon, his faith but not his speech wavers: "it is the lot of every man who has to speak for the satisfaction of the crowd," the narrator concludes in words not so different from Tito's own reflections on public speaking, "that he must often speak in virtue of yesterday's faith, hoping it will come back to-morrow" (LXII, p. 521).

The distinction between Savonarola's private and public voice is explored through Baldassarre, who becomes, in one more of his roles, a parody of the public Savonarola. In their different effects on Romola and Baldassarre, Eliot implies the moral difference between Savonarola's private and public visions. In one very important respect, Savonarola and Baldassarre are in no way alike, as Eliot suggests in the very different demands each makes on Romola. Although both begin with a recognition of suffering as a premise—and Baldassarre is indeed the only pagan figure in the book who shares at least so far in the Christian vision that he accepts pain as an irremediable fact of existence—they arrive at antithetical conclusions. To Baldassarre, "it seemed that pain was the order of the world for all except the hard and base. If any were innocent, if any were noble, where could the utmost gladness lie for them? Where it lay for him—in unconquerable hatred and," as is appropriate for this Bacchic figure, in a vengeance that was "triumphant" (L, p. 448). It is on this assumption, and in the belief that Romola shares his view, that Baldassarre asks her to help him take their common revenge on the man who had betrayed them (chap. LIII). To Savonarola, as he had told Romola in the conversion scene, suffering justifies not revenge but sympathy. Yet this truth seems clearer to him in his private than in his public role, for it was not sympathy Savonarola urged in Bernardo's case, but indeed revenge. And this implication in Savonarola's voice, concealed from everyone, including Savonarola himself, had been first perceived by Baldassarre.

Fleeing the French soldiers from whom he had escaped, Baldassarre had taken refuge in the Duomo, and the Advent sermon of 1494 that had first inspired Romola to her Christian conversion had been heard by Baldassarre as well, but in a very different light. In her chronology of Savonarola's life, Eliot had entered into her *Quarry* that the subject of this Advent sermon in 1494 had been the Book of Haggai. That prophet's call for the rebuilding of the Temple, one that was to be less splendid materially than Solomon's but greater in spiritual glory, is interwoven in Savonarola's sermon with a more political concern as Savonarola at the same time welcomes Charles VIII of France as the *Gladius Domini* who will bring divine retribution on Florence. While Romola had listened to the glories of the Temple, Baldassarre had heard only the promise of vengeance to come. In that, it had seemed to him not only that Savonarola addressed himself to his own case but that in Savonarola he could see his own reflection. Baldassarre is not entirely mistaken, for in one respect at least, the two figures are structurally parallel. Each a votary of one of the chief gods of the book, each in one of their roles an agent of retribution, Baldassarre and Savonarola mirror the private and the public versions of the same point.

Here again, the two mystery cults confront one another and prove to be, in form, one another's reflections. The great Duomo in which Savonarola preaches, and the Temple of which he speaks, are mirrored in Baldassarre's own body, which he regards as the "temple of vengeance" (XLIV, p. 398). To Baldassarre, as to Savonarola, that vengeance is a "sacred fire" (L, p. 440). When Baldassarre says to Romola, "My mind goes—everything goes sometimes—all but the fire. The fire is God; it is justice; it will not die" (LIII, p. 465), he envisions himself as much the special instrument of a divine purpose as Savonarola does when he tells Romola that the cause of his party is the cause of God's kingdom. If Baldassarre is driven by a Bacchic *mania,* Savonarola is driven by "divine frenzy" (XLI, p. 379). The mysteries are, once again, very similar, and if not restrained by the reason and humanism of the pagan mask that Piero di Cosimo had placed between the Bacchic and the Christian emblems in his sketch, both will escape into those regions of enthusiasm that stand by their very natures beyond the limits of civilization. Thus, both Tito's and Savonarola's ends come about as a result of the latent perversion concealed in their mysteries. In their stories, Eliot plays out their implications to the end, and each relives the ritual of his god. As Tito dies in a reenactment of the *sparagmos,* the last rite of the Bacchic worship, so Savonarola dies in a sense like Christ crucified. Yet the final irony is that even as they fulfill the rituals of their gods, Tito and Savonarola betray them. For their lives are empirical evidence in Eliot's argument that only when ritual is internalized, only when religion becomes mythology, do we share in the divine mystery. This will be Romola's last discovery, and in making it she will enter into the modern era.

9.

The Birth of Modern Man

Romola's marriage to Tito had effectively ended in a final moral rupture over her father. Her marriage to Savonarola ends similarly in a moral rupture over her godfather. When she had fled Florence the first time, she had found herself in a situation somewhat similar to that of the husband she was then leaving. When she flees Florence the second time, Romola discovers that hers is now very much the problem that her spiritual husband is confronting. Savonarola's dilemma, as Romola how formulates it to herself, is to understand "where the sacredness of obedience ended, and where the sacredness of rebellion began" (LVI, p. 483). Both obedience and rebellion are duties (LV, p. 471). Threatened with excommunication by the pope, Savonarola seems to have before him the choice of obeying God—as he conceives God's will—or obeying his embodiment on earth, the church. It seems obvious here that it is not only in one of Romola's stages that Eliot suggests the Protestant era, but in Savonarola himself. It is, in a sense, Savonarola's tragedy that he is a Protestant without knowing it, that he is a figure in an age of transition through whom history changes its course. And it is because, unlike Romola, he does not realize that the moment of transition has come that Savonarola is now, as Bardo had been before him, historically doomed. Ironically, therefore, as Romola dissociates herself from Savonarola, she follows his example, although ironically yet again, by disobeying him.

As Savonarola chooses to remain true to his own vision against that of the church, Romola yields to her own inner conviction to leave not only Savonarola but Tito as well, to break the bond to which Savonarola had earlier returned her. The "outward law" that binds her to Tito Romola acknowledges as "a widely ramifying obligation," but for the first time she sees the superior claim of the "inner moral facts." The "sanctity attached to all close relations, and, therefore, pre-eminently to the closest, was but the expression in outward law of that result towards which all human goodness and nobleness must spontaneously tend; that the light abandonment of ties, whether inherited or voluntary, because they had ceased to be pleasant, was the uprooting of social and personal virtues. What else had Tito's crime towards Baldassarre been?" But her marriage to Tito had become "simply a degrading servitude" (LVI, p. 483), and one therefore that conscience itself could not sanction. So too had her second marriage to Savonarola. To both Romola and Savonarola "there had come one of those moments in life when the soul must dare to act on its own warrant, not only without external law to appeal to, but in the face of a law which is not unarmed with Divine lightnings—lightnings that may yet fall if the warrant has been false" (LVI, pp. 483-84).

As Romola leaves Florence now, she feels "orphaned" (LXI, p. 520). This is literally the case, since all her fathers have been lost to her in succession. But Romola is orphaned in a far more symbolic sense as well, the symbolic sense that is implied in the literal. Although in her first flight Romola had felt alone, she had been mistaken, for there had been still a wealth of human knowledge and experience she had not yet assimilated. When Romola leaves Florence the second time, she is truly alone. There are no fathers now to act as her teachers and heroes because in having relived in her life the history of civilization Romola has at last caught up with the cultural heritage of mankind. It is at this point, therefore, that Romola realizes most fully the image of Antigone, the moral pioneer, and that she takes metaphorically from Savonarola's hand, as she had taken the crucifix literally from Dino's, the cross of the "genius of the future."

In Romola's dilemma now, Eliot raises another historical question, the perennial conflict between tradition and change. We have long been accustomed to think of Eliot as a political conservative who, like so many Victorians, perhaps in the wake of the bloody French Revolution and the unbloody but no less traumatic industrial revolution, feared the rebellion of the masses and the upheaval whose seed Karl Marx was soon to sow. Eliot did think of herself as a conservative, but she meant the word, surely, in an etymological sense. She knew as well as Matthew Arnold that to annihilate culture, in its broadest historical sense, was to choose anarchy. Culture, in the sense of legacy, is precisely the point of Eliot's epic, and the political as well as moral anarchy Tito brings about is implicit in the repudiation of that legacy. That is why Eliot argued not only that we remember history lest we be condemned to repeat it, but indeed that we assimilate it into our own consciousness, as Romola assimilates it. There is nothing incompatible here with radicalism, however, which Eliot embraced as well, again I think in an etymological sense. Readers who have long been puzzled by the subtitle of *Felix Holt, The Radical,* and have often concluded it to be a very misleading introduction to the social and political position of its protagonist, have thought of radicalism in its looser sense and not as an attempt to probe to the "root" of a problem, an attempt that favors neither tradition nor revolution for its own sake but that looks to tradition, to culture, as the touchstone that must determine whether conservation or revolution is in order. As Romola had discovered, both obedience and rebellion may be duties; it is only culture, in its broadest sense, that can say which is the duty of the hour.

In this sense, Romola is, as I think Eliot was, both a conservative and a radical, assimilating the past but always willing to break with the past for the promise of a better future. That future begins for Romola the loneliest part of her pilgrimage, which takes her into territory unmapped by social exploration. Here, the individual and the community are no longer in step. Society is created by tradition, on which it relies for its coherence. Progress, however, is the work of individuals, of those who see, as Antigone does, ahead of their time. In time, as the future becomes the past, their visions, as Romola's will, become the common tradition of mankind, to be challenged again by the next incarnation of the moral pioneer.

In terms of another dominant metaphor in the book, at this moment Romola has come at last to hear her own inner voice. In her argument with Savonarola over Bernardo, Romola had, in a sense, proclaimed her freedom. You "yourself declare," she had said, "that there comes a moment when the soul must have no guide but the voice within it" (LIX, p. 506). But Romola does not yet hear what that inner voice prompts. "What force was there," she asks herself, "to create for her that supremely hallowed motive which men call duty, but which can have no inward constraining existence save through some form of believing love?" (LXI, p. 515). When he had converted her, Savonarola had commanded Romola to find and observe the duties that belonged to her name. But these Romola has now despaired of finding (LXI, p. 515). All her experiments seem now to have proved false. Romola's spiritual state recalls Bardo's intellectual crisis at the beginning of the book. She has, as he had, reached the end of analysis but stands only on the threshold of synthesis. And that threshold she does not know, any more than Bardo had known, how to cross.

In Romola's mind, this last experiment seems to close the range of possibilities, and with that, once again, the possibility of life itself. She has reached the second center of indifference. But this time she has lost more than her will to live. The heroism she had relied on in Savonarola had inspired her to believe in her own ability to rise to a higher life. His fall degrades her with him. With "the sinking of high human trust, the dignity of life sinks too; we cease to believe in our own better self" (LXI, p. 517). While "she could not directly seek death," Romola can "wish that death would come" (LXI, p. 517), and it is with that wish that Romola gets into the boat she happens to find on the shore of the Mediterranean and drifts away.

The chapter called "Drifting Away" reminds us of the chapter called "Borne Along by the Tide" in *The Mill on the Floss,* and like Maggie Tulliver, in the face of an apparently irreconcilable conflict, Romola wants to be freed from the burden of choice (LXI, p.

519). Drifting on the water, Romola had begun to long "for that repose in mere *sensation* which she had sometimes dreamed of in the sultry afternoons of her early girlhood, when she had fancied herself floating naiad-like in the waters" (LXI, p. 517; my italics). She had begun to wish, that is, as the word *sensation* suggests, for a return to Bacchic ease when life was, if less meaningful, at least simpler. Tito had in fact once said that he would "like to dip" Romola "a little in the soft waters of forgetfulness" (XXIV, p. 239), and it is that very "Lethe" existence (LXVIII, p. 566) that Romola finds on the waters on which her boat drifts, symbolically unguided. But what appears to be at first a pagan state of forgetfulness, one that recalls Tito's and Baldassarre's, is only a suspension of consciousness that returns her to that state of passivity in which Savonarola had converted her to Christianity. For Romola is about to be converted again. In a moment of apparent inaction, the choice she feels unable to make consciously is being made unconsciously in what will prove to be the period of her most intense moral activity.

Symbolically, this final transformation is enacted in the village to which the boat drifts. Floating on the waters, Romola had not, after all, found the repose in mere sensation that she had sought. Unlike Tito's and Baldassarre's, Romola's Lethe of forgetfulness had been disturbed by memory, memories "which hung upon her like the weight of broken wings that could never be lifted—memories of human sympathy" (LXI, p. 519).

Although she does not yet realize it, all her experiences have been for Romola a preparation for this moment. Eliot wrote that this scene and the "Drifting Away" that precedes it were the earliest she thought of in conceiving the book *(Letters,* IV, 103-4). Indeed, this is the end toward which the images of the book have persistently pointed. The symbolic plague that Dino had accused Bardo of ignoring had already become a real plague in Florence. At that time, while Romola had remained in the city to minister to its victims, Tito had taken up residence outside it to avoid contamination (LV, p. 473). His flight had, of course, echoed the work of another Florentine, Boccaccio, whom, in fact, Eliot was reading through a second time between August and November 1862 (Yale MS 3), undoubtedly in her own well-marked copy of his works (no.

251 in the Eliot/Lewes library). It is the story of Gostanza in Boccaccio's *Decamerone* that Romola remembers when she, like Gostanza, has not the courage to take her own life and commits it instead to the fortunes of the boat in which she sets out to sea (LXI, p. 518). But unlike Boccaccio's characters, it is not from but to the plague that Romola is being taken, the second plague that realizes Dino's earlier metaphor. In his metaphor, Dino had implied the meaning of both literal plagues: to be born is to be born to pain; joy is possible, but sorrow is certain.

It may seem true on the novelistic level that, as Avrom Fleishman argues, Romola rejects history in this second flight from Florence in the typical fashion of the late Victorian historical novel for the sake of a nonhistorical higher life.[1] But here as always the meaning of the novel must be drawn from the epic that informs it, and on the epic level Romola's flight is not a rejection of history but a return into the mainstream of history. This plague-stricken village, in which Romola finds her ultimate perception of meaning, is not to be seen in contrast to the historical life in Florence, not to be isolated as another and distinct world, but in fact to be identified as the same world symbolically represented in its most essential features. We recall that when Romola enters the boat she falls asleep, and from that moment the narrative is like a dream sequence; everything that happens between Romola's flight from Florence and her return to it is a dream, the dream of a medieval allegory in which real events are stripped of their complexity and ambiguity and appear truly in their most fundamental relations in a world in which time is perceived in the context of eternity.

It is just such a sleep and such a dream that begins the *Inferno* of Dante's epic. To recall Dante is to realize that like Dante's dream Romola's is the conventional epic descent into the underworld. Eliot reenacted that obligatory scene, not because it is formally required, but because, like Homer and Dante and every epic poet, Eliot knew that to confront death is to confront one's vision of life in its most radical form. It was just that, as Eliot herself tells us, that Romola finds in the village. "In Florence," the narrator observes, "the simpler relations of the human being to his fellowmen had been complicated for" Romola "with all the special ties of marriage, the State, and religious discipleship, and when these had disappointed her trust, the shock seemed to have shaken her aloof from life and stunned her sympathy" (LXIX, p. 576). In the village, however, the simple and urgent human need sweeps away moral perplexity and theoretic doubt. The immediate empirical fact generates its own compelling solution. In Florence, Romola had felt "without bonds, without motive." Here, no motive is necessary, for there is a distinct reason for action in the misery before her that no one else can alleviate. The conscious self-sacrifice to which Savonarola had urged her as a theory of life had taught her to seek satisfaction in the reflection that she had helped to lighten sorrow. She had found satisfaction in such reflection, but not enough. Unlike Dino, Romola had never been able to wholly transcend the personal, and Savonarola's universal love had not proved for her a sufficient reason for living. But in the village, "reasons for living, enduring, labouring" do not take "the form of argument." The habit of sympathy Romola had acquired in Florence finds its unreflecting strength in an "energetic impulse to share the life around her, to answer the call of need and do the work which cried aloud to be done" (LXIX, p. 576). Romola's experience in the village, then, like the dream of the allegory or the descent into the underworld of the epic, is a metaphor in which all her experiments are synthesized, in which all her historical legacies are brought to the ultimate test of action.

As many have suggested, Romola arrives here at something that recalls Comte's Religion of Humanity. When she had declared to Savonarola that she preferred to stand with the beings she loved outside God's kingdom, as he had represented it, she had in effect announced her separation from institutions of religion, as shortly she would announce her loss of faith. In a very important sense, therefore, this second flight from Florence marks the end of the Christian epoch in history and the beginning of the modern age, the age that Comte called the Positive (scientific and secular) period of history. But it is certainly to a far richer and subtler, and in some respects even different, end than Comte imagined that Eliot brings Romola.

Bernard Paris characterizes one important aspect of Romola's last transition when he observes that in the village "direct experience" replaces reflection.[2] It is toward a confrontation with direct experience that Romola has long been moving. The knowledge that began in myth ends with the knowledge that needs to pass through no structural translation. It is both the same and a different knowledge. In one sense, this knowledge is the inarticulate meaning of the mythic symbol, but to the degree that the meaning and the symbol are categorically distinct, the knowledge is also different from its formal expression.

This is the last antithesis of the novel—the empirical as opposed to the reflective experience of life—and it is the most important antithesis of form and substance, since it brings us at last to the irreducible fact. Reflection may comment on life, but it is not the same as life. Experience cannot be translated. It is not the wisdom gained in experience, therefore, that Romola has attained, although she has attained that also, but the wisdom that is experience itself. Piero di Cosimo had once said to Tito that "a philosopher is the last sort of animal I should choose to resemble. I find it enough to live, without spinning lies to account for life" (XVII, p. 197). Philosophy fares no worse in Piero's remark than its inherent distinction from life makes necessary. Philosophy spins lies, not because it speaks what is untrue, but in a sense because it speaks at all.

It is significant that it is the artist of the book who holds this opinion. The basis of Eliot's persistent argument that art transcends philosophy is the point of Piero's observation. Unlike philosophy, art confronts the reader not with theory but with life, life exactly as it is lived, and differing from it only in that the artist reveals in his work that which the reader may not be able to perceive in life for himself. It is not, certainly, that theory is unnecessary, for life does raise questions. And unreflective goodness, if such a thing exists, is not what Eliot suggests as a pattern of life. Tessa, whose sweet disposition makes her gentle and generous, is not an acceptable moral model. But in contrast to Tessa, Tito's sophisticated knowledge of the theoretic arguments concerning good and evil has little effect on his conduct. Nello observes of Bratti that he "has a theory, and lives up to it, which is more than I can say for any philosopher I have the honor of shaving" (III, p. 30). Philosophy alone, and under that rubric Eliot here includes all theory, seldom issues in action. Thus, although Eliot recognizes the validity of the theoretic question and even of the search for an answer to it in Romola's epic journey through all possibilities, she recognizes theory as meaningful and useful only if it is brought at last, as it is for Romola in the village, to an empirical synthesis whose end is action. The conclusion to which Eliot takes Romola is very like the conclusion to which Thomas Mann takes Hans Castorp in *The Magic Mountain* when, after his long residence in the world of possibilities, Hans is brought down from the mountain into the real world of action and decision. Curiously perhaps, while experience itself requires only the stimulation of the senses, as we saw in Tito, the empirical world becomes meaningful only in a detour through reflection.

But, as Romola learns herself, the detour must be just that. Unlike Dino, we must return from our digression to the world of experience, from the underworld again to life. This view of theory does not, of course, answer the puzzling questions the book raises. But that was precisely Eliot's answer, as indeed it was Comte's, that the questions cannot always in fact be answered, that human existence is, after all, not entirely intelligible. Something of this is suggested in the group of characters to whom we return in the Epilogue. There is little consensus in this group, and indeed more doubt than resolution. All we can conclude is that with the help of Monna Brigida's common sense and warm motherly heart; with the help of Nello's pagan rationalism, his skepticism, and his good nature; and finally with the help of Piero di Cosimo's artistic vision, his integrity, and his unreligious but reverential sense of life, Romola, as the spirit of historical progress, can guide Tessa and her children, and the children especially, since they are our projection into the future, toward a better age, further yet along the night-student's circle of light and glory.

These characters gather in the Epilogue on the twenty-second of May 1509, to commemorate on its eve the anniversary of Savonarola's death. Although Romola had long ago altered her estimate of and her relationship to Savonarola, his heroism once more inspires her, as the memory of the great inspires mankind, as indeed Eliot meant Romola herself to inspire the reader. But there is a more direct link between Savonarola's presence here and Romola's last vision. While the historical Christian era has come to an end, Romola rescues from her disillusionment with religion the spirit of the Christian conversion to sympathy. In an entirely mythical sense, Christ remains still the "genius of the future." This too is made clear in the imagery.

Romola had been awakened from the sleep into which she had fallen in the boat by the cry of a child (LXIX, p. 576). This child's voice is the last important voice in the book. It is the voice of suffering and, moreover, an inarticulate voice that can express only the raw sound of pain. The book lists and alludes to a number of children among its characters, but symbolically they are all manifestations of the same child. Piero's sketch, on which had been foreshadowed the rest of Romola's life, had also prepared for the conclusion that Romola's thematic progress through the three experiments would come to rest at last in a transformation of the Christian vision in the fact that the three masks had lain on the lap of a little child whose gaze it had become customary for painters to give to the divine Infant. That this is the same infant who awakens Romola now is implied in his history, which parallels Christ's, for the "Hebrew baby" is temporarily adopted by Romola in her role as the Virgin and becomes in time a Christian (LXVIII, p. 575).

Ironically, the chapter that immediately follows Romola's rupture with Savonarola and her departure from Florence returns to Savonarola just at the moment at which he speaks the words of absolution over Florence: "*Benedicat* vos omnipotens Deus" (LXII, p. 523; my italics). The chapter is appropriately called "The Benediction," but Romola is not one of those whom Savonarola blesses, for in passing beyond Savonarola's vision, Romola has found her own absolution, enacted in the most etymological sense of the word in her baptism on the waters. And she has found, therefore, her own benediction as well, in her encounter with Christ in this child who, at his baptism, comes to be called Benedetto, the "Benediction" (LXVIII, p. 575).

Earlier, the narrator had remarked that the guardianship of the Eumenides would become needless when "all outward law has become needless," when "duty and love had united in one stream and made a common force" (XI, p. 122). This synthesis is symbolically represented in the Christ child, to whom Romola has been brought quite literally on a "stream," and whose metaphoric significance Eliot had suggested as early as the Proem, where she observed that "little children are still the symbol of the eternal marriage between love and duty" (p. 9).

In the act of picking up and carrying this Christ child, Romola of course undertakes again the role of the Virgin, and it is indeed as the Virgin that the villagers receive her. The youth who first spots her thinks that she is the Virgin (LXVIII, p. 571); and the priest, less credulous, concludes that while she is a living woman, her embassy must be from God (LXVIII, p. 573). The villagers quickly fall into the habit of thinking of her as the "blessed Lady" (LXVIII, pp. 575, 578), or the "sweet and sainted lady" (LXVIII, p. 575), or the Madonna (LXVIII, 579). And when Romola at last leaves the village, she travels, like the Virgin, on a mule (LXVIII, p. 578).

The entire period from her drifting in the boat to her departure from the village is identified by the narrator as Romola's "baptism" (LXVIII, p. 567). Romola had passed through many sacraments in the course of the narrative, as Tito had passed through parodies of them, but it is curious at first that her last sacrament in the book should be the one that is logically prior to them all. But both mythologically and historically, "baptism" is the right word here. Romola had fallen asleep in the boat wishing for death. And having indeed passed through death, she returns to life—she is reborn. Unlike Tito, whom John the Baptist had disowned when he had leaped into the waters of the Arno, Romola is accepted into the Christian fellowship. This is confirmed in the calendar. Eliot leaves it to us to calculate that in reaching the Mediterranean shore, where she finds the boat, on the eighth day after the execution of Bernardo del Nero (LXI, p. 515), Romola begins drifting on the waters on August 29, the day on which is commemorated the martyrdom of John the Baptist. It is appropriate, therefore, that the boat which Romola had at first hoped would become her coffin proves to be the "cradle of a new life" (LXVIII, p. 567), a life to which the Chirst child symbolically awakens her.

It is curious too at first that the moment of Romola's "baptism" should be the moment of her apostasy. In the order of sacraments, baptism is followed by confirmation. Romola does not, however, confirm her faith; she denies it. "If the glory of the cross," Romola declares, "is an illusion, the sorrow is only the truer" (LXIX, p. 576). The assumption of the conditional clause is at the very least agnostic, and very likely, if read in another way, atheistic. But in its metaphoric sense, in Eliot's view baptism is possible only and just when faith is abandoned. For it is only then that Romola understands that the real meaning of Christianity lies not in the religion but in the myth. She understands Christianity, that is, as Eliot herself understood it, not as a system of faith but as a symbolic articulation of the inarticulate. Just a month after she had finished *Romola,* Eliot wrote in a letter: "It seems to me the soul of Christianity lies not at all in the facts of an individual life, but in the ideas of which that life was the meeting-point and the new starting-point. We can never have a satisfactory basis for the history of the man Jesus, but that negation does not affect the Idea of Christ either in its *historical influence* or its great *symbolic meanings"* *(Letters,* IV, 95; my italics). In another letter, written at Christmas in 1862, while she was still working on *Romola,* Eliot had remarked: "What pitiable people those are who feel no *poetry* in Christianity!" *(Letters,* IV, 71; my italics). Christianity does not require historical evidence for the life of the man Jesus, or belief in his divinity. It requires only the imagination that can perceive it as poetry, as a historical force, that is, and as a symbolic meaning. It is as poetry that Christianity has been the subject of Eliot's book, and it is as poetry that Romola herself at last recognizes it.

Thus, the habit of the nun, in which Romola again leaves Florence, is once more both a true definition and a disguise. Romola herself thinks of it as a disguise, as she had the first time, and claims to be indifferent to the deception (LXI, p. 515). But perhaps this time the word has a special significance. For what Romola has discovered is that the Christianity to which Savonarola had converted her in that same habit was itself a disguise, a formal expression in religion of a substance entirely human. Although belief in the formality had been useful to Romola as a discipline, in Savonarola she had learned of its dangers. In drawing away, then, the veil of form to behold the hidden substance, Romola in her apostasy experiences a purification, a cleansing that is appropriately identified as a baptism.

Romola's baptism in this sense is the historical birth of modern man. Romola is, after all, what Eliot's readers have always suspected she was, a thoroughly contemporary figure, the Victorian intellectual struggling to resolve the dilemmas of the modern age. Her history, which has been the history of mankind, has been in its entirety like a dream, a dream that is the collective consciousness of the race, and a dream therefore which every individual relives as that consciousness is transmitted to him, and that every age must recall if it wishes to be reborn, not in Tito's image, but in Romola's.

When Romola awakens in the boat, she has completed the largest historical and mythological circle of the book and has assumed her most encompassing epic role. Long before, Tito had, in his pagan idiom, fallen into the romantic habit of calling Romola his "goddess" (see, for example, XVII, pp. 185, 189). But the goddess with whom Romola is identified is described with more content by the narrator as a "nature goddess, who was not all-knowing, but whose life and power were something deeper and more primordial than knowledge" (IX, p. 100). Embodying these primordial forces, Romola is returned here to ancient earth cults, perhaps to the most ancient earth cult of all, the cult of the earth mother.

The rituals of such cults were secret mysteries, for, like the sensibilities of which the narrator speaks, what they celebrated was inarticulate. For those who had been initiated, no words were necessary. For those who had not, no words were sufficient. As the participant became wholly identified with his god, and through the god with nature, and through nature with life itself, he transcended his own individual consciousness and shared in the common experience of the tribe. That transcendent moment comes to Romola at the moment of Bernardo del Nero's death when she gives way "to an identification of herself with him in these supreme moments" in which she feels "the full force of that sympathy with the individual lot that is continually opposing itself to the formulae by which actions and parties are judged." And at that moment, she experiences "that intensity of life which seems to transcend both grief and joy—in which the mind seems to itself akin to elder forces that wrought out existence *before the birth of pleasure and pain*" (LX, p. 513; my italics). Thus, in her last stage, Romola closes the circle not only of history but of prehistory as she assumes once more, although at a different level, a mythic image more ancient than Bacchus and Christ, an image in which pleasure and pain are not at war, nor reconciled, but undifferentiated because in the transcendent mystery all have become one with the form and substance of the universe. In reliving all of human history, Romola has achieved, at least in her own consciousness, Savonarola's dream, the dream he himself could not realize, of a world united in sympathy.

10.

Resurrection

The ending of *Romola* is either satisfying or not, depending not only on the reader's personal convictions, but equally on which of the book's ambiguous implications he chooses to stress. Literally, the ending may be less than adequate, and we are perhaps justified in concluding that as a novel *Romola* does not end well. It is above all difficult to accept Romola's last choice, to acquiesce in the tasks to which she commits herself, at twenty-three, for the remainder of her life. For it seems clear that Eliot does not foresee any life for Romola beyond the book's last pages other than the one she undertakes at the end, to care for Tessa and her children.

It may be, as some have suggested, that having never herself overcome, at some level, her own guilt over her union with George Henry Lewes, Eliot punished Romola by condemning her to the loneliness of a perpetual widowhood. It may be for that personal reason that Eliot found attractive the perpetual widowhood on which Comte insisted in his detailed regulations for the life he envisioned in the Positivist era, for it does seem to be to this Comtean end that Eliot brings Romola. We know that in her readings Eliot was often concerned with discussions of the indissolubility of marriage. At the back of her copy of *Die Familie,* for example, Eliot jotted down the page numbers of Riehl's examination of that subject, and similarly, in the Eliot/Lewes library volume of Vico, she jotted down the pages that take up the question of the sacredness of marriage. Indeed, as many have commented, it was perhaps Eliot's reluctance to dissolve the marriage bond that prompted Savonarola's arguments to Romola when she first determined to leave Tito.

But Romola does leave Tito in the end, and perhaps the conclusion of the book is not as uncritical or as simple as it at first appears. In the conflict of Christ and Bacchus, the "clashing deities," a perfect balance is difficult to achieve, and Romola had failed to discern it at many earlier points. The "strict and sombre view of pleasure," the narrator had observed of the passionately Christian Romola, tends to repress poetry in the attempt to repress vice. Sorrow and joy have each their peculiar narrowness; and a religious enthusiasm like Savonarola's, which ultimately blesses mankind by giving the soul a strong propulsion towards sympathy with pain, indignation against wrong, and the subjection of sensual desire, must always incur the reproach of a great negation. Romola's life had given her an affinity for sadness which inevitably made her unjust towards merriment. That subtle result of culture which we call Taste was subdued by the need for a deeper motive" (XLIX, pp. 436-37). Like Hawthorne's Goodman Brown, in discovering sin Romola has all but lost her faculty for pleasure. Although Eliot regrets it, it is of the two the preferable imbalance. For this may indeed be the price we must pay for sympathy. As Romola tells Lillo later, the capacity to share in the sorrows of others leaves little room for joy, for the sorrow of the world is great. "We can only have the highest happiness," she says, "by having wide thoughts, and much feeling for the rest of the world as well as ourselves; and this sort of happiness often brings so much pain with it, that we can only tell it from pain by its being what we would choose before everything else, because our souls see it as a good" (Epilogue, p. 598). In this sense, as in the mystery of the primordial earth cults, pleasure and pain are indistinguishable.

This reminds us that we must not read the end entirely, or even primarily, on a literal level. Laurence Lerner remarks that in

Romola's return to Florence and in her adoption of Tessa and the children, "we have not even what symbolic force the drifting in the boat had managed to generate, but merely a worthy and moralised Victorian ending." [1] This is far from the case, for the ending is as symbolic as the book has been thoughout, and the literal ending of the novel is wholly informed by the poetic ending of the epic.

When Romola returns to Florence, it is once more, and for the last time in the book, Easter, the same Easter whose beginning had seen Tito's death but whose end will see Romola's resurrection. It is April 14, 1498, when Romola passes once again through the gates of Florence to rejoin within its walls the human community in its progress (LXX, p. 579). It is Holy Saturday, and on the next morning she begins her search for Tessa and the children (LXX, p. 581), a task appropriate for this Easter Sunday, since it fulfills a number of promises, both literal and figurative.

When once she had found Lillo lost and roaming the streets of Florence, Romola had returned him to his home and promised Tessa that she would always take care of her and her children if she needed it (LVI, p. 480), as indeed she had earlier taken care of her during the Anathema. Never has Tessa been in more need than now of someone to care for her. Entirely helpless in every respect, Tessa has no one else to turn to when Tito dies. The need is mutual, however, for in a very different way Tito's death has left a void in Romola's life as well. It is not sympathy alone that compels Romola to look for Tessa now, but her own overwhelming desire to have "something she was bound specially to care for" (LXX, p. 582), an object, that is, that would synthesize for her the call of love and duty, and thus implement in the real world the symbolic lesson she had learned in the plague-stricken village. Tito's "widow," with whom she feels, despite the peculiarity of the situation, a natural identification, is Romola's only connection now to Florence, to the concrete life around her.

The narrator had earlier remarked that the child was still the symbol of the marriage between love and duty, and Tito's other family, which now becomes Romola's, are in fact all children, Tessa included. Although sixteen when the book opens, nearly the same age as Romola, Tessa has not—and never will—outgrow infancy. She is invariably called a "baby"; her features are always described as those of an infant; and her nature and manner are suggested in the animal imagery that characterizes her: a tiny fish, a little bird, a kitten, a little goose, and—recalling the image of the fertility goddess in her addiction to nuts—a squirrel. It is this childlike quality that makes Tessa a cherub (X, p. 111), an image that associates her with the divine Infant of Piero's sketch and that once more defines Romola's relationship to her as that of the Holy Mother.

This last relationship Tessa shares with her children, but especially with her son Lillo. Tessa and Tito had been "married" on the Eve of the Nativity of the Virgin; on a subsequent *Nativitá,* Lillo was born (XXXIII, p. 306). Indeed, Tessa thinks Lillo is very much like the "little Gesù," and believes that in recognizing the similarity the "Santa Madonna would be kinder" to her (XXXIII, p. 309). Thus, while Tessa is the real mother of Lillo, it is Romola who is destined to be his symbolic mother. If Romola's marriage to the fertility god proved barren, her marriage to Christ has proved fertile indeed: Tito's children, including Tessa, are now the offspring of her union with Christ, the children of her compassion.

In one symbolic sense, a sense which is stressed in that they share a common husband and his children, Tessa and Romola are really the same woman, as the fertility goddess and the Virgin are the two faces, the sexual and the spiritual, of the ancient earth mother. This dissociation of the two aspects—one embodied in the Virgin Mary and the other in Mary Magdalen—with both of whom Romola has been identified, has been characteristic of Western culture since the beginning of Christianity and was especially characteristic perhaps of the nineteenth century, as Thomas Hardy suggested in *Jude the Obscure* in Jude's dissociated attraction on the one hand to the earthy and seductive Arabella Donn and on the other to the genderless, "epicene," Sue Bridehead. Although that dissociation was never the ultimate center of her fiction, Eliot was no less aware of it than Hardy. A large part of Maggie Tulliver's tragedy in *The Mill on the Floss,* for example, is her inability to reconcile flesh and spirit, one embodied for her in Stephen Guest and the other in Philip Wakem. Similarly, it is a more mature and wiser Dorothea Brooke in *Middlemarch* who, after the death of her ghostly first husband, whom she had mistakenly envisioned as the answer to her spiritual passion, comes to recognize her own complex needs when she chooses a more normal union with Will Ladislaw. Perhaps in bringing Tessa and Romola together in this way at the end of the book, Eliot acknowledged the necessity of integrating these two forces in a symbolically common identity.

In another symbolic sense, however, the Virgin remains the historically pivotal image. For in identifying Romola with the Virgin, Eliot recalls the earth mother that was the Virgin's ancient, pagan, form, and, as U. C. Knoepflmacher suggests, points at the same time to the Comtean emblem of a woman holding a child and preaching the gospel of love.[2] Thus, Eliot's last portrait of Romola is a synthesis of superimposed images in which the whole history of civilization, from prehistoric times to the modern epoch, is implied, implied indeed in the pagan, Christian, and Comtean contexts through which Eliot has throughout traced Romola's epic journey.

As the season which ends the book promises, that journey must lead at last to salvation, and it is that salvation that is symbolically realized in Romola's adoption of Tessa and the children. As the character who has been from the beginning Tito's antithesis and touchstone, Romola has been time and again called on to redeem the world from the moral chaos that follows in Tito's wake. "If we are united," Romola had once said to Tito, "I am that part of you that will save you from crime" (XLVI, p. 418). It is Romola, for example, who, by discovering Tito's first plot against Savonarola, saves him from Tito's treachery (XLVI, pp. 412 ff.). This event takes place on October 30, 1496, the day the statue of the Madonna dell' Impruneta is brought into the city, the day on which Romola enacts the role of the Holy Mother made visible. On this same day, Romola saves not only Savonarola but Baldassarre, who, stricken with hunger, disease, and weariness, lies as though dead, in a symbolic imitation of the fate to which Tito had abandoned him. It is Romola who finds him and, as Tito should have but did not long before, rescues him to a new life. Thus, in the role of the Virgin, Romola fulfills the image of Ariadne, not as Tito had defined her on the triptych, but as the guide who leads us out of the moral labyrinth and in whom, therefore, are embodied both Antigone and Christ. It had been as a savior that Romola had entered the plague-stricken village. She had come there upon a scene that had seemed like "a village of unburied dead" (LXVIII, p. 569), and she had brought the village back to life.

It is, therefore, as a final extension of her role as the savior that Romola adopts Tessa and the children. And as she does so, the historical and universal currents of the epic are brought at last to coincide completely. Here the "Florentine lily," who had come to represent mankind in becoming fully identified with the human community symbolically embodied in Florence, the "Lily of the Arno," assumes the role of the Christian savior at Easter, the season whose flower is the lily, on the day, in fact, of the resurrection.

The last thought with which the book leaves us however is not a statement but a question, and a somewhat ironic one at that. The symbol of Christ on which the book comes to rest recalls the Infant Jesus of Piero's sketch, and that Infant in turn recalls Lillo, whom Tessa had identified with the Christ child. Yet in Romola's last conversation with Lillo, it is clear that this child is already tempted by the ease and pleasure that had seduced his father. On this day that commemorates Savonarola's martyrdom and celebrates, therefore, the essential and symbolic truth of the Christian myth, Lillo casts a satanic shadow, as his father had over the entire book. Earlier, Monna Lisa had said of Lillo that he would turn out to be "as cunning as Satan before long" and had added, with no sense of paradox, "and that's the holy truth" (LVI, p. 476). Undoubtedly, Romola's influence will have its effect on Lillo. The world moves forward, however slowly. That had been one of the chief projections of the epic. But it is difficult to forget the sinister prophecy in Lillo's character. The perennial conflict, we suspect, goes on. Somewhere, another Romola waits for this new, and perhaps slightly better, incarnation of the god of joy to initiate her into the world of sorrow.

Manuscript References

Quarry

Entitled "George Eliot's Notes for Romola," this manuscript, Additional Manuscript no. 40768 at the British Library, London, was in fact only one of Eliot's quarries, the other being her *Commonplace Book* (see below). Eliot seems to have kept it primarily for notes from her wide readings in the Florentine Renaissance.

Yale MS 1

A journal for the years 1854-61, this manuscript also contains: Recollections of Weimar, 1854; Recollections of Berlin, 1854-55; Recollections of Ilfracombe, 1856; Recollections of the Sicily Isles, 1857; Recollections of Jersey, 1857; How I Came to Write Fiction; and the History of "Adam Bede." Some of these Recollections have been published in various volumes, but for the student of *Romola* the manuscript is useful chiefly for its journal entries. The manuscript is now at the Beinecke Library at Yale University.

Yale MS 2

This manuscript contains a journal of Eliot's trip to Germany in 1858 and Recollections of Italy, 1860, a journal of her first trip to

Italy and Florence. Although portions of the Recollections of Italy were published by John Walter Cross in *George Eliot's Life as Related in Her Letters and Journals,* many entries that are especially pertinent to the composition of *Romola* were not. This manuscript is also at the Beinecke Library at Yale University.

Yale MS 3

The journal Eliot kept between July 1861 and December 1877, in its earlier entries are to be found if not a complete at least a very ample record of Eliot's studies for *Romola,* as well as many comments on the stages and trials of its composition. This manuscript too is at the Beinecke Library at Yale University.

Yale MS 6

This is Eliot's *Commonplace Book* a very large portion of which is devoted to notes for Romola. Although like the *Quarry* it contains some entries from Eliot's readings in the Florentine Renaissance, much of the *Commonplace Book* was apparently reserved for entries on material pertaining to the symbolic imagery of the book. It is here, for example, that Eliot entered her Attic calendar. This manuscript too is at the Beinecke Library at Yale University.

Yale MS 18

This tiny volume at the Beinecke Library at Yale University is marked "Quarry" and consists of a chronology of ancient history. It is undated, and to my knowledge no one has yet divined Eliot's purpose for it.

Notes

Chapter I: Introduction

1. *The George Eliot Letters,* ed. Gordon S. Haight (New Haven, 1954-55), VI, 312.
2. Perhaps it was because *Romola* was Eliot's favorite among her own books that she chose Frederic Leighton's illustrations for it, illustrations I will discuss later, to hang, as Charles Eliot Norton reported after visiting her home, on the walls of her drawing room (see Gordon S. Haight, *George Eliot: A Biography* [New York, 1968], pp. 409-10).
3. Although Eliot had had a preliminary correspondence with Blackwood over her plans for *Romola,* it was not in the end Blackwood—who had published the first three and was afterward to publish the last three of Eliot's books—to whom Eliot entrusted *Romola* for publication, but to George Smith. It was not, however, because Smith offered her the unusually large sum of £10,000 for the book, nor because, as Eliot added, Smith could print the book in larger installments in the *Cornhill Magazine,* that Eliot abandoned Blackwood for the only time in her career. The exception seems to me rather to be consistent with the fear and agitation that marked every aspect of the book's composition, and that made nearly everything connected with it unique.
4. *The Truthtellers: Jane Austen, George Eliot, D. H. Lawrence* (New York, 1967), p. 249.
5. *Essays of George Eliot,* ed. Thomas Pinney (New York, 1963), pp. 432-36.
6. We hear of Eliot's plans for this book for the first time in a letter from John

Blackwood who wrote to Eliot during her visit to Munich in June 1858 that he thought she would find many studies for heads in the Munich Gallery that would be useful for "the Italian story you have in view" *(Letters,* II, 463).

7. Yale MS 3. For fuller information on this and all subsequent manuscript references, please consult the page of "Manuscript References" at the back of the book.
8. John Walter Cross, *George Eliot's Life as Related in Her Letters and Journals* (Cabinet Edition), II, 244.
9. In *Critical Essays on George Eliot,* ed. Barbara Hardy (London, 1970).
10. "Romola," *A Century of George Eliot Criticism,* ed. Gordon S. Haight (Boston, 1965), pp. 28, 29.
11. *George Eliot* (London, 1940), p. 126.
12. P. 29.
13. "Romola," *George Eliot and Her Readers,* eds. Laurence Lerner and John Holmstrom (London, 1966), p. 57.
14. *"Romola:* A Reading of the Novel," *Victorian Studies,* VI (1962), 31.
15. P. 142.
16. *Romola,* ed. Viola Meynell (Oxford University Press, 1949), p. 1. Available editions of Romola are few, another symptom of neglect. I use the Oxford edition because it seems to be the most easily available, but cite chapters to simplify references to others.
17. *The Novels of George Eliot* (New York, 1961), p. 82.
18. Browning's enthusiasm had prompted him to write to Eliot before he had finished reading *Romola.* On finishing, he felt disappointed that Eliot had not made the cause of Italian liberty her central theme.
19. "Polly" was one of Lewes's pet names for Eliot. Another pet name that is particularly interesting in connection with the imagery in this book, as in Eliot's others, is "Madonna."
20. The first appeared in *College English* (January 1970), the second is included in *The Theory of the Novel: New Essays,* ed. John Halperin (Oxford University Press, 1974).
21. Although he gives a very incomplete and partial account of Eliot's debt to the classics, Vernon Randall does at least convince us that Eliot had a good foundation in the study of the ancients. See "George Eliot and the Classics," reprinted and more easily available in *A Century of George Eliot Criticism,* pp. 215-25.
22. P. 351.
23. In the same letter, Eliot settled what was then, and for many readers remains today, the stubborn question of pronunciation. The name of the heroine and of the book, Eliot tells Alexander Main—who was one of the few to have guessed it correctly—is to be pronounced not Romōla but Romŏla.
24. William Baker, *The George Eliot-George Henry Lewes Library: An Annotated Catalogue of Their Books at Dr. Williams's Library, London* (New York, 1977), no. 943. Since many of the books that Eliot and Lewes owned have been widely

dispersed and can no longer be traced, and since many others have not yet been found, identified, or catalogued, Baker's collection does not by any means tell us what Eliot and Lewes had in their library. It is the best catalogue we have, however, and it often provides an insight into Eliot's and Lewes's interests and readings for which we have no other evidence. Hereafter, references to this work will appear in parentheses in the text. I will not include here volumes that were published or acquired after Eliot had completed *Romola.* (In most cases, I cite the titles as they appear in Baker without comment.)

25. Felicia Bonaparte, *Will and Destiny: Morality and Tragedy in George Eliot's Novels* (New York University Press, 1975).
26. Perhaps we hear in this image an echo of a line by one of Eliot's favorite poets, the line "Yet all experience is an arc," from Tennyson's "Ulysses."
27. For a brief discussion of the importance in Eliot's fiction of this view, and indeed of this very remark in her letters, see Thomas Deegan's "George Eliot's Novels of the Historical Imagination," *ClioW,* I (1972), 21-23.
28. Haight, *Biography,* p. 351.
29. P. 79.
30. P. 31.

Chapter II: The Greek, Roman, and Christian Worlds

1. "The Sketch of the Three Masks in *Romola,*" *Victorian Newsletter,* 41 (1972), 9-13.
2. P. 60.
3. Eliot was, of course, very well acquainted with Strauss's work, having already translated his *Leben Jesu,* a book to which I will return later.
4. *Nineteenth Century Fiction,* XXVI (1972), 390-405.
5. Actually, Shaw's play shares considerably more with Eliot's book than I have had reason to discuss here.
6. Although I agree with J. B. Bullen's study of Positivism in *Romola* to some extent, my own view is that the Comtean framework is rooted in the far more important mythic context, and that, as I will suggest later, in one vital respect at least Eliot rejected the Comtean vision (see "George Eliot's *Romola* as a Positivist Allegory," *Review of English Studies,* XXVI [1975], 425-35).
7. Trans. J. H. Bridges (Stanford, n.d.), p. 252. Eliot herself knew Bridges and greatly admired his translation.
8. Haight, *Biography,* p. 345.
9. Geometry and mathematics generally are amply represented in the Eliot/Lewes library, and the works were undoubtedly of interest to both Eliot and Lewes. The library, in fact, includes even a copy of Lobachevsky's *Geometrical Researches on the Theory of Parallels,* in a French translation from the German (no. 1310), the highly radical work published in 1840 in which Lobachevsky

revolutionized the field by challenging Euclidean geometry, thus inaugurating the modern geometry that led, among other things, to the theory of relativity.

Chapter III: The Clashing Deities

1. The image of Antigone haunted Eliot's imagination and often inspired her conception of characters even when there is no direct allusion to the mythological figure. Such allusions are, however, frequently explicit. One is reminded, for example, of Dorothea Brooke, who is in some sense a reincarnation of Romola at a later date. Just as the artist of *Romola,* Piero di Cosimo, confers the mythological title on Romola, so the artist of *Middlemarch,* Adolf Naumann, confers it on Dorothea when he tells Will Ladislaw that Dorothea seems to him a Christian Antigone (chap. XIX), a term that could well describe Romola in her Christian period and that seems indeed an echo of Piero's subsequent reference to Romola as "Madonna Antigone." It is significant that in *Middlemarch* too Antigone and Ariadne are joined, for when Adolf Naumann first sees Dorothea, she is standing in the Vatican in front of the sculpture of the reclining Ariadne, an image that takes on special meaning when we recall the images of the labyrinth that define Casaubon.

Chapter IV: Bacchus and Ariadne Betrothed

1. Some aspects of Eliot's use of Ovid in *Romola* are discussed by Edward T. Hurley in "Piero di Cosimo: An Alternate Analogy for George Eliot's Realism," *Victorian Newsletter,* 31 (1967).
2. As Hurley suggests, Tito's instructions hint at fraudulence in another way as well, since he describes to Piero a highly selective version of Ovid's account, and thereby corrupts Ovid's intention.

Chapter V: Tito and Florence—A Prophecy

1. The imagery of this passage was to be echoed a few years later in *The Spanish Gypsy,* in the lines "the vine-wreathed god/ Fronts the pierced Image with the crown of thorns." The two works have one important point in common, as I will discuss later.
2. In "Villari's *Life and Times of Savonarola:* A Source for George Eliot's *Romola,*" *Anglia,* 90 (1972), Gennaro A. Santangelo suggests that in Villari's account of the immoral life that characterized the Florentine in that period, Eliot found a source for her characterization of Tito. I will discuss Villari later, in connection with Savonarola, but my own view is that while Villari contrib-

uted, among many others, to Eliot's knowledge of the period, and was particularly important in her study of Savonarola, for Tito himself, as I have been suggesting, it is not to Villari that Eliot was indebted.

3. Although it was Lewes who marked their library copy of J. R. Gertel's *Hades* (no. 797), it seems likely that Eliot was also acquainted with it.

Chapter VI: Bacchic and Christian Mysteries

1. P. 40.
2. See XII, p. 133; XXXV, p. 324; XXXIX, p. 360; XLVII, p. 421; LIV, p. 468; LXIII, p. 536; and LXV, p. 549.
3. See vii, p. 85; XVI, p. 170; XVII, p. 191; and XXII, p. 224.
4. *The Spanish Gypsy and Poems by George Eliot* (Illustrated Cabinet Edition), I, 25-30.
5. "Piero di Cosimo and the Higher Primitivism," p. 399.
6. "Piero di Cosimo and the Higher Primitivism," p. 404.

Chapter VII: Conversion

1. (Berkeley, 1972), p. 49.
2. Although Eliot by no means agreed with Carlyle in every respect, she was, like so many in her century, profoundly indebted to him. It was perhaps to acknowledge that debt, and certainly to express her admiration, that Eliot sent Jane Carlyle presentation copies of *Scenes of Clerical Life* and *Adam Bede,* hoping no doubt that, despite his refusal to read any more novels, the volumes would find their way into Carlyle's hands.

Chapter VIII: Creon and Antigone

1. I am indebted to Professor John Geerken of Scripps College, Claremont, for some suggestive hints on this subject.
2. P. 94.
3. *Essays of George Eliot,* pp. 263, 265.

Chapter IX: The Birth of Modern Man

1. *The English Historical Novel: Walter Scott to Virginia Woolf* (Baltimore, 1971), pp. 161-62. While I do not think that Romola is here rejecting the historical life, I do agree with Fleishman when he concludes that this higher life is essentially the vision of an individual who must, therefore, pursue his individual

perception independently of the state. If *Romola* were only a novel, it would be necessary to distinguish, as Fleishman does, between the individual and the stream of history. But the epic identifies Romola with the stream of history, and the distinction is therefore neither necessary nor true, on the epic level or on the novelistic level, which derives its meaning from the epic.

2. *Experiments in Life: George Eliot's Quest for Values* (Detroit, 1965), p. 222.

Chapter X: Resurrection

1. P. 249.
2. *Religious Humanism and the Victorian Novel: George Eliot, Walter Pater, and Samuel Butler* (Princeton, 1965), pp. 40-41.

Index

Date Due

7-10-88